HIDDEN HERETICS

PRINCETON STUDIES IN
CULTURE AND TECHNOLOGY

Princeton Studies in Culture and Technology
Tom Boellstorff and Bill Maurer, series editors
This series presents innovative work that extends classic ethnographic methods and questions into areas of pressing interest in technology and economics. It explores the varied ways new technologies combine with older technologies and cultural understandings to shape novel forms of subjectivity, embodiment, knowledge, place, and community. By doing so, the series demonstrates the relevance of anthropological inquiry to emerging forms of digital culture in the broadest sense.

HIDDEN

באהאלטענע אפיקורסים

HERETICS

Jewish Doubt in the Digital Age

AYALA FADER

Princeton University Press   *Princeton and Oxford*

Published by Princeton University Press
41 William Street, Princeton, New Jersey 08540
99 Banbury Road, Oxford OX2 6JX

press.princeton.edu

First Paperback Printing, 2022
Paperback ISBN 9780691234489

The Library of Congress has cataloged the cloth edition of this book as follows:

Names: Fader, Ayala, 1964- author.

Title: Hidden heretics : Jewish doubt in the digital age / Ayala Fader.
Description: 1st. | Princeton : Princeton University Press, 2020. | Series:
Princeton series in culture and technology | Includes bibliographical
references and index.
Identifiers: LCCN 2020001342 | ISBN 9780691169903 (hardback) | ISBN
9780691201481 (ebook)
Subjects: LCSH: Ultra-Orthodox Jews—New York (State)—New York—Cultural
assimilation. | Judaism and secularism—New York (State)—New York. |
Social media—Religious aspects—Judaism. | Ultra-Orthodox Jews—New
York (State)—New York—History—21st century. | Ultra-orthodox
Jews—Relations—Non-traditional Jews.
Classification: LCC BM198.4.N49 F33 2020 | DDC 296.8/32097471—dc23
LC record available at https://lccn.loc.gov/2020001342

British Library Cataloging-in-Publication Data is available

Editorial: Fred Appel and Jenny Tan
Production Editorial: Leslie Grundfest
Text Design: Pamela Schnitter
Production: Erin Suydam
Publicity: Kate Hensley and Kathryn Stevens (UK)
Copyeditor: Aviva Arad

Cover photo by Luc Kordas
Cover design by Faceout Studio, Lindy Martin

This book has been composed in Adobe Text Pro and Eurostile LT Std

In honor of my mother, Yael Chipkin Fader,
whose memory is already a blessing.

With gratitude and love to
my father, Laurance Fader, and
my in-laws, George and Evelyn Idelson

With love and gratitude to
Adam, Simon, and Talia

CONTENTS

ACKNOWLEDGMENTS

Spending years in ultra-Orthodox Jewish communities in New York has been a privilege, one made possible by the generosity of different people and institutions. It is a pleasure to thank many of them here, even if anonymously.

My gratitude to the *ofgeklerte* (open-minded), the hidden heretics, those living double lives of many kinds. They impressed me with the courage of their convictions and their loyalty to their families and communities. I wish I could thank them here by name, but I cannot, so I will have to assume they know who they are. I will not name the therapists, rabbis, and life coaches who tried to help those with life-changing doubt either. However, the courage of their very different convictions was equally impressive and often moving. I thank them as well.

Special thanks are owed to Shimon Steinmetz, whose vast knowledge of Judaism, history, and the ultra-Orthodox world was an incredible resource throughout this project. He showed me connections and nuances in Jewish texts and ideas I would not have recognized. Shimon also expertly helped me negotiate a minefield of secrets and his advice on every step was invaluable.

Special thanks also go to Yoelish Steinberg, whose insights into the Hasidic world are unparalleled. Over many years, he patiently answered my questions, pointed me in fruitful directions, and creatively introduced me to many who became central figures in this book. He has been a generous teacher and thoughtful translator of ideas.

Special thanks to the WhatsAppville Yinglish group, whose members must remain anonymous. Over many years, group members explained, explained again, told me frankly when I was wrong, and have kept me updated on the latest goings on in the ultra-Orthodox world. Their insights, the material they shared, their good will, humor, and patience have all been much appreciated.

Ethnography takes a long time, so I had ample opportunities to present portions of this book to various academic and nonacademic audiences, where I received very helpful feedback. These included: Indiana University's Borns Jewish Studies Program (especially title help); the University of Michigan's Frankel Center for Judaic Studies and the Department of Anthropology; the City University of New York's Jewish Studies Program; the New York University Center for Religion and Media and Department of Anthropology; UCLA's Department of Anthropology; Georgetown University's Center for Jewish Civilization; the Oxford Institute for Contemporary and Modern Judaism; the Religious Studies Department of the University of North Carolina at Chapel Hill; Cornell University's Jewish Studies Program; Young Israel Congregation of New Rochelle; Chulent; and Footsteps.

Generous institutional support of different kinds made the research and then the writing of this book possible. Fordham University sponsored my initial research with a Faculty Fellowship, and a Memorial Foundation for Jewish Culture Senior Grant made a leave possible. Thanks to Faye Ginsburg, a long-time mentor, for inviting me to be a visiting scholar at the NYU Center for Religion and Media and for so generously including me in the wider New York scene. A National Science Foundation Senior Grant (#1357556) supported the research, and program officer Jeffrey Mantz was especially supportive. A National Endowment for the Humanities Fellowship (FA-251802) allowed me to focus exclusively on writing the manuscript. I am especially grateful for these agencies' support when government funding for the humanities and social sciences is in peril.

At Fordham University, I owe a special debt to Celinett Rodriguez and Kris Wolff at the Office of Sponsored Programs for expertly navigating complicated federal and Fordham bureaucracies over years. Annmarie O'Connor efficiently and cheerfully provided administrative help. Lindsey Karp and Kristin Treglia helped me with WhatsApp technology. Kevin Munnelly made many things possible. I'm also grateful to Magda Teter for making the Fordham Jewish Studies Program such an exciting place to be.

Friends and colleagues read parts or all of the manuscript and provided invaluable support. Special thanks to my longtime friend, Chris Walley, who heroically read a first draft of the whole manuscript. Her kind and rigorous notes both encouraged and pushed me. Boundless gratitude to the North Square Writing Triangle: Omri Elisha and Karen Strassler. Their insightful reading of my work was formative and their own writing inspired me. Matthew Engelke and his Columbia University graduate seminar read a later draft of the whole manuscript and shared valuable insights especially on media and mediation. Emma Tarlo's writing pushed me to experiment with my own. Life-long adviser and friend Bambi Schieffelin consulted on everything, as usual. Jeffrey Shandler has been a real friend and mentor over the years, always supportive and so helpful with historical and editorial advice.

Thanks to those who helped with the analysis of the data, especially Yiddish translation and transcription. Isaac Bleaman was a terrific research assistant and is now a terrific colleague. Katherine Rofey creatively collated and categorized all the popular magazine data and helped with bibliographic references. Translator Rose Waldman expertly consulted on Yiddish translations and was an excellent research associate. Emily Rivke Canning and Rebecca Galpern helped with transcriptions and bibliographic work. Sandra Chiritescu expertly checked the Yiddish in the manuscript, patiently discussing the delicate, often political, challenge of romanizing Yiddish and Hebrew.

Princeton University Press peer reviewers Janet McIntosh and Jonathan Boyarin were insightful, sensitive readers and made excellent suggestions. I am grateful to both of them.

Princeton editor Fred Appel gave me space when I needed it, critical attention when I needed that, and always brought his intelligent, experienced eye to all. He has consistently been there for me, and I am grateful to work with him on this project. Aviva Arad was an efficient copyeditor, and working with Dave Luljak on the index was a pleasure. Leslie Grundfest ensured that the book production went smoothly and prioritized quality over schedule.

Family and friends provided all kinds of support, including diversion and reminders to go outside. Thanks to Jeanne Flavin, who is always ready to read a chapter and take a walk. My comrade-in-arms for the New York Working Group for Jewish Orthodoxies, Orit Avishai, read, listened, supported, and along the way became a true friend. Thanks to Lotti Silber for her longtime friendship through thick and thin, in all kinds of media on all kinds of topics. I am grateful for Stacey Lutz and Barbara Miller, whose long-term friendships are sustaining. Valerie Vann-Oettl makes Wednesday mornings special.

The extended Fader and Idelson clans gather for holidays, vacations, and all significant events, including very recently my mother's memorial. No matter where we are, there is always love, arguing, and a lot of laughing. At home, my partner, Adam, calls me on too-long sentences, vague ideas, and buried ledes among many other foibles. He read every single chapter of this book, and I could not live without him.

My children, Simon and Talia, are almost grown now and living their own very interesting lives. During the writing of this book they endured my distraction, moodiness, and tuna melts for dinner with good humor and loving support. I am very proud of them, and I think they know that they (and their dad) matter more to me than anything else.

HIDDEN HERETICS

1

Life-Changing Doubt, the Internet, and a Crisis of Authority

Yisroel was an earnestly pious boy growing up Hasidic in Brooklyn, New York. With his side curls grazing his shoulders, thick plastic glasses, and big black velvet yarmulke, he looked like all the other boys in his yeshiva, where he studied the Torah and its commentaries from early in the morning until late at night. But when he was thirteen, Yisroel began to notice contradictions that troubled him in the religious texts he was studying. He didn't initially doubt the truth of ultra-Orthodox Judaism, but he had problematic questions—what are called in Yiddish *emuna kashes* (questions about faith). Only once did he timidly confide in his teacher, a rabbi, who angrily warned him that such questions came from the sin of masturbation. From then on, confused and ashamed, he kept his questions to himself and tried, as he told me, to "push them under the rug." At eighteen he got married, and he and his wife, Rukhy, whom he barely knew but grew to adore, had five children in quick succession. To support his growing family, Yisroel eventually stopped studying Torah and began, as many Hasidic men do, to work in information technology.

However, in 2003, when he was twenty-nine, his questions began to nag at him again. And this time, thanks to his work with computers, he turned to the internet, secretly searching for and reading forbidden scholarly articles on theology, biblical criticism, and science. He hoped to finally find answers to his questions about faith in these non-Jewish sources, but they only provoked more questions. He decided then, he told me, that he had to "take his questioning all the way."

Late at night, sitting alone in the kitchen after everyone had gone to bed and the only sound was the humming of the two dishwashers (one for meat and one for dairy), he began reading some of the then-popular heretical ultra-Orthodox blogs, like *Hasidic Rebel* and *Shtreimel.* These led him to online forums of the day, where writing under a pseudonym in Yiddish and in English, Yisroel debated with ultra-Orthodox Jewish doubters and even some who had openly left Jewish Orthodoxy altogether to go "OTD," or "off the *derekh*" (path). He tried to convince them (and himself) that they were wrong. All of his searching, he told me, remembering his anguish, "tortured" him, but he could not stop.

Eventually, his questions gave way to doubt in the central premise of ultra-Orthodox Jewish authority: that God revealed the Torah to the Jews at Mount Sinai through Moses. Yisroel was in such agony at this heresy (*kfira*) that he secretly began to make phone calls to consult rabbis outside of his community who specialized in answering questions of faith. Their arguments failed to convince him. Despite continuing to observe the *mitsves*, the 613 prohibitions and commandments that had always directed every aspect of his life, he began to doubt their divine truth.

The first time he ever violated one of the commandments was on a Sabbath evening in 2012. His youngest was crying, and he knew that turning on the musical mobile above her crib would calm her down. Observant Jews do not turn electricity on or off during the Sabbath. He stood alone in the dark with his hand on the switch for a long time—yes, no, yes, no, yes, no? And then he switched it on. Each time he broke another commandment, like using his phone on the Sabbath, or skipping daily prayers, or even eventually sneaking nonkosher cold cuts into the pocket of his jacket to nibble on at home, he told me, he felt a sense of "freedom," finally "in control of his life."

That was when he became one of a growing number of what most ultra-Orthodox call in English "double life" or "ITC" (in the closet), or what Yiddish-speaking ultra-Orthodox call *bahaltena apikorsim* (hidden heretics), those who feature in this book: men and women who practiced religiously in public, including at home, but who often violated the commandments in secret because they no longer believed them to be God's words to his chosen people. Yisroel and others like him kept their double lives secret to protect their families and for fear of being cast out in a world they were ill-prepared to navigate.

In 2014, after Yisroel had developed a growing network of double-life friends on social media and in person, his wife, Rukhy, finally confronted him. She had noticed that in the intimacy of their bedroom, he had stopped "washing *negl vasser*," the ritual handwashing upon waking each morning. She asked him if he still prayed. If he kept the Sabbath. Did he still believe? Hiding in their bedroom closet and whispering late at night, so their children would not hear, he told her everything. She was devastated and told me she cried for three days straight. Then, just a few months later, the *vaad ha-tsnius* (the Committee on Modesty), a group of self-appointed activists and rabbis, contacted Yisroel through his brother-in-law. They somehow knew that he had just bought a book on science from Amazon for his twelve-year-old daughter, which included a section on the theory of evolution, which Hasidic Jews reject.

Yisroel's world was literally falling apart, and that was when I met him. A mutual contact, Zalman, who had been forced to leave his own ultra-Orthodox community a few years earlier for heresy, introduced us, knowing I was conducting anthropological research with those living double lives and those who tried to help them. Over the next year, Yisroel and I met periodically in a wooden booth in the back of a dark bar on Manhattan's Upper West Side, amid the safe anonymity of Columbia University students. He still had his long side curls along with a long beard, thick glasses, and a big black velvet yarmulke. However, as a small personal rebellion, he had taken off the high black velvet hat most Hasidic men wear, and instead of the usual Hasidic men's long black jacket, he always wore a cardigan or a parka.

Yisroel told me his story as it was unfolding. Although he was always anxious about protecting the anonymity of his family, he seemed to need to talk, often asking me about his legal rights, something I knew little about. When we couldn't meet, we communicated on WhatsApp, the secure phone messaging app that so many ultra-Orthodox Jews used. He told me how he and his wife were trying to figure out how to make their life together work again. He had promised her that he would keep practicing in front of the children. He hoped it was enough.

With her permission, he gave me Rukhy's number, and I began to talk with her, too, on the phone and on Facebook. Rukhy, who used to rely on her husband for spiritual guidance, told me how his doubt had begun to affect her: how she worried about her own faith *glitshing* (slipping); how she had begun to reach out to other women in similar situations online; and about her new sense of responsibility for the *rukhnius* (spirituality) in their home, traditionally the authority of the husband. Yisroel's secret was hers now too. She could tell no one, not even her mother or her sisters who lived across the street. She told me she was scared, angry, and heartbroken all at once.

The Committee on Modesty wanted Yisroel to sign a contract promising he would stop using any social media, part of the growing effort by the ultra-Orthodox to control the internet and protect the community from what was increasingly called the "crisis of *emuna*," or the crisis of faith. This made Yisroel angry, and he brought up his constitutional right to privacy, having only recently learned about the existence of the Constitution at all. He was not rebellious, he insisted. He was simply following his conscience. Then the committee threatened to expel his children from school and to tell Yisroel's parents unless he and Rukhy agreed to see a religious therapist, someone who worked with a rabbi and then reported back to the committee. Many ultra-Orthodox Jews believe that religious doubt might be symptomatic of an underlying mental illness, perhaps depression, a trauma, or anxiety, something that could be treated and cured. Afraid, Yisroel and Rukhy tried a number of different therapists, religious and secular, but none helped Yisroel regain his faith.

What Yisroel called his "journey" was still unfolding. Would he and his wife stay together, and if they did, would her faith continue to slip? Would the religious authorities and institutions be able to control the decisions Yisroel and his wife made? Would they expel his children, which would have serious repercussions for the entire family's life, especially when it came time for matchmaking? Where did his responsibilities as a parent lie, especially as his children got older? Was there anyone, a therapist or a rabbi, who could help Yisroel regain his faith, something he still wished for?

Yisroel's story was but one of many, the uncharted territory of ultra-Orthodox hidden heretics living double lives where belief and practice were at odds; these were men and (fewer) women, who no longer believed in the literal truth of divine revelation at Mount Sinai. Nevertheless, they felt bound by love and a sense of moral responsibility to stay with their still-religious spouses and children. Keeping secrets from those they were closest to, double lifers upheld the public appearance of adhering to ultra-Orthodoxy, even as they explored forbidden worlds, online and in person, beyond their own.

Those living double lives are part of a broader twenty-first-century generational crisis of authority among the ultra-Orthodox. Despite their robust demographic growth, there have been increasingly loud struggles over competing knowledge and truths. The internet facilitated the formation of a public oppositional voice, one that included anonymous expressions of life-changing doubt and validated radically changing perceptions of oneself in the world. Gender was key to the experience of and possibilities for living double lives, since gender structures authority in both ultra-Orthodox life and its alternative public. Begun in online spaces, but soon crossing over to meetings in person, this alternative public gave a platform to dangerous questions: Who should have the authority for making life choices? What and who defined Orthodox Judaism or self-fulfillment or an ethical life? The pages ahead ask what double lifers' everyday struggles can tell us about religious doubt and social change in the digital age.

* * *

Until recently, ultra-Orthodox Jews experiencing the kind of life-changing doubt that Yisroel did had trouble finding others like themselves. One might suspect from outside signs that a cousin or friend was doubting—maybe he had hidden an English book in his Hebrew prayer book in *shul* (synagogue) or maybe her skirt had gotten an inch shorter—but reaching out meant possibly risking everything. Back then, living a double life was very lonely unless you had the means to venture out of your community. For example, Tsvi, a Hasidic man in his sixties who had lived a double life for decades, told me he had found kindred spirits among less observant Jews he met in public libraries or Jewish seminaries in Manhattan. Women living double lives, especially with children, generally had much less independence than someone like Tsvi, so they were even more alone than men.

Since the early 2000s, however, the internet has created new possibilities for those living double lives to find each other and build secret worlds together. Through blogging and then later on social media (forums, Facebook groups, and texting platforms like WhatsApp), many began to anonymously critique, parody, and mock what they called "the system," the structures of rabbinic authority and their affiliated insitutitions, such as schools, synagogues, charities, kosher businesses, and summer camps. They also wrote about and discussed, in gendered varieties of Yiddish and English, their changing sense of themselves in the world. Once they trusted each other, they met up in person too, secretly exploring their new desires, ideas, and feelings in and around New York City.

Those living double lives formed an anonymous public with its own morality. This public, selectively rooted in North American liberal morality, included ideals of individual autonomy, choice, and self-fulfillment. Double-life women had fewer avenues for participation in this public, however; they had less access to new technologies, less mobility for getting together, and were sometimes less comfortable speaking up or writing in mixed-gender groups.

In reaction to this growing chorus of anonymous critics, ultra-Orthodox Jewish rabbis, rebbes (Hasidic leaders), educators, and self-appointed communal activists (*askonim*) began to rethink their approaches to what they called "the internet" or, in Yiddish, *tekhnologia* or *keylim* (devices), and especially smartphones. They came to the conclusion that the internet was more dangerous to Jewish continuity than the Holocaust. As a public poster that circulated on WhatsApp warned: "The Holocaust burned our bodies, but the Internet burns our souls."

At the same time, rabbinic leadership began describing the contemporary period as "a crisis of faith." They claimed that exterior material signs and embodied practices (*khitsoynius*)—for example, distinctive clothing (*levush*), head covering, ritual practice such as prayer—could no longer assure, as they had in even the recent past, the cultivation of shared interior faith, one strong enough to resist the temptations of the Gentile world. As a rabbi noted in the popular ultra-Orthodox magazine, *Ami*, "Before *levush* was enough. . . . Nowadays we have the Internet, where everyone is anonymous and no *levush* can act as a shield." To staunch what many worried was a growing wave of secret doubters and those leaving the faith, rabbinic leadership began speaking explicitly about how to protect and cure Jewish interiority (the *pnimiyus*)—hearts, minds, and souls.

Rabbinic leadership's public talk and writing about interiority integrated two different authoritative bodies of knowledge, or what anthropologist Talal Asad called "discursive traditions":[1] Jewish theology and American popular psychology. To protect Jewish souls against the corruption of the internet, rabbinic leadership began holding fiery anti-internet rallies (*asifes*), including the 2012 event in Citi Field Stadium in Queens, which drew over forty thousand men and boys. In rallies, leaders denounced the internet for disrupting the healthy struggle of each Jew to defeat the innate inclination for evil (*yeytser hora*), including a willingness to submit to hierarchies of religious male authority. They posted edicts limiting access to the internet and enlisted the ultra-Orthodox school systems to support them.

However, when life-changing doubt was revealed or confessed, rabbinic advisers almost always referred the person to a religious (*frum*) therapist or less formal satellites—Orthodox Jewish life coaching or outreach (*kiruv*) rabbis. Religious therapy as a discipline was founded in the nineties, and there was a wide range of professionalization: some held master's degrees from reputable universities, while others practiced without licensing or training. Some therapists cast life-changing doubt as a symptom, either of insufficient spiritual education or of underlying emotional issues.

They pathologized doubt using medicalized models of emotional health, which designated faith the normative default. This was a change from decades past, when those who left or doubted were seen less as a threat and simply as weak and undisciplined, in thrall to their evil inclination or Satan.

In this latest chapter of North American ultra-Orthodox life, the crisis of *emuna* and struggles over the internet should be understood as a wider crisis of authority. On the heels of political, economic, and social conflicts, in the context of exploding population growth, a small, homegrown generational backlash has begun challenging the authority of ultra-Orthodox leadership and their claims as the legitimate arbiters of tradition (*mesoyra*). In this social drama, the internet became a lightning rod for wider communal debates about religious authority through public discourse about interiority. While numbers of those living double lives and fellow travelers arc not reliably known, with individual estimates varying from a hundred to tens of thousands worldwide, they increasingly figure large in the ultra-Orthodox imagination.[2] Using the public yet intimate anonymity of the internet, those living double lives rejected the heightened religious stringencies of their communities following the Second World War and wrote their changing interior lives into being. Ultra-Orthodox leadership, in contrast, defined the contemporary crisis of authority as the latest threat—the most recent in a long history of such threats—to the very survival of the Jewish people.

Arriving in the 1950s after the Holocaust as refugees, primarily from Eastern Europe, ultra-Orthodox Jews today make up about 10 percent of the estimated 5.3 million Jewish adults in the United States, with 89 percent living in the Northeast, especially Brooklyn and upstate New York. In the eight counties that make up the New York area, 22 percent are ultra-Orthodox, roughly seventy-two thousand households. Despite public talk about the crisis of faith, in fact, demographically ultra-Orthodox Jewish communities continue to grow, owing to so many having large families (48 percent have more than four children).[3] There was a growing fear among many ultra-Orthodox that as they have grown increasingly comfortable in the United States, further from the trauma of the Holocaust with its moral imperative to rebuild, new dangers from outside and within were gathering force, most concretely from the internet.

In many ways more similar politically and culturally to Christian Evangelicalism than to other denominations of American Judaism, ultra-Orthodox life is all-encompassing despite so many living in the middle of New York City. Children attend private ultra-Orthodox gender-segregated schools affiliated with rabbinic leadership, with different curricula and languages for boys and girls. These schools later feed into arranged marriages, often brokered transnationally. With limited secular and English education, especially for Hasidic boys who speak primarily Yiddish, ultra-Orthodox married men often continue their religious study for some years until they go to work, either self-employed or in cash businesses that do not require degrees or even proficiency in English, such as accounting, real estate, information technology, local and online business, or teaching in ultra-Orthodox schools. And as I learned in the research for my first book, *Mitzvah Girls: Bringing Up the Next Generation of Hasidic Jews in Brooklyn*, ultra-Orthodox women often work as well, even as they rear large families. Their greater fluency in English helps them negotiate the secular world, so that men and boys can study the Torah undistracted and with pure hearts, which hastens the coming of the messiah for all.

Ultra-Orthodox men and women in New York participate in the economic, political, and recreational life of the city, but only in order to build up their own communities, not from a shared sense of citizenship; instead, religious leaders, educators, and parents endeavor to create communities for their children and themselves where they can be protected from knowledge, technologies, or people that might corrupt, distract, or challenge their commitment to an ultra-Orthodox way of life. They might live and thrive in the diversity that is New York thanks to federal, state, and city policies, but the ultra-Orthodox are sure that they alone are God's chosen people, waiting, as they have for over two millennia in diaspora, for the final redemption.

To tell the story of the contemporary crisis of authority, I organized this book around two ultra-Orthodox perspectives: (1) men and women living double lives, primarily married adults in their late twenties, thirties, and forties and their friends and families, and (2) rabbis, educators, and activists who tried to protect the faithful from doubt and those who treated doubt once it became intractable: Torah therapists, outreach rabbis, and Jewish life coaches. Those living double lives fell along a continuum of doubt, with implications for their belief and their practices. Further, men and women double lifers had very different opportunities and experiences, so that gender shaped the experience and enactment of doubt. Outreach rabbis, religious therapists, and life coaches made a living using therapeutic and religious talk to strengthen faith, to cure doubt, and to reinscribe gendered hierarchies of authority. In their struggle over definitions of ultra-Orthodoxy, those living double lives and the faithful both appealed to an idealized shared Jewish past and drew on contemporary North American and Jewish theological discourses of the interior self.

An ethnography of a relatively small population of ultra-Orthodox Jewish doubters, those who tried to help them, and the role of the internet raises all kinds of questions about dramatic personal and social change. These questions are relevant not only for scholars of religion or of media, but for anyone interested in how people struggle to live morally meaningful lives in the digital age. What, for example, were the ethical dilemmas of those living double lives, who publicly practiced a religious life they no longer believed in and secretly violated? How did they talk about their doubts and keep secrets from their spouses, and how did their rabbis and therapists respond? What can ultra-Orthodox struggles over the internet—which double lifers used as a lifeline, while rabbinic leadership claimed it contaminated Jewish souls—tell us about the possibilities and dangers of digital media? And how did those living double lives subtly try to teach their children what they called "tolerance" and "critical thinking," negatively valued as moral relativism in their own communities? To develop an anthropology of life-changing doubt, this book examines semiotic forms and practices—language, the body and clothing, digital technology, food and activities (like bike riding or praying)—to tell the story of the everyday moral compromises and dilemmas of those living untenable contradictions.

The Anthropology of Life-Changing Doubt

Ethnographically studying doubt productively complicates conceptions of religious lives and how anthropologists might study them.[4] I distinguish between two kinds of doubt. The first is doubt that defines or refines faith. Anthropologist Tanya Luhrmann, for example, has shown that for contemporary Evangelicals that she studied in the United States belief in God was "made real" through playful, ongoing narrative expressions of doubt and skepticism.[5] For ultra-Orthodox Jews it was the discipline of religious practice—the adherence to the commandments and prohibitions (*mitsves*)—that ensured that interior *emuna* would always return, despite what all agreed was the inevitability of doubts, questions, and uncertainties across the life cycle. That kind of doubt remained private and contained, never acted upon and rarely spoken about, though one could and should seek out *khizuk* (moral strengthening) from books or listen to *shiurs* (inspirational lectures) given by respected rabbis.

My focus in this book is another kind of doubt, what I call "life-changing doubt." This was a kind of doubt that dramatically troubled a person's faith in the truth of all they had grown up believing, maybe even obliterating it for good. Life-changing doubt was so profound that it could no longer be contained inside, unspoken, not acted upon. People experiencing life-changing doubt sought out new truths with other doubters, which led them to change how they perceived themselves and their worlds. And just as with the doubt that defines faith, few anthropologists of religion have studied life-changing doubt.[6]

Life-changing doubt almost always provokes individuals to make larger, public changes in their everyday lives, with social and institutional repercussions. For example, religious studies scholar Philip Francis wrote about this kind of doubt in his study of a college "semester-away" program that exposed Evangelical young adults to poetry, literature, art, and music. The experience of listening to Bob Dylan or seeing a Rothko painting in a London museum led some students to experience life-changing doubt and subsequently leave Evangelicalism altogether. Francis notes that leaving did not just entail "tinkering with belief" or making an intellectual adjustment, but rather involved a "recreation of one's being in the world."[7]

The ultra-Orthodox Jews living double lives that I write about experienced similar life-changing doubt, and they too re-created their lives. But they did not leave. They felt they could not. There was no rupture of everyday life, like those Evangelicals, Mormons, or even other ultra-Orthodox Jews who have had crises of faith and then left, a kind of reverse conversion story.[8] Those living double lives stayed, and they kept their doubting secret, even as they made gradual and subtle changes to their everyday ultra-Orthodox lives, eventually including secretly breaking many of the religious commandments that had been part of the very fiber of their being since birth.

This kind of life-changing doubt became threatening to ultra-Orthodox leadership because it was a doubt that refused to remain in individual interiors where it belonged. One man living a double life remembered his Orthodox therapist "screaming" at him impatiently, "Why can't you be like everyone else and just keep these doubts to yourself? . . . Your *emuna* will return if you just keep practicing [the *mitsves*]!" The crisis of authority, then, was not about life-changing doubt per se, but about interior individual doubt that became social and discursive. That is, those with life-changing doubt discussed it together and shared and explored other ways of being and living. They did so at first anonymously and secretly online, but eventually in person as well.

Once interior doubt became a discursive social practice, it also became public, which was the most threatening to rabbinic leadership of all. By public I mean that life-changing doubt was made real with others across all kinds of technologies, in written and spoken languages (Yiddish, English, and *loshn koydesh*: sacred Hebrew and Aramaic), on changing bodies where beards were trimmed or hair grew long, in changing clothing and in everyday practice. Those with life-changing doubt moved through unsanctioned spaces, such as social media platforms like WhatsApp and Facebook, as well as New York City parks, restaurants, private homes, or Broadway plays. People and digital texts went to places they should not be, doing things they should not do, arguing about the existence of God, falling in love, or taking off their wigs in the subway on their way to Manhattan bars. And because those living double lives continued to look and act mostly the same to their families and communities, it was the new medium of the internet that was initially blamed for enabling those with life-changing doubt to form an anonymous heretical public that was so frightening and challenging to rabbinic authorities.[9]

Both secret and public, life-changing doubt morally threatened the very integrity of ultra-Orthodox religious authority and, as such, it needed an explanation.[10] Double lifers had grown up exposed to the truth and beauty of ultra-Orthodoxy. How could that not have protected them from growing *kalt tse yiddishkayt* (cool to Judaism, i.e., vulnerable to doubt)? Those living double lives could not be dismissed merely as what were called, bums or *bumtes* (feminine, bum), or for yeshiva boys, *tshillers* (chillers), that is, ultra-Orthodox Jews who were lax about religious practice not because of intellectual questioning, but just because they wanted to have a good time and were too weak to fight their inclinations for evil, their own *tayves* (lusts, desires, urges). Bums and *bumtes* were open about their "lifestyle," repenting every year during the high holy days, though they and their families were marginalized accordingly, especially in matchmaking. Double lifers were different. They had questions that could not be answered, questions that made it impossible for them to continue living as they always had. This was unfathomable and disturbing to the faithful. I remember visiting a community college class catering to Orthodox Jews, invited by a double-life professor of sociology. At the end of the class, a Hasidic student asked me eagerly, "What have you found? What really makes these people lose their *emuna*?"

There were, in fact, few consistent predictors of why a person raised in ultra-Orthodoxy experienced life-changing doubt. Esty, a Hasidic woman who appears frequently in this book, brought up this example. Her friend had told her that once she read Louisa May Alcott's *Little Women*, that was it. Her world changed, and she eventually left. "But," Esty said with a shrug, "I read *Little Women* too, and I was as *frum* as ever until much later in life."

Almost all of the men and women I spent time with remembered having had doubts and questions as teens, but many ultra-Orthodox teens do. That is the kind of doubt that defines faith. Most of them had had good reputations before they were married, and came from "good" families. Few had been labeled "at risk," a category that lumps questioning in with other pathologized behaviors such as addiction, promiscuity, or self-harming. Almost all steered clear of any connection to Footsteps, an organization that counsels those who are questioning or have left their ultra-Orthodox communities. None that I met claimed to have been sexually abused— those who have more often leave altogether. The majority of those I met living double lives were also not gay or queer, something that can make staying, one woman told me, impossibly lonely. Most reported that as teens they had been merely *naygerik* or curious, not rebellious, though perhaps a few were called "*ongelaynt*" (suspiciously well-read), class clowns or cynics (*letsonim*). What those living double lives did share was that at the particular time of the life cycle, married with young children, that their *emuna* was supposed to be getting more and more *ernst* (serious), as their parents' and grandparents' had, their earlier questions and doubts resurfaced. However, this time the doubts and questions refused to be denied, and this time there was an online public to support them.

The life-changing doubt of those living double lives was not uniform or consistent. Not all became atheists, as I had assumed at first. There was a continuum of doubt, complete with nuanced local Yiddish, Hebrew, and English categories that shaped religious practice or lack thereof. At one pole were the *ofgeklerte* (enlightened), those who had become more "open-minded" about religious doctrine and exposure to diverse perspectives (Jewish and non-Jewish). For example, *ofgeklerte* individuals might dip into academic articles about biblical criticism or evolutionary biology, along with religious texts not sanctioned by their own community (e.g., the writings of Rav Kook, founder of religious Zionism, taboo for Satmar Hasidim who reject the State of Israel). Their reading might eventually lead them to break some Jewish laws in private, but not necessarily.

In contrast, *apikorsim* (skeptics), were more explicitly critical of ultra-Orthodoxy and its leadership. They publicly denigrated the sages and rabbis, read all kinds of heretical literature, and even rejected certain core ultra-Orthodox doctrines, such as belief in the resurrection of the dead upon the arrival of the messiah (*tkhiyes ha-meysim*). *Apikorsim* were boundary pushers and social critics, but they were not necessarily atheists either. *Kofrim* (heretics) were similarly critical of ultra-Orthodox leaders and the system, but that was because they had more broadly come to reject the truth of the divine revelation at Sinai (*matn toyre*), which brought the entire narrative of ultra-Orthodoxy tumbling down. Even so, some heretics continued to believe in God of some kind. Both skeptics and heretics often violated Jewish laws, though only in secret as well.

At the far end of the continuum of life-changing doubt were atheists or agnostics (terms used in English), who rejected belief itself. Atheists might not feel obligated by Jewish law or believe in God, but some, not all, still retained an emotional attachment to what they called the "lifestyle" of ultra-Orthodoxy with its close-knit ties and sense of shared purpose, especially in contrast to their perceptions of the emptiness of other ways of life.

These were not hard-and-fast categories, since real people never fit so neatly into boxes. And time was a factor too. Some living double lives stayed put at one end of the continuum of doubt, while others moved along it over time. When I first met Yonah, he was *ofgeklert*, still committed to keeping all the commandments, what is called "Orthoprax," but not necessarily believing that those commandments were truly God's words. A few years later, though, I realized he was texting me on WhatsApp on the Sabbath, something he had never done before. What the internet and, later, social media offered, all double lifers agreed, was a safe space to gather with like-minded others. This made them feel less alone and fear a little less for their sanity.

The continuum of doubt denied women even the possibility of intellectual doubt, since it referenced exclusively male categories. For example, some men living double lives called themselves *maskilim* (Jewish Enlighteners), the male Jews who challenged rabbinic authority in an earlier crisis of authority, the eighteenth- to nineteenth-century Haskalah (Jewish Enlightenment). Women I met did not use that term for themselves, nor did they generally call themselves *ofgeklerte*, *kofrim*, or *apikorsim*, words that appear in religious texts men study. Women I met often claimed they were "spiritual" even if they no longer believed in the system or the divine revelation at Mount Sinai. Though there were fewer women living double lives for structural reasons of mobility, opportunity, and access, even when a woman expressed life-changing doubt, male authorities (husbands, rabbis, fathers, therapists) almost always blamed emotional problems, dissatisfactions, or sexual promiscuity. As Shmuel, a Yeshivish blogger who figures prominently in the pages to come, wrote to me on WhatsApp: "Women [double lifers] are below the radar to the authorities. . . . [They] would probably ignore a woman's profession of doubts as the real issue and attribute it to a wandering uterus if you know what I mean."

Living a double life happened over real time and was sometimes enacted before my very eyes, since ethnography happens over real time too. For example, in our first meeting at the Atlantic Avenue subway stop in Brooklyn, thirty-year-old Hasidic Gavriel asked me to walk several yards ahead of him, so no one would see us together in public. We slunk into a nearby Starbucks, where he tentatively tried a cappuccino, his first. He looked nervously over his shoulder the entire time and spoke practically in a whisper, asking me not to use my tape recorder. When I met with him again, a year and a half later, at my university cafeteria, he was still living a double life, but he was, as he said, "less paranoid," since he had come clean to his wife, and she had decided not to divorce him. He seemed relaxed and confident, eating whatever was being served that day (not worrying about what was kosher), and talking openly, though he still asked me not to record him. For some, living a double life was temporary before they decided to finally leave altogether or were kicked out. For others, those in this book, there were more incremental changes over years, a process of making ethical compromises, often with a still-religious spouse, but ultimately remaining in their ultra-Orthodox communities. Those communities have experienced dramatic changes over the past twenty years or so, which ignited the contemporary crisis of authority.

Jewish Orthodoxies in Crisis

Ultra-Orthodox Jews are part of the New York City landscape. Men's distinctive black and white dress, their beards and side curls, yarmulkes and hats have been featured on subway murals, television, and in movies. Women's and girls' modest clothing and hair is less marked, until the summer months, when their stockings, long skirts, and buttoned blouses are suddenly very apparent amid shorts and tank tops. Ultra-Orthodox Jews share city spaces, resources, amenities, and citizenship with the diversity of New Yorkers, but their interactions are limited: bumping elbows on crowded streets, voting, buying electronics or renting apartments, invoking nostalgia for tourists and more liberal Jews, or instigating conflicts over resources and real estate.[11]

Ultra-Orthodoxy is quite different theologically from more liberal Jewish denominations, such as Reform, Conservative, and Reconstructionist, especially in terms of belief and practice. In the Reform Judaism I was raised with, for example, belief meant belief in God, not belief that God literally gave the Jews the Torah at Mount Sinai. And belief in God was something to be discussed not assumed. In the Hebrew school classes I attended, Jewish laws seemed, at least to me, like ethical suggestions rather than obligations. I learned that Judaism was a religion of questioning authority, not a religion of submission. It was only in graduate school, as I prepared to do research with Hasidic Jews, that I read about the history of Reform Judaism, as a legacy of nineteenth-century German Jews' efforts to make Judaism align with emerging European modernity, something it ironically shared with earlier struggles over Jewishness.

What is now called ultra-Orthodoxy was a traditionalist movement that arose in eighteenth-century eastern Europe in response to the rapid social changes modernity provoked.[12] Contemporary ultra-Orthodoxy includes two major strands of Ashkenazic (European) Jewish Orthodoxy, Hasidic and Yeshivish.[13] These were originally opposed to each other, with each claiming traditional authority.[14] After the Holocaust, though, as ultra-Orthodox Jews successfully rebuilt thriving communities in the United States, Canada, South Africa, England, Belgium, and Israel, to name a few places, Hasidic and Yeshivish communities grew less oppositional, especially in contrast to the American rise of Modern Orthodoxy, a denomination that attempted to balance adherence to Jewish law with full participation in the world.

Nevertheless, there remain significant differences between and among Yeshivish and Hasidic ultra-Orthodox Jews. For example, different Hasidic communities who most often trace their lineages to towns and cities in eastern Europe are each led by a rebbe, the spiritual leader of a Hasidic court (*hoyf*). In contrast, Yeshivish communities are organized around a prominent rabbi, a *rosh yeshiva* (head of a yeshiva), and the yeshiva itself. Hasidic and Yeshivish communities are further distinguished by religious practice, education, language, and exposure to the *goyish* (Gentile) world and its media. For more about distinctions between the Hasidic and the Yeshivish, particularly about multilingualism and educational practices, as well as my transcription conventions, see the appendix. The glossary that follows provides definitions of key terms and concepts.

Ultra-Orthodoxy is an admittedly vague and even judgmental term, as in who says who is "ultra" or even Orthodox? Ultra-Orthodoxy also masks important Jewish Orthodox diversity of many kinds. However, I still decided to adopt the term for a number of reasons. First, it is commonly used by many community members themselves.[15] Second, in order to protect the anonymity of those living double lives, I was unable to name particular communities beyond Hasidic or Yeshivish lest I accidently "out" someone, so the wide-ranging, often subtle distinctions among the ultra-Orthodox are somewhat muted here. Third, despite its shortcomings, I have found that the term ultra-Orthodoxy encourages a wider category of analysis than has been common, one that accounts for diversity and debates across Jewish orthodoxies as they happen on the ground. Finally, my use of the term should be understood as an approach to religious life that foregrounds the importance of ethnographically examining competing claims to correct belief (*doxa*), which I consider a form of religious practice (*praxis*). This approach puts struggles over authority front and center, in addition to the more common terrain of religious law, canon, and ritual. This allows me to recuperate the notion of interiority, especially belief or faith, showing that in moments of social change interiority can become public and political, made visible and audible in technology, in writing and reading, and on and through bodily practice.[16]

While there is the ever-present temptation to see ultra-Orthodox Jews as throwbacks to a lost past, as communities that resist modernity, social scientists including myself have unequivocally shown otherwise. Ultra-Orthodox Judaism could exist only in a place and time where religious difference was tolerated, where the structure of the state provided support like food stamps or subsidized housing, which many ultra-Orthodox Jews rely on, and where participation in democracy made the ultra-Orthodox a powerful interest group.

Ultra-Orthodox Jews, as I have argued, are better understood as part of an alternative religious modernity, whose leaders have increasingly used the authority of religious stringency rather than leniency in observance of Jewish law to bolster their claim to Jewish authenticity. An example of religious stringency can be traced through the prosaic example of head coverings. Married women are obligated to cover their hair, and in the 1960s many merely wore a wig over their hair. However, those same women's daughters and granddaughters are now often obligated by male authorities within families, schools, and rabbis to wear wigs covered by a hat or a kerchief. Wigs and hats were merely one way that ultra-Orthodox authorities built more and higher "gates" (*gedorim*) around every aspect of life, hoping to protect their communities from the influence of Gentiles.

Over the past twenty years, those living double lives have tapped into a wider generational backlash of men in their late twenties, thirties, and early forties, Hasidic and Yeshivish, who were frustrated by these religious stringencies, which limited their educational and economic opportunities in what has become a very expensive way of life. Leyzer, a Hasidic double lifer texted me, "What we're seeing now in my generation is a rebellion." He elaborated that he and some of his peers (fourth generation in the United States) were rebelling against leaders who treated them as children, incapable of setting their own moral limits (my translations in brackets):

> Like, first of all, stop telling me that goyim [Gentiles] are all pigs and wanna kill me. Stop telling me that an iPhone is gonna make me burn in hell. Stop telling me that making eye contact with a woman is gonna make me have sex with her. Stop telling me those things because you're disempowering me. You're not allowing me to have choices. Don't tell me that the only thing I can do in this world is to sit and learn [i.e., study Torah and Talmud] . . . it's demasculating [*sic*].

The wider political and social context of this generational rebellion is important for understanding the contemporary crisis of authority. The turn of the twenty-first century brought the end of a generation of important Hasidic rebbes and Yeshivish rabbis born in Europe, who wielded moral authority by dint of charisma and/or their ties to a lost European past. Their death led to public political infighting over succession, with a number of major Hasidic groups in particular splintering off.[17] The very visible and human political machinations over resources, wealth, and power made some ultra-Orthodox, especially certain groups of Hasidim, quite cynical about their once-revered leaders.

This cynicism occurred just as populations, real estate prices, and the cost of everyday life in New York soared. Many men expressed frustration that they had not been prepared to support their large families (birth control was forbidden), including never learning much English or math.[18] Ultra-Orthodox life became increasingly expensive, with private school payments, special clothing, kosher food, and conspicuous displays expected for holidays and frequent family celebrations, such as weddings and bar mitzvahs. Without even high school diplomas and with strict adherence to the Jewish holiday calendar, options for employment were limited if married men did not or could not continue to study Torah full-time. Most relied on work in ultra-Orthodox or Orthodox Jewish businesses or social institutions, while some were self-employed. Women, who often did have high school diplomas, worked as teachers, or in offices or stores, until they had a few children, after which many stayed home with their families. Despite extensive and active ultra-Orthodox charitable organizations (*gmakhim*) and participation in federal and state aid programs, such as food stamps or Section 8 housing, making a living in New York could be a challenge.

Along with economic challenges, public charges of sexual abuse especially in boys' yeshivas, which broke in the Jewish and mainstream presses in 2006, added to a growing disillusionment for some. The coverage followed other exposés of sexual abuse in the Catholic Church, the Boy Scouts, elite private schools, and football teams. An anonymous ultra-Orthodox blogger kept running lists of well-known Hasidic and Yeshivish rabbis accused of impropriety but never prosecuted. The *New York Times* reported on the Brooklyn district attorney's complicity with Agudas Yisroel, the leadership and policy organization of ultra-Orthodox rabbis, to try the accused in their own religious courts. All these cases involved struggles over a great deal of money, public perception, and the political power of some institutions to reject the authority of the federal, state, and municipal legal systems. The broader media coverage, in particular, forced ultra-Orthodox parents to acknowledge that their leaders had put the reputations of accused rabbis before the protection of their children.[19]

The loud and increasingly popular Jewish blogosphere, including such bloggers as DovBear, Rabbi Natan Slifkin, and Hasidic Rebel, mocked and parodied ultra-Orthodox leadership as materialistic, corrupt, and power hungry. As their followers eventually printed out the blogs for them to read, rabbinic leaders, in turn, slowly began to rethink their internet policies, formulated ad hoc in the mid-1990s. Controlling internet access, however, proved more complicated than any other new medium or technology had since the invention of the printing press in Europe centuries before.

The ultra-Orthodox strategy for a new medium of communication has historically been either to transform and control the content or have rabbinic leadership censor it altogether. Every community has its own standards and rules, and often as new media become available, the old media come to seem more "kosher." For example, newspapers, magazines, and novels in Yiddish and English with Jewish content became readily available to all groups from the 1950s on. Television was banned in the 1960s, though many from that time remember watching it at their grandparents' homes. Tape recorders, which were originally forbidden by some Hasidic communities, had become kosher by the time CDs and DVDs made their appearance in the early 2000s.[20] Making a medium of communication Jewish was quite similar to the process of making a language Jewish. Linguistic and technological transformations were possible because of a semiotic ideology, a cultural and religious belief about signs, that almost any medium could be redeemed and put in the service of Jewish intention. In practice, this meant that if a medium (such as novels or CDs) carried Orthodox Jewish content or actually changed its form by adopting Jewish signs (such as using Hebrew letters for English words or a Yiddish accent in English), it could become kosher.

The internet was different. It was difficult to censor, and it remained critical to the growth of ultra-Orthodox communities. Men without degrees, for example, found work in information technology companies; the internet was used for independent small businesses; and federal aid programs could only be accessed online. (Food stamps were accessed online, for example.) Ultra-Orthodox politics and news were increasingly reported online, and shopping, wedding lists, and charities all were shared online. Even ties across national borders among extended families were kept up on social media.

From the 1990s on, there were efforts to make the internet kosher, much as other new media had been uplifted and made Jewish. There were increasingly online Orthodox news sites, inspirational lectures, and all-men's forums where any *kfira* (heresy) was blocked. WhatsApp texting was regularly used by all kinds of families to share invitations and special news. For example, one Hasidic mother sent all of her children, living in Brooklyn and Israel, a weekly WhatsApp message with a picture of a single red rose, reminding them the exact time to light candles and wishing them a joyous, peaceful Shabbes.

Different ultra-Orthodox communities had their own policies about internet use. Lubavitcher Hasidim, for example, were unusual as early adopters of the internet, although they have drawn the line recently at social media, such as Facebook for girls. Satmar Hasidim, in contrast, tried to limit the internet to men's "business" (i.e., work) in offices and keep it out of homes. Yeshivish Jews were much more open to the internet initially, as they have been to other innovations. More recently, however, Yeshivish activists in Lakewood, New Jersey, have become the center of efforts to control the internet through their organization, Ichud Ha-Kehillos LeTohar HaMachane (Union of Communities for the Purity of the Camp). Since 2006, they have been holding rallies against the internet and its dangers to *emuna*. They also developed a well-funded filtering service, Technology Awareness Group (TAG), that anyone owning a smartphone was increasingly expected to adopt. All of this anti-internet activism was good for the ultra-Orthodox economy, since it created new jobs for ultra-Orthodox men and revenue streams from filtering, which had become a requirement for any parents wishing to send their children to ultra-Orthodox schools.

The time period of my research was particularly volatile, when Hasidic and Yeshivish leadership began to join forces to try to control the internet, especially smartphones. By the mid-2000s, many began to equate the internet, embodied in the material object of the smartphone, with outside contamination that led to the slippery slope of religious doubt, part of the wider fear that more and more were leaving ultra-Orthodoxy. I first learned about the crisis of faith and its relationship to the internet when I met Toby through a mutual friend. Originally, we had planned to discuss my first book, which she had just read. Instead, we ended up talking about her double life and the wider crisis of faith, something I had never heard of despite my years of fieldwork. I realized then that ultra-Orthodoxy was changing in all kinds of ways, and I wanted to know more.

Ethnographic Collaborators or "Guinea Pigs"?

Writing about secrets, authority, and the internet shaped how I conducted ethnographic research. Anthropologist Graham Jones, writing about secrecy, notes that anthropology as a discipline is itself premised on the revelation of secret or invisible knowledge to its readers, which gives anthropologists their own kind of authority.[21] I would add to this that conducting research "at home," which for me was also New York City, in shared online and in-person spaces added other layers to the politics of fieldwork, discussed by so many other anthropologists.[22] These included who defines what constitutes data and the object of study; responsibility for ethical representation; and the problematics of collaboration between anthropologists and those with whom they work.

A conflict—the crisis of *emuna*—organizes this book, and it also shaped my fieldwork. Many sociological and anthropological accounts of ultra-Orthodoxy have tended to portray discrete, bounded communities rather than the messy actuality of urban movement and diversity. In contrast, I followed networks of friends, relatives, and professionals; I crossed lines of ultra-Orthodoxy and Orthodoxy when and where they did.[23] Many, though not all, of the double lifers I got to know were Hasidic, including the very different groups or "courts" of Satmar, Pupa, Belz, Lubavitch, and Bobov. Most often, those who tried to help double lifers were Yeshivish or Modern Orthodox rabbis, educators, and therapists. To protect anonym-

ity, I do not use the real names of any people I met (except two public
figures) or the names of specific Hasidic groups, and I have changed all
personal details or kept some of them intentionally vague, especially ultra-
Orthodox New York neighborhoods and double lifers' jobs and educational paths. I am always aware that my primary mandate must be to write
in a way that does not compromise anyone's double life.

The crisis of *emuna* was lived in online and face-to-face spaces, which
meant my research crossed those boundaries too, which is not at all un-
common in anthropological research. Many anthropologists these days
include posts from social media in their ethnographies, while some con-
duct fieldwork exclusively online. Digital fieldwork, especially with a
smartphone, does erase any lingering illusions of the discreteness of home
and the field, something I experienced, for example, watching a Hasidic
music video posted on Facebook in between making dinner or writing
this book.

Anthropologist Tom Boellstorff suggests—and my experience supports
this—that ethnography in online spaces is not that different from fieldwork in person.[24] However, there were times I wondered what kind of
fieldwork spending time on Facebook or texting on WhatsApp actually
was. What exactly was I observing and participating in when I responded
to someone's blog or read as a comment thread unfolded? Digital material
has its own insights and limitiations, as do, of course, field notes taken
after participating in an event or an audio-recorded interview. To clarify
these different kinds of data I initially decided to focus on the medium that
both the digital and the face-to-face share: language, written, printed, or
spoken. However, I quickly realized that while language was certainly important, what was more interesting was the ways that language intersected
with other semiotic forms, such as material culture, the body, and practices (like skiing or having a beer). To account for this wider semiotic lens,
I drew on writing in popular magazines, on blogs and social media, as well
as participant observation in real life events, interviews (often with the
same people over years), formal lectures, rallies, conferences, celebrations, and also embodied and material forms of social life, such as clothing
or children's anti-internet trading cards. I came to understand that while
the internet was indeed a new medium for the twenty-first century, the
ultra-Orthodox world had struggled with new media in prior historical
eras, each with its potential for introducing heretical ideas and challenging
existing structures of authority. I recorded and transcribed where I could,
which was primarily in public events and individual interviews. When I
quote people's speech it was either in a text, recorded speech, or occasion-

ally, reproduced from memory in my field notes. By integrating field notes, transcriptions, and digital data, mine is an account of life-changing doubt where and how it was lived.

The ultra-Orthodox faithful and those living double lives each had their own agenda for my research and its eventual publication as a book. The ultra-Orthodox who tried to help those with doubt did not want to expose their methods or even the existence of doubt to public scrutiny, non-Jewish or Jewish. As one ultra-Orthodox life coach told me, she did not want to "air dirty laundry," especially to someone who was not ultra-Orthodox, a fact about myself that she quickly sussed out when she asked what my husband did (he's a television producer). I turned instead to publicly available recorded and live events, which were plentiful. In contrast, many professional religious therapists were curious about my research, generously opening up their conferences, seminars, and listservs.

Those living double lives had different investments. Many hoped my research might show them to be moral people with legitimate intellectual doubts, not mentally ill or in thrall to their evil inclinations. Others hoped a book might help bring about social change to ultra-Orthodoxy itself. Their investments made access to double-life networks surprisingly easy. Some had already read my first book and as autodidacts were interested in talking to a professor. Others told me that an interview was like therapy, offering relief in narrating their lives. They referred me to their friends and even some of their still-religious kin, who had their own reasons for agreeing to speak with me. There were some living double lives who refused to talk with me or come to events if I was there. For years, for example, I tried to gain access to a closed Facebook group for those living double lives. There were, I was told by an insider, discussions about me, but some did not want any outsiders on the site. One person posted, "I don't want to be a guinea pig," a refrain I heard in various guises at many other events I attended.

As I began to get to know a loose network of double lifers, our relationship changed from anthropologist and her "informants" to a kind of collaboration. To avoid being "guinea pigs," those living double lives took the lead in our encounters, and I followed. When, for example, I realized that the circulating posts on WhatsApp groups would be rich places for ethnography, I asked Zalman if he would invite me to join a group of his. In fact, I asked many times. Finally, his girlfriend said to him, "Have pity on the poor woman." So Zalman made a mirror group of one of his groups, naming it "WhatsAppville Yinglish." He used an icon of a woman, who even looked a little like me, listening at her computer.

Later he changed the image to two Hasidic men in deep conversation.

Description
Genizeh for Yinglish Cultural Ongoings and Trends
Sharable on Social Media

Zalman introduced the group this way (my translations):

1/7/14, 12:41:43 PM: This is a group to copy and paste text and WhatsApp messages as it is used in Hassidic circles, from simche [celebration] and fundraising announcements, personal or group communications (as much as you feel comfortable sharing, with personal information omitted), to messages making the rounds on news and gossip in the community. From Yiddish to yinglish to English, in both Hebrew and English characters. Ayala would be looking at both the language and subject matter. Please advise if you wish to leave the group. Any additional members joining would have to be agreed upon by all members. Feel free to simply say, "I would rather not," no explanations necessary.

In effect, those on WhatsAppville Yinglish curated the messages, images, audio, and video they received from their own WhatsApp groups, along with their commentary for my research purposes and for themselves too. Members controlled my access by choosing what they felt was meaningful to post or repost, much as people do in face-to-face interviews. WhatsAppville Yinglish members created, then, a digital public, what Zalman described on the icon as a *geniza* (a repository for written Hebrew texts) of about fifteen people, a living window onto what they considered the wider ultra-Orthodox public and its critics, as they interacted among themselves and with me.

WhatsAppville was an ongoing resource to the research. I crowd-sourced questions, bounced around ideas, and tested hypotheses. When, for example, I got interested in Hasidic theological ideas of the soul, I had a group of thoughtful and knowledgeable Hasidic men and women to ask. I also got to know many of the group members in person, interviewing and hanging out with some. The members of WhatsAppville kept me on my toes, reminding me that they were never guinea pigs. For example, in the exchange below, Shmuel and Motti joke (sort of), that they were "studying" me too, echoing back my own words I had used to reassure them:

> [1/21/2016, 9:06 AM] Shmuel: Ayala, what you don't know is that we're also amateur anthropologists studying anthropologists.
> [1/21/2016, 9:19 AM] Ayala: Shmuel I'm afraid!
> [1/21/2016, 10:24 AM] Shmuel: 😜 🤪
> [1/21/2016, 10:37 AM] Motti: Don't worry, Ayala. We'll show you everything we want to publish beforehand.
> [1/21/2016, 11:02 AM] Ayala: Witty!
> [1/21/2016, 11:04 AM] Motti: 😜

Sometimes those I worked with disagreed with my analyses or writing choices. This was even true of the term "double life" that I decided to use (except in the title) after much deliberation. Some of those on Whats-Appville Yinglish and beyond complained that they did not like the term because it had "duplicitous connotations." At the same time, others did not feel that the increasingly common "ITC" (in the closet) completely represented their experience either, given its provenance in LGBTQ communities. Only Yiddish-speaking Hasidim used the term *bahaltena apikorsim* (hidden heretics) or the abbreviation אנ״ש (אנש׳ שלומנו, mean-ing "us" or "people like us"). I learned from Dovid that in Israel, the He-brew term *anusim* (the forced), that is, forced to be religious, was used. My own experience was that despite many people's ambivalence, the term "double life" was quite common, for both Hasidic and Yeshivish ultra-Orthodox. I decided to use it since I felt it foregrounded the moral complexities of lived experience when what you believe no longer aligns with what you do. As for the "duplicitous connotations," I would just note, as the Urban Dictionary does, that spies and lovers lead double lives, but so do superheroes.

In my efforts to collaborate and always aware of the primacy of protect-ing anonymity, I asked two double lifers, Shmuel and Chavi, to read drafts of talks and articles before I went public. I realized how important this kind of collaboration would be when once, at an academic lecture I gave, I accidentally "outed" someone, in my anxiety to acknowledge his contribution. The ensuing conflict ended our relationship, since the person immediately heard about the slip from a community member at the talk, who posted about it on that same closed Facebook group, where it then blew up. After that, Shmuel agreed to read a draft of this whole book to ensure that no one's identity would be compromised, and of course, to give all kinds of feedback. In fact, over the years I have gotten messages on Facebook and WhatsApp, and phone calls, asking me how the book was going, wondering when it was going to be published, or in some cases worried that my account of religious therapy might be too negative. I remain very aware, as I write, that double lifers and those who try to help them will be carefully reading, though of course, this account of the crisis of authority remains my own.

Cast of Main Characters and a Road Map

I talked to and spent time with all kinds of ultra-Orthodox and Orthodox Jews, but a smaller circle of friends became key figures. Many in this circle were also at some point on WhatsAppville Yinglish and often spent time together. **Shmuel**, for example, a Yeshivish intellectual, seemed to know everybody and everything. **Zalman**, the OTD Hasid I mentioned, was a similarly well-known figure in double life and OTD circles, especially friendly with double lifers **Leyzer**, **Boruch**, **Menashe**, and **Shimon**. There were long-term double-life Hasidic couples who had "flipped" their spouse, like **Tamar** and her husband or **Pinny** and his wife, and long-term double-life lovers, like **Blimi** and **Moishy**, each married to still-religious spouses, feeling they had the best of all possible worlds. Some couples were unhappily in "mixed marriages" with a still-religious spouse, like **Dovid** and **Shoshana**, **Miriam** and her husband, and **Tsiri** and **Aron**. Some women, like **Chavi, Toby, Sheyndie,** or **Esty**, looked outside of their communities for fulfillment of different kinds, including higher education. **Yitsy, Motti, Yonah,** and **Gavriel** were Hasidic male friends who all hung out regularly. Chavi had a traumatic experience with religious therapists, outreach rabbis, and life coaches, as did Miriam, Esty, and Pinny. **Leyeh** was Toby's teenage daughter, who had a lot to say about her mother's longtime double life.

I also got to know a number of religious therapists well, one of whom, **Nosson**, had experienced life-changing doubt himself. **Eitan** was a well-trained Yeshivish therapist who was critical of the system, while never losing his faith. **Dr. Rosenberg**, a Modern Orthodox psychologist, patiently answered many questions despite our never meeting in person, and his comments on the listserv were always informative. **Rabbi Tessler** figures prominently and is an influential and very well-known psychiatrist and rabbi. Shimon, who felt hurt by an extended exchange with him, asked that I use the rabbi's real name, but I decided that would be both inconsistent and unethical. I frequently cite a column by **Mashy Blum** in *Mishpacha* magazine as public musings on the dilemmas of religious therapy. Finally, I was able to talk with two life coaches, the Lubavitcher **Mrs. Klein**, and Modern Orthodox **Coach Levine**, each of whom so generously shared their insights.

The book is divided into two parts. Part I follows the trajectory of the crisis of authority as it has been unfolding over struggles about the internet. From the turn of the twenty-first century to 2019, I tack between perspectives of those living double lives and rabbinic leadership. Chapter 2 ethnographically traces the contemporary crisis of authority to the Jewish blogosphere in the mid-2000s, which created an alternative, anonymous heretical public both online and in person. This public referenced an earlier crisis of authority, the Jewish Enlightenment (mid-eighteenth to mid-nineteenth centuries in Europe), when a generation of Jewish men exposed to the European Enlightenment used innovations in print culture to take on traditional Judaism and its leadership. Chapter 3 follows contemporary rabbinic leaders, who increasingly blamed the crisis of authority on an external Gentile medium: the internet, particularly social media. In public rallies and printed edicts, they declared that the internet corrupted innately pure Jewish souls, leaving them unable to fight their own inclinations for evil and infecting them with invisible doubt. To protect the faithful and preserve the coming generations, rabbinic leaders attempted to leverage schools and mothers to enforce emerging standards for kosher filtering, which simultaneously reinforced existing male hierarchies of authority.

Part II focuses on the experience of life-changing doubt and its implications for families, friends, religious authorities, and institutions. Chapter 4 turns to the diversity of those living life-changing doubt and their still-religious spouses, especially the distinctive experiences and implications for men and women. Double lifers elaborated and navigated a changing morality influenced by liberal values, often in conflict with the ultra-Orthodox morality of their still-religious spouse and children. Chapter 5 follows those whose life-changing doubt was discovered by or confessed to a spouse and the therapeutic professionals who tried to help them, especially Jewish life coaches, outreach rabbis, and religious therapists. The profession of religious therapy was itself in the midst of a moral struggle as to which authorities they owed their allegiance: their own religious orthodoxy or their clients' individual autonomy.

Chapter 6 recounts the secret social lives of double lifers as they experimented with other ways of living, writing, and feeling in digital and face-to-face spaces. The inescapable changes these experiments wrought on exterior forms—on bodies and clothing, in writing or speaking—were efforts by those living double lives to feel more comfortable in their own skins and hints to their loved ones that they were slowly changing inside. Chapter 7 focuses on the moral implications for children of parents living double lives. Despite keeping their life-changing doubt secret, double life parents often tried to subtly introduce new ideas to offer their children more of a "choice" than they had had. This led to ethical and emotional dilemmas, especially for ultra-Orthodox teenagers.

I have spent many years as a mostly secular Jewish anthropologist attempting to understand ultra-Orthodox life in New York, the city where I was born and brought up and have now, with my husband, brought up our own two children. This led to the intellectual questions I explore in this book, such as what and who defines moral responsibility; how age and gender shape ethical judgment; what the politics of ethnographic fieldwork are in shared online and face-to-face spaces; how media of many sorts—bodies, languages and technologies, material culture—can create publics with their own authorities; and the ways that new digital media might actually be changing human interactions, expression, and concentration as we know it.

But there are emotional questions at play too. The stories of those living double lives and those who minister to them are about moral struggles over change—generational, technological, spiritual, intellectual—and they are filled with human pain, contradictions, and unexpected discoveries. My hope is that they speak to a wide audience, as they have so eloquently to me, so that this particular historical moment in Jewish ultra-Orthodoxy might provoke conversations about the moral ambiguities of humans attempting to live ethical lives in the digital age, whatever and wherever those might be.

PART I

2

The Jewish Blogosphere and
the Heretical Counterpublic

In 2011 *Ami Magazine*, an ultra-Orthodox English-language publication, put out an article that many readers found shocking, entitled "Imposters among Us." The pseudonymous author, Rafael Borges, warned readers about an invisible threat lurking in the ranks of the ultra-Orthodox: men who were "externally ultra-*frum* [religious]" but who had "sworn off the basic tenets of Jewish belief." Borges called them the "Orthoprax" because though they practiced Jewish Orthodoxy, they no longer believed it to be true.

As ultra-Orthodox rabbinic leadership was increasingly doing, Borges blamed the internet for Orthopraxy, calling it "a breeding ground for an ominous rebellion against the Torah." He compared the contemporary Orthoprax and digital technology to mid-eighteenth- and nineteenth-century European *maskilim* (Jewish Enlighteners), who, influenced by European Enlightenment philosophy and literature, experimented with writing and print technology to critique rabbinic leaders and the nascent Hasidic movement:

> The old-time *apikorsus* [heresy] has been updated for the 21st century because of new technology that has made covertness much easier for those harboring and espousing heretical views, and yeshivas and *kol-lels* [yeshivas for married men] . . . are not more immune from these fifth-columnists than they were in Europe.[1]

Ironically, many men living double lives also invoked the Jewish Enlightenment, calling themselves *maskilim* too, though for very different reasons. They claimed that they, just like the European *maskilim* before them, were developing the "purest form" of Judaism, which they contrasted to the extremism of what they called today's "Taliban Judaism."[2]

In long talks with Shmuel, Zalman, Toby, and others, I learned that the connection between secret life-changing doubt and the internet began roughly in 2002–2003, when disillusioned Modern Orthodox and ultra-Orthodox Jews began to blog. The Jewish blogosphere or "Jblogosphere," as it came to be called, gave anonymous public voice to a range of private, interior life-changing doubt. Not all Jbloggers lived double lives, but many did, so that writing and reading on the Jblogs in English, Yeshivish, and Yiddish came to mediate life-changing doubt. By "mediate" I mean the processes by which invisible life-changing doubt was made visible and audible, discursive and public.[3] Over time, posts on the Jblogs, along with buzzing comment threads and eventual in-person meet-ups, created invisible networks of secret doubters across digital and face-to-face spaces. The Jblogosphere became an increasingly loud heretical site until roughly 2009, when many moved their conversations over to social media, just as the rest of the world did.

The Jblogosphere set the stage for the contemporary crisis of authority. Jblogs formed what I call a "heretical counterpublic," that is, a marginalized group's assertion of an alternative discourse in conflict with the dominant public sphere. All modern life is made up of many such publics and counterpublics.[4] In this case, the Jblogosphere created a heretical discourse that attacked the ultra-Orthodox religious public sphere, those real and imagined spaces controlled by male hierarchies of religious authority, who claimed the right to interpret God's will for their followers. As Shmuel, himself a prominent blogger back in the day, remembered, "Before maybe you were thinking this, maybe your friend or your neighbor was thinking this, but now here are these hundreds of people. Who are they? It was like a sucker punch to the solar plexis for the rabbis."[5] Women were less prominent in this heretical counterpublic, unofficially limited to observing and commenting from the sidelines, much as they were in the ultra-Orthodox religious public sphere. Men had easier access to computers, were fluent in Jewish religious scholarship, and were more comfortable expressing themselves in public. Some women living double lives or those with doubts read and posted comments, however, only a handful had their own blogs, and even fewer met up in real life. They had, some told me, too much to lose, especially custody of their children if their husbands divorced them (see chapters 4 and 6).

Men's blogging was particularly threatening to rabbinic authority because of the central place of Jewish male literacy in Orthodox life. Men's Torah study—their reading of sacred *loshn koydesh* (holy language, ancient Hebrew and Aramaic) texts and commentaries of the sages discussed with a partner—is fulfillment of their covenant with God (*avoyda* or *avoda*), and as such it hastens the coming of the messiah. However, Jbloggers who participated in the heretical counterpublic "wasted time that could have been spent studying Torah" (*bitl toyre*). Worse, they used that wasted time to challenge ultra-Orthodox authority with posts that undermined criticized, parodied, and mocked rabbinic leadership. As one prominent Jblogger, Hasidic Rebel, posted in 2003, "Today's Chasidic Rebbes are of no stronger moral character than the rest of us, the piety attributed to them is a farce, and their learnedness and scholarship is for the most part unimpressive." In secret and without consulting a rabbi, Jbloggers relied on their individual authority to explore different truths and forbidden knowledge with other kindred spirits. Equally troubling was that many Jbloggers' posts were in the familiar languages and discourse of learned ultra-Orthodox men, but the content and intent smacked of questioning, doubting, engagement with secular knowledge, and individual transformation. In a way, the Jblogs were leading a linguistic kind of double life just like the "imposters": they looked ultra-Orthodox on the outside, but they were heretical on the inside. The familiar languages and forms of interaction used on the new medium of the blog to express life-changing doubt ultimately challenged ultra-Orthodox understandings of digital technology, language, and mediation itself.[6]

As the crisis of authority gathered force over a decade, Jbloggers living double lives and rabbinic authorities both appealed to shared ultra-Orthodox beliefs about the arc of Jewish history, tradition, and the nature of humanity, but they came to different conclusions. For some, writing and reading online loosened their ties of religious obligation, leading them to embrace different truths with their own form of authority.[7] In contrast, for rabbinic leadership the medium of the blog became the message:[8] digital technology posed a threat to the very existence of Jewish ultra-Orthodoxy. Over time, the unruly heretical counterpublic made it increasingly clear to Jbloggers and rabbis that there were, indeed, "imposters" among them.

The Morality of Time, Tradition, and New Technologies of Communication

Both double lifers and rabbinic authorities compared the contemporary crisis of faith to the Jewish Enlightenment in central and eastern Europe, asserting historical continuities and revisiting old battles over claims to Jewish Orthodoxy. In fact, both the contemporary period and the Jewish Enlightenment were historical moments of technological, political, linguistic, and religious change, so the parallel was apt. In particular, Jbloggers and Jewish Enlighteners were each living in times with unprecedented opportunities for participation in the non-Jewish world and access to diverse bodies of knowledge. This led both to experiment with language choice, genre, and literary style to address expanding reading publics, thanks to changes in technologies of communication, print or digital.

An implicit shared ideology about time and tradition undergirded contemporary comparisons to the Jewish Enlightenment. The alternative modernity of today's ultra-Orthodox Judaism was premised, in part, on the moral decay of each successive generation, since each was further removed from the moment of divine revelation at Mount Sinai; the concept is called *yerides ha-doyres*, decline of the generations. This understanding of history inverted modernist ideologies of progress with its freedom from coercive authority. Instead, contemporary ultra-Orthodox Jews described freedom as a selfish, immature lack of discipline. In this regressive notion of history, frequently invoked with rosy glasses as a destroyed, pre-Holocaust eastern European shtetl (small town), all Jews in the past, even the heretics, were at a higher moral level. Simultaneously, another version of history circulated, one that conflated all threats to Jewish existence regardless of time or place. For example, biblical Egypt, the Jewish Enlightenment, the later twentieth-century secularizing European Jewish youth movements and radical politics, and even the Holocaust were all equivalencies in that they threatened the Jewish people. That is why contemporary ultra-Orthodox rabbinic leadership could assert that the new medium of the internet was actually not that new at all; it was just their particular generational challenge, their *nisoyen ha-dor*, and those doing the challenge were not even at the same level of past heretics.

Jbloggers, in contrast, aligned themselves with *maskilim* and the Jewish Enlightenment in their eagerness to prove that their life-changing doubt was an intellectual critique of the system and did not stem from emotional problems or uncontrolled lusts. That is, double-life bloggers positioned themselves with what all ultra-Orthodox Jews agreed was a morally superior generation of critics from a morally superior time. Me-nashe, a member of WhatsApp Yinglish, defined today's *maskil* for me, "A thinker, a cynic, someone learned, not accepting the haredi [ultra-Orthodox] narrative or dogma. . . . Maskilim today like those in the past were Jews in their own way, not abandoning religion or their communities at least outwardly."

Jbloggers used some of the very same literary forms, genres, and lan-guage choices as Jewish Enlighteners had to express their changing sen-sibilities. With their individualized, reflexive voices, Jblogs were strik-ingly similar to the new autobiographical writing of Jewish Enlighteners in the context of the emergence of the modern subject. This was not by chance. Shmuel told me that many Jbloggers actually read these old au-tobiographies and came to feel a real kinship with their authors. The En-lightenment autobiographies were readily available in Brooklyn Jewish bookstores, where rows upon rows of religious texts could provide a cover for men to safely explore and hang out. In fact, frequenting Jewish bookstores was much more socially acceptable than going to the public library, which everyone knew was a dangerous, forbidden place stuffed with heretical books.

Gendered language, then and now, shaped access to and participation in heretical counterpublics. Despite male *maskilim*'s knowledge of Yiddish and *loshn koydesh*, the majority chose to write either in a European lan-guage (German, Polish, or Russian) or a unique variety of Hebrew they created as a modern link to a glorious lost civilization. Their language choices should be understood in the context of cultural beliefs about lan-guages and what they are good for, what are called "language ideologies."[9] Jewish Enlighteners in Europe were writing at a time of nation building when languages were believed to convey the spirit of a people. One of the aims of the Jewish Enlightenment was to redefine Jews and Judaism as a people, a nation like any other, with its own literary heritage, as historian Marcus Moseley explains.[10] Yiddish was considered a *zhargon* (jargon, not a real language) and the *loshn koydesh* of the Torah was considered a sa-cred language, not suitable for individual expression in modern literary genres. Of course, this had consequences for participation, again, since women had less access to Hebrew of any sort.[11] One of the first Jewish Enlightenment autobiographies, for example, was by a prominent and in-fluential German Jewish *maskil*, Solomon Maimon, who chose to write his *Lebensgeschichte* (1792) in German, explicitly modelled after the autobiog-raphy of the Enlightenment philosopher Rousseau. Inspired by Maimon, the Vilna *maskil* Mordekhai Aharon Ginsburg later wrote *Avi'ezer* (1863), a Hebrew-language autobiography, which established the genre. It included critiques of traditional Jewish institutions of socialization, an account of religious doubt that led to conflicting beliefs and practice, and an eventual crisis of faith brought on by exposure to European Enlightenment reading and writing.[12]

Jblogs were similar to Jewish Enlighteners' autobiographies in content and form. Jbloggers also chronicled their negative experiences in ultra-Orthodox institutions. For example, Shaigetz (a negative word for a Gentile or a Jew who looks/acts like a Gentile) wrote in October 2007:

> My years in yeshiva in Israel were the most miserable of my life. . . . The study of Talmud, although in fact difficult enough to be a satisfying challenge, was carried out under such duress and with such dogmatic simplicity that I spent every waking moment dreaming of what I would do when I was old enough to assert my independence and live in the way I saw fit.

Like *maskilim*, Jbloggers also posted about their doubts and questions and their crises of faith, similarly brought on by their reading in secular science, biblical criticism, and psychology.

Jbloggers' language choices were significant too, but distinctive from that of *maskilim,* since languages and their ideologies had shifted significantly in contemporary New York. The establishment of the State of Israel with its own secular variety of Modern Hebrew (*ivrit*) made Hebrew not suitable for ultra-Orthodox Jewish sensibilities (although some used *loshn koydesh* to write poetry). Instead, the majority of Jbloggers, who were Yeshivish, chose to write in their vernaculars, standard English and Yeshivish English, to reach across Jewish audiences and inhabit new ways of being, even while they referenced their deep knowledge of religious texts and comfortable ultra-Orthodox Jewish male ways of interacting. For some Hasidic Jbloggers, in contrast, there was ambivalence to their own Hasidic Yiddish and its limitations for secular expression, very much like *maskilim*'s dismissive attitudes to Yiddish in the mid-nineteenth century.[13] However, this has been changing with the development of what I call "Enlightened Hasidic Yiddish," written on social media and beyond, something I discuss more below and in chapter 6.

Technological innovations of the day and the politics surrounding them were critical catalysts for the production and spread or suppression of new genres of writing in mid- to late nineteenth-century eastern Europe and twenty-first-century New York. The material qualities of each technology—print or digital media—what are called its affordances, shaped (not determined) how people used them.[14] During the Jewish Enlightenment published books, printed pamphlets, journals, chapbooks, and handwritten letters circulated across geographic distances among growing networks of European Jews of many sorts, feeding the growing consumer market for texts along with new privatized reading practices. Various government censorship of Jewish publishing houses, as well as internal struggles over Judaism (e.g., the Hasidic movement, the Haskalah) further constrained or encouraged production and circulation of texts.[15] Blogs similarly created anonymous, international networks of readers and writers, but they were produced much more quickly than printed texts and were easily accessible to anyone with a computer. Further, the blogs included comment threads, where readers could debate and interact in real time. With the availability of free templates, like Blogger or WordPress in the early 2000s, blogging became even more accessible, so that anyone with very basic computer skills could set up a blogging account, which led to the surge in participation in blogging more generally.[16] However, distinctions among Jbloggers were important. There were differences of religious orthodoxy, linguistic fluencies, and gender, which all shaped the ways that the heretical counterpublic took on the authority of ultra-Orthodox rabbis to be moral arbiters of truth.

The Authority to Control Knowledge

Yeshivish and Modern Orthodox Jewish bloggers, who initially had fewer restrictions against technology than Hasidic Jews, began to post blogs in reaction to banned books and rabbinic sexual abuse scandals reported in Jewish and mainstream media. In this way, the new medium of the blog was a way to express dissatisfaction with rabbinic control of media more generally, especially censorship of ideas by the powerful, whose hypocrisy had proven them to be corrupt. For example, one of the early bloggers was Failed Messiah, a Lubavitch returnee to the faith (*baal tshuva* or BT), who was disillusioned by, among other things, the ongoing sexual abuse scandals. His blog had a running public list (a "wall") of rabbis accused of sexual abuse, who had never been prosecuted but were instead either moved to other yeshivas or even allowed to continue where they were. In a few cases, charged rabbis were moved out of the country altogether to avoid prosecution. Failed Messiah fashioned himself as a watchdog for the wider Orthodox and ultra-Orthodox, providing information on predators that he felt was being covered up by ultra-Orthodox rabbinic leadership.

It was this same rabbinic leadership who had the authority—according to some Jbloggers unjustifiable authority—to control access to innovative religious interpretations and secular knowledge. For example, Rabbi Natan Slifkin wrote an English-language book, which attempted to reconcile Torah with evolution. Soon after, a large group of predominantly Yeshivish ultra-Orthodox rabbis publicly banned the book as heresy.[17]

In response to the censorship of Slifkin's book, a blogger named Not the Gadol HaDor (Not the great leader of the generation), who unbeknownst to Slifkin turned out to be his own brother, began posting critiques of what he defined as Jewish "fundamentalism." Shmuel told me that Not the Gadol HaDor devoted a lot of space to defending Slifkin and "wrote withering satire of the ultra-Orthodox rabbis." Ultimately, Not the Gadol HaDor had a very public crisis of faith, which he blogged about. For example, in 2005 he wrote (my translations):

> My mind has reached the point where it is holding with fairly equal tenacity on to two conflicting sets of ideas. One set of ideas is skeptical, rational, logical and cynical and is not particularly prone to believe in any mumbo jumbo. The other set of ideas, a culmination of a lifelong absorption in Orthodoxy, with a good portion of that spent in the Yeshivah world, is all about Torah, Avodah [service], Gemillus Chassadim [acts of loving kindness]. A long term liveable situation?

Shmuel remarked to me, "Many people, especially the closeted Orthodox . . . flocked to this blog. . . . He was one of the stars of the Jblogosphere . . . and he and his blog were a source of consternation . . . to establishment types."

Blogs are linguistic artefacts, not only technological ones. Yeshivish blogs, for example, were written in standard English with influence from Yiddish grammar and incorporation of religious Hebrew terms, sometimes translated but more often not, much as Yeshivish Jews speak. Beyond language choice, posts on blogs were often intricate talmudic-like, logical argumentation about science, Torah, faith, and Jewish history. Bloggers referenced the Jewish writings of Rav Kook, Maimonides, the Kuzari proof,[18] and even modern Jewish thinkers like Rabbi Abraham Joshua Heschel, along with Western philosophers and scientists. To an outsider like myself, the Yeshivish blogs seemed like an unlikely coffee klatch of men in yeshivas talking with graduate students in philosophy. I actually had a hard time following some of the posts with their references to insider talmudic legal debates, histories, and concepts, rarely translated or explained. These kinds of posts hinted that Jbloggers were having lively debates among themselves about Jewish Orthodoxy even as some were simultaneously reading skeptic Mormon blogs or the parallel Islamic blogosphere.

Perhaps the sense of a digital yeshiva space, where Orthodox men argued over *loshn koydesh* texts in English, made blogs feel like Orthodox Jewish male public space, even if it was heretical. For example, one of the early Yeshivish bloggers, DovBear, imagined his blog as a virtual ultra-Orthodox Sabbath table; his innovation was to include the voices of those critical of ultra-Orthodoxy, which were generally silenced through censorship and social pressure. He posted (my translations), "Please consider this blog, for lack of a better metaphor, a very large *shabbos* [Sabbath] table, where we sit together and discuss the *parsha* [weekly Torah portion], the news, and other events of the day." Note that women at ultra-Orthodox Sabbath tables rarely if ever discuss the *parsha*; they are busy listening, serving food, and cleaning up. Nevertheless, the virtual male space of the Jblogs was amplified for men and women readers by the material properties of the new medium.

The Affordances of Blogging for the Heretical Counterpublic

The affordances of the Jblogs included anonymity, gendered pseudonyms, standardized spatial organization, and for Hasidic Jews, the use of gendered varieties of language. These affordances allowed Jbloggers living double lives to express the changes they were going through, while hiding their identities, though many nodded ironically to them in their pseudonyms or "niks." For example, a Hasidic blogger I discuss below called himself Shtreimel, which is Yiddish for the high fur hat worn by Hasidic married men on holidays and the Sabbath. One of the few Hasidic women

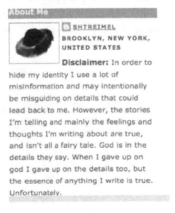

About Me

SHTREIMEL
BROOKLYN, NEW YORK, UNITED STATES

Disclaimer: In order to hide my identity I use a lot of misinformation and may intentionally be misguiding on details that could lead back to me. However, the stories I'm telling and mainly the feelings and thoughts I'm writing about are true, and isn't all a fairy tale. God is in the details they say. When I gave up on god I gave up on the details too, but the essence of anything I write is true. Unfortunately.

bloggers' pseudonym was Shpitzle Shtrimpkind—a *shpitsl* is a piece of rolled up material worn under a headscarf for married Hasidic women, giving the illusion of hair; *shtrimp* are stockings; and *kind* is a child (alluding to Astrid Lindgren's *Pippi Longstocking*). These kinds of inside jokes or references contributed to the sense that there was a vital heretical coun-

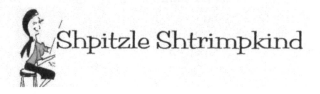

terpublic of others, which reassured double lifers that they were neither alone nor crazy.

The organization of the Jblogs created a visibly recognizable genre of heretical blogging. Most used a freely available blog template, Blogger, with a heading, a gendered pseudonym with a subheading, and a short "about me" section with a contact email on the lower corner of the page. For example, one of the few to blog in Hasidic Yiddish, Katle Kanye's pseudonym (meaning idiot or fool) was in Hebrew orthography and included the subheading in Yiddish, which he translated (at my request), "Merry like a hasid, ponderous like a *maskil*, angsty like a human." All blog

posts were journal-like entries with titles and dates. They were written in the first person, except when short fiction was posted or a poem. There were also archives of previous posts, generally by year and month on the side, creating an archive of postings.[19]

Below the archives were links to other blogs, the majority of which were also ultra-Orthodox double lifers or those who had left altogether, marked by names like Frum Heretic. This made the counterpublic a space of what literary critic Michael Warner calls, "stranger-sociability," that is, the blogs were a digital site to write and read postings that were very intimate, but in their anonymity, impersonal.[20] The ability of readers to link to other blogs created a sense of shared community despite the necessity for this anonymity. As blogger Hasidic Rebel explained to me, "I encountered it [the Jblogosphere] mostly when it encountered me. When I started blogging, lots of other blogs linked to me, and there were cross-blog conversations, which made me feel part of a community rather than just a lone voice." The organization of blogs, especially the links, gave the sense that individualized postings spoke for a bigger counterpublic, an anonymous yet critical mass of heretics and doubters.

Postings on the Jblogosphere in the mid-2000s got to be so popular that they began to seep into ultra-Orthodox spaces too. For example, in 2013 the Hasidic blogger Shtreimel wrote about his own nostalgia for the "blogging of yore, when posts generated comments in the 100's. Back when posts were talked about in *shul* [synagogue], in *mikve* [here, men's ritual baths], and even at family *shabbos* tables." Blogs circulated beyond computer screens to penetrate some of the most sacred ultra-Orthodox, male-dominated spaces, private and public.

As the Jblogs spread, Hasidic rebbes, who were not (officially) online, slowly became aware of the growing heretical counterpublic. Shmuel remembered hearing about advisers to Hasidic rabbis and rebbes who resorted to printing out physical copies of the Jblogs in order to alert them to the scope of the threat that the heretical counterpublic was beginning to pose. This led some to mock rabbis' and rebbes' very notions of the dangers of heretical reading. For example, in 2009, Jblogger Baal Habos wrote this sarcastic post (translations are mine):

> I once had a rebbi in bes medresh [synagogue], who often stated that Kefira [heresy] Material, anything that contradicts the Torah, is like a hole in the head. Get exposed to it, even accidentally, and you've damaged your brain with a tiny hole, spiritually speaking that is. Do it often enough and you've got hundreds of holes; effectively you're damaged goods. Not that the Torah is false (CH"VSH) [*khas ve-sholom*, God forbid], just that you as an individual are no longer capable of resisting the falsehoods of the world.

Hasidic Bloggers: Multilingual Blogging and the Mediation of Heresy

There were fewer Hasidic bloggers than Yeshivish or Modern Orthodox on the Jblogosphere, because, as I noted, technology was more restricted for Hasidic Jews by their leaders. Nevertheless, there were four—three men and a woman—who were quite prominent, and all were living or had lived double lives: Katle Kanye, Hasidic Rebel, Shtreimel, and Shpitzle Shtrimpkind. All chronicled the interior changes they were going through in their blog postings, but used different languages. Katle Kanye, whom I never met in person but corresponded with on Facebook, wrote in men's Hasidic Yiddish, what I call Enlightened Hasidic Yiddish. Shtreimel and Hasidic Rebel, both of whom I spent time with, used standard English. Shpitzle Shtrimpkind, whom I also spent time with, wrote in Hasidic English, her vernacular.

These bloggers' posts all challenged a central Hasidic cultural belief about signs, what anthropologist Webb Keane calls a "semiotic ideology": that essentialized Jewish intention, mediated by language, content, or form could elevate and redeem any Gentile medium.[21] This semiotic ideology had allowed Hasidic Jews to consistently adapt and adopt useful media of all kinds by making it Jewish, including (at first) the internet. Hasidic bloggers, in contrast, often used Jewish languages, religious scholarship, or insider knowledge of ultra-Orthodoxy to express heretical ideas and their life-changing doubt, challenging the very nature of ideologies of language and media for double lifers and for rabbinic authorities.

Katle Kanye: Enlightened Yiddish for Hasidic Men

Katle Kanye was one of the very early Hasidic bloggers, who was deep in the closet and continues to be. It was reputed that no one had ever met him in real life. Or maybe one person had. Or maybe he just lived in England, so no one in Brooklyn knew him. He told me in a private message on Facebook that he wrote frequently and "at all hours of the night," juggling his work and family life. He wrote exclusively in Hasidic men's Yiddish, with its shadow of holiness cast by its use as a language of discussion for religious learning, its nostalgic ties to pre-Holocaust eastern Europe, and its form, which included *loshn koydesh*, talmudic references, and Hebrew orthography. This was a Yiddish that was primarily accessible to other Hasidic men, not Hasidic women or even other ultra-Orthodox

Jews, the Yeshivish, who do not use Yiddish as a vernacular at all.[22] Hasidic Rebel explained Katle Kanye's Yiddish writing to me, which I found too hard to read without help:

> He's difficult. He's staggeringly brilliant. But he uses very gendered language, the language you don't hear among [Hasidic] women, only among [Hasidic] men. Men will use homiletic expressions, *loshn koydesh.*

Katle Kanye used men's Yiddish to experiment with a taboo genre: parody. As Hasidic Rebel explained, "Katle Kanye is modeling his writings on [Jewish] scholarly language, but it is a parody of scholarship." His parody of Jewish scholarship was premised on deep knowledge turned inside out, making irreverent fun of the whole system. In fact, the heretical counterpublic came to be such a threat particularly because of *leytsones*, mockery of leadership, institutions, and ways of life. *Leytsones* was not just rude or disrespectful, though. In Psalm 1:1, *leytsones* is actually conflated with sin and wickedness.[23] As Katle Kanye wrote to me, "I like subversion more than anything and for that I have an unfair advantage writing for an easily mocked community."[24]

Katle Kanye critiqued the system, even while he chronicled his intimate daily life. For example, he described today's rebbes as "fools and knaves." Yet he also wrote about being a Hasidic father and a man, posting about matchmaking for his son, "This is the first time that I am not fantasizing about a woman for myself, but sizing her up for my son."[25] Katle Kanye explained to me in a Facebook message, "My thrill was and is in conveying our life in an authentic yet heretical voice." And he used the Yiddish of Hasidic men's study to do just that.

Katle Kanye had other linguistic aspirations for Yiddish as a language. In some posts, he experimented with resignifying Yiddish, telling me he wanted to create a more literary, not necessarily religious language, "by us and for us" (meaning Hasidic Jews). Hasidic Jews do not usually read, and some are even unaware of the large secular Yiddish literature from prewar eastern Europe. Indeed, some living double lives were quite angry to discover that a whole secular Yiddish literature even existed. However, though Katle Kanye did know and was inspired by this literature, he did not necessarily turn to it on his blog in his effort to create an Enlightened Yiddish for Hasidic men. Instead he experimented with translation of the American literary canon into Yiddish, providing an individualized, aesthetic experience for readers. For example, in one post Katle Kanye translated Robert Frost's "Stopping by Woods on a Snowy Evening"

(בײַם וואַלד אָן אַ שנייעקער נאַכט, *baym vald on a shnayeker nakht*) into Yiddish. However, he titled the blog post with the Frost translation not as "evening" but "*mayrev in vald*" (*mayrev* in a wood), where *mayrev* is the time of the Jewish evening prayer service. In effect, Katle Kanye's post sacralized Robert Frost and secularized the Yiddish language. The very act of translation from English to Yiddish was transgressive and transformative: a secular poem about life choices translated into Yiddish could offer male Hasidic readers an emotional resonance to the theme of life choices that so many double lifers were grappling with.

Further, his translation offered Hasidic men the chance to experience Yiddish reading as an aesthetic leisure activity. Hasidic men were not expected to do much of this kind of reading, as I noted, since it wasted time that could be spent studying Torah (*bitl toyre*). The Yiddish translation of Frost's poem also had the potential to connect Hasidic readers to a wider English literary public. And it was this shared public that troubled the essentialized, moral differences so many ultra-Orthodox believers elaborate between Jews and Gentiles. In making Frost's poem accessible to Hasidic readers using the familiar Hasidic men's Yiddish to express enlightened ideas, Katle Kanye offered them a way to rethink the very purpose of ultra-Orthodox men's reading and of Yiddish, too.

Years later, on WhatsAppville Yinglish, Gavriel and Zalman remembered how shocking it had been to read Katle Kanye's posts, which had such enlightened content but were written in their own male Hasidic Yiddish. Gavriel wrote, "When I first read Katle Kanye I was traumatized for a day or two." Zalman agreed, "KK shook me to the core." I wrote back asking what it was about Katle Kanye's Yiddish in particular that had been so disturbing. Zalman explained, "It's because we're trained to dismiss a secular source. . . . But when it's written in a heimish [homey, i.e., ultra-Orthodox] Yiddish that only a person from within can, someone like me, that gets your attention and it's disturbing. . . . It made me think. A lot."

Shtreimel and Hasidic Rebel: English and Language Purism

Shtreimel and Hasidic Rebel each lived double lives for a long time, though both now have been forced out of their communities. When they were blogging, each chose to post in Standard English rather than Yiddish, even though Shtreimel, at least, was not fully fluent in English when he began (Hasidic Yiddish was his primary language). Both reported writing at their offices (a store and a tech company), where they had more privacy, and posting a couple of times a week. Hasidic Rebel began early in 2003, stopped for a few years, and then started again. Shtreimel was inspired by Hasidic Rebel's posts and started blogging soon after in 2004.

Metapragmatic commentary, or talk about talk, suggests that ideologies of Yiddish and English changed for men like these two. Shtreimel and Hasidic Rebel each used Standard English, with no mixing or code-switching from Yiddish or *loshn koydesh*. They used English to reach a new audience, a public of fellow doubters and, for Hasidic Rebel at least, an imagined intellectual public of non-Jews. For example, Hasidic Rebel, who had unusually been reading in English since he was a child, was very pleased when he posted some of the reader responses to his fluency in Standard English:

> Since I started this blog, I've gotten a couple of emails from people doubting that I'm really a Chasid . . . most say my writing style is impossible without growing up in a secular environment. . . . Wow! These people actually flatter me.

The ability to write in Standard English was a sign for some readers that Hasidic Rebel was not really Hasidic, perhaps merely posing as Hasidic to lead others astray.

In contrast, Shtreimel described how difficult his first posts were because he had not had much exposure to English. Initially he wrote in English because he did not have a Hebrew keyboard. Later he wrote in English for other reasons. He posted in 2007, "My grammar was horrendous—I had never really learned to write. . . . Soon I found good fellows who took their time to correct my English and teach me how to be more articulate." Eventually both Shtreimel and Hasidic Rebel were contacted and interviewed by a non-Jewish reporter, who facilitated an in-person meeting between the two. Standard English eventually became a lingua franca for Hasidic Jews living double lives to communicate not only with non-Jews, but perhaps more important with Yeshivish and Modern Orthodox Jewish doubters.

Eventually, beyond the blogs fluent Standard English became a sign of doubt or at least *ofgeklerte* (enlightened) leanings. If a Hasidic man's English was "too good," that is, too fluent and too colloquial, those around him might suspect that he was reading secular material in English. This was troubling since men should not be wasting time reading English and that kind of reading could lead to ideas that might corrupt. Indeed, men's lack of fluency in English was often public confirmation, a sign, that they were immersed in Torah study and sheltered from the world. In fact, Motti, a young man leading a double life, told me that when a first match was proposed, his prospective wife felt uncomfortable with how good his English was. It made her wonder about his level of religiosity, and she did not accept the match.

Jblogging in Standard English began to influence language ideologies of Yiddish more generally for those living double lives, ideologies which contrasted with those of Katle Kanye. Both Hasidic Rebel and Shtreimel asserted in conversations with me that Hasidic Yiddish had inherent linguistic limitations in addition to a limited readership. For example, Hasidic Rebel explained, "The Yiddish I was reading was never about ideas, never about critical ideas. So the language of critical ideas was English." Shtreimel told me that in Yiddish, "You can't transmit ideas. You can't talk about anything but really, really simple." When I noted that some were indeed blogging in a sophisticated Yiddish (e.g., Katle Kanye), he suggested that they had to rely on *loshn koydesh* borrowings, though in fact the Hebrew and Aramaic components of Yiddish have always been part of the language. Men like Shtreimel began talking about language using a discourse of purity that I had not heard articulated by Hasidic Jews before. I had always found it interesting that for a community that essentialized the difference between Jews and Gentiles and men and women, there was so little concern for language standardization or language mixing between Yiddish and English.[26] On the Jblogs, though, for some there was a growing appreciation for standard language, perhaps influenced by their use of Standard English and its association with secular education and literature, which many Hasidic boys had limited access to.[27] This emerging ideology of language purism would eventually influence the new variety of Enlightened Hasidic Yiddish, which developed on social media and has spread to print (see chapter 6).

The comment threads on Hasidic Rebel and Shtreimel's blogs reveal that with the exception of a few non-Orthodox explorers who introduced themselves, the majority of participants were other ultra-Orthodox Jews. Many seemed to be Hasidic, marked by their pseudonyms (e.g., "Also a *Chusid*" [Hasidic Jew]). Nevertheless, almost all of the comment threads on these blogs were attempts at Standard English. For example, one commenter wrote a post in Yiddish, and another responded, "Such a beaitful [*sic*] post, why not write it in English so everyone can understand it?" Some comments were by the faithful trying to dissuade doubters and bring them back to belief, again mostly in English. As an anonymous poster wrote on Shtreimel's blog: "I hope you return [i.e., to religion]." Another wrote, "I hope you choose to stay *frum*." Other posts signaled insider status, writing in English but code-switching to mention a month in Hebrew (Elul) or ending their English post, *"kol tuv"* (all the best), without any translation at all.

English has always been complicated ideologically since it could not simply be rejected as the language of Gentiles. Many Hasidic Jews, especially Hasidic women and the Yeshivish, use varieties of English, and some English was often critical for many men's economic livelihoods, even when they worked for other ultra-Orthodox Jews. Indeed, part of the contemporary backlash against rabbinic leadership included a generation of men angry that their yeshiva educations had not taught them enough English or math. In the comment thread of one of Shtreimel's posts, for example, one poster apologized, "And since English is a language we did not leat [*sic*, learn] in CHEIDER [Hasidic elementary school], please forgive my misspellings."

Standard English on the Jblogs was not so much about adopting the Gentile language, however. Instead it became an ultra-Orthodox Jewish men's medium of choice for articulating forbidden thoughts, desires and emerging new selves. Shtreimel and Hasidic Rebel's English posts, for example, were filled with theological debates and discussions, ones that would have been impossible to air in the ultra-Orthodox public sphere without severe sanctions for oneself and one's family. For example, in a post titled "Atheism" Shtreimel challenged his readers:

> On a previous post I asked if there is anyone here who thinks that they could PROVE to me that there is a god out there to step forward. If you can send me an email with an argument I promise to post it, discuss it and comply with the conclusions.

Similarly, on their blogs Hasidic Rebel and Shtreimel experimented with changing beliefs, tastes, and ideas. For example, both wrote long responses to secular books that they were reading, movies they secretly saw, and current events, especially conflicts over Israel. Shtreimel wrote about his first experience of eating on Yom Kippur, the Jewish Day of Atonement. He also described an experience hanging out with some girls on a pier in Manhattan, which made him reflect on the gender segregation in his Hasidic community. Similarly, Hasidic Rebel wrote about how his discovery of the Beatles, the Beach Boys and Abba, did not have to exclude the popular Hasidic music he had loved as a teenager. In 2003 he also wrote about how his new dreams for exploring the wider world conflicted with his still-religious wife's lack of interest:

For years I've been dreaming of touring Europe. The history, the culture, the art, the sights, the romance. Problem is, my wife doesn't much care for Europe, or any other place for that matter, besides our little Chasidic ghetto here.

While theological debates were common on the Jblogs, so were posts that described the personal emotional pain of living a double life. For example, Shtreimel wrote on September 2005:

Living a lie might be a sport, a bragging point to a welcoming blogging audience, but at the end of the day it is me who is going through sheer hell trying to keep up with my old good kid image combined with my new rebellious self-image. I can assure you that it is no easy task at all.

In the ultra-Orthodox religious public sphere, Shtreimel continued to conform. It was on his English blog on the heretical counterpublic that he could reveal his rejection of that sphere, as well as explore his own emotional sense of self. In the post above, he compared his "rebellious self-image" online to his "old good kid image." This juggling of selves— virtual rebel blogger and in-person Hasidic Jew—included a third, less visible aspect: the pain and difficulty of "living a lie," which paralleled the "cognitive dissonance" described by Jewish Enlightenment autobiographies so long ago. The English blog was a digital, written manifestation of the disjuncture between Shtreimel's virtual self and his public Hasidic self, his double life made discursive and public through language and technology.

Jbloggers used Jewish languages and English, but they confounded the speakers these languages were commonly associated with. Writing in Standard English with some *loshn koydesh* to address other ultra-Orthodox men or writing in men's Yiddish to express new enlightened or heretical ideas created an ultra-Orthodox counterpublic, where male reading and writing did not bring the messiah closer, as religious study did. Instead, Jewish men's reading and writing on the Jblogs undermined the authority of contemporary ultra-Orthodox leadership by questioning a key semiotic ideology: that Gentile media could be made Jewish by infusing it with Jewish form, intent, or content. Jbloggers and the heretical counterpublic showed instead that Jewish form, intent, and content could be used on a new medium to actually undermine ultra-Orthodoxy itself.

A recent post on an all-male Yiddish language forum, *Kave Shtibl* (coffee/break room in a yeshiva or synagogue) warned of the danger to ultra-Orthodox authority when a Jewish language was the medium to express heretical ideas. The writer used *loshn koydesh*–inflected Yiddish to claim that the real danger of the blogs lay in the medium of language, not the technology of the blog (Yiddish translation, Rose Waldman):

> Katle Kanye was the first to cold-heartedly use our mame loshn [mother tongue] to make fun of all that is holy. Already in 2002, when the internet was still in its diapers, he had already sharpened his sword and stabbed his readers with toxic poison, simple dry bones that came alive beneath his colorful language and schmaltzy [literally, chicken fat, corny] Yiddish.[28] His mocking words entered everyone deeply—this was still before the time we'd become immunized to the heimishe [ultra-Orthodox] smart-alecky words on internet blogs, and it's impossible to say that they did not leave an impression forever on refined souls. May he live happily, but it's good that he folded.[29]

Katle Kanye's Enlightened Hasidic Yiddish was what made his blogging so "toxic." Yiddish, that intimate Hasidic masculine language, was like sheep's clothing that hid the wolfish danger of his mockery to pure Jewish souls, something that Shpitzle Shtrimpkind's feminine Hasidic English blog did too.

Shpitzle Shtrimpkind: Feminine Hasidic English

Shpitzle Shtrimpkind's blog, like men's blogs, was a space for self-expression, along with sarcasm and mockery, which gradually led her to challenge and question religious authorities and the system. However, unlike male Jbloggers, she documented her transformation from believer to heretic in Hasidic English (what she calls English or Yinglish), which juxtaposes and plays with Yiddish, Hebrew, and English words and orthographies. In May 2013 she explained to me why she chose to use Hasidic English on her blog, rather than Standard English or Yiddish:

> I am definitely fluent in Yiddish, but I always wrote in English. . . . women are like that. When I wrote my blog . . . I felt mixing Yiddish and English was a way to speak insiders' jokes. I was entirely unconcerned with reaching a wide audience or making the mix of languages more readable. I thought English was a good language for expression . . . but I felt it was crucial to include lots of Yiddish to make the English heimish.

Haymish (heimish) literally means homey, but it has become a local term that emphasizes shared sensibilities among ultra-Orthodox Jews, rather than their differences of practice or belief (i.e., those who would get her "insider's jokes").[30] For Shpitzle, writing in a *haymish* language not only carved out a particular audience of readers, it added a sensory dimension to reading and commenting on her blog—the feeling of cozy Hasidic women's domesticity. As she continued to blog, Shpitzle, like Hasidic male bloggers, engaged the Hasidic semiotic ideology of making a Gentile medium feel, sound, and look familiarly ultra-Orthodox, but again for the subversive purpose of expressing her growing heretical ideas that undermined ultra-Orthodoxy.

Shpitzle's blogging emphasizes the importance of considering how technology gets gendered, with implications for the ability to participate in a digital counterpublic and beyond. Unlike male bloggers, Shpitzle initially had to rely on her husband to post her blogs on his Blackberry, which she wrote first in email at an office where she worked as a secretary. Shpitzle told me she began posting online initially to convince other Jbloggers that they were wrong about their critiques of the system. She did so with her husband's approval and technical assistance. Over the course of a few years, her writing reflected a series of virtual snapshots of a believer's changing sense of herself. On her blog, life-changing doubt was a public process, not an invisible interior state, mediated by gendered language.

Shpitzle quickly drew quite a following on the Jblogosphere, though she suggested to me that despite being a subversive space, ultra-Orthodox gendered hierarchies remained intact. Indeed, some men bloggers did not take her seriously. For example, on his own blog Katle Kanye wrote in Yiddish: "Toyre by Shtreimel, praktik by Shpitzle" (Torah at Shtreimel's blog and the practical/everyday at Shpitzle's). Shpitzle explained to me that this statement slotted her blog into the gendered realm of practical knowledge rather than any deep intellectual journey, marked by the colloquial use of *toyre* as deep philosophical thought, which readers could find on Shtreimel's blog.

As Shpitzle began to have religious doubts, her very language use made her emerging double life visible. In this way, as digital culture scholar Carmel Vaisman suggests, the blog postings became objects to be "looked at, not only through for their meaning."[31] Shpitzle's written posts were objects, which reflected in their switch in orthography the distinction between her publicly visible body and her changing interior. For example, in 2007 Shpitzle wrote this post, which subverted the truth of a common Yiddish proverb:

In all, the underground Internet community is probably growing. It's marvelous because it allows you צו טאנצן אויף ביידע חתונות [*tsu tantsn af bayde khasanas*, to dance at both weddings].

In fact, the Yiddish proverb states, "mit ayn tukhes ken men nisht tantsn af tsvey khasanas" (with one behind, you *cannot* dance at two weddings). By removing the "not" Shpitzle claimed that she was actually able to dance at two metaphorical weddings: being a Hasidic wife and mother in one world and exploring a new world online. The juxtaposing of the English and Yiddish alphabets was a material sign of her emergent double life. Her newly critical voice instantiated in the writing and digital medium of her post contradicted the "truth" of *haymish* Jewish folk knowledge.

Shpitzle did not call herself a *maskil*, but she did use the term "enlightened" as she began to experiment with a mocking, sarcastic tone and parodies of women's narrow concerns in Hasidic life.[32] She chronicled her own transformation by showing, through metapragmatic commentary (talk about talk), how her style of writing further mirrored her interior transformation. For example, in the introduction to her now-archived blog, she wrote in 2007 after she had left:

> When the writing here is followed in chronological order, you can watch my tones and positions evolve. Whereas I began the blog innocently thinking it will serve to speak for the good in the Chassidic life, I soon found myself lamenting about the bad. I learned new things daily that ate away the fabric of my old understanding. In the archives you'll find my first ever piece, a heated and unfortunate defense of Satmar to be a far cry from my later posts—sarcastic criticism on my Satmar/chassidic community. On the Shpitzle blog I went from committed chassidic mother and wife to enlightened bum.

Sarcasm has become a marked feature of a religious doubter, regardless of the kosher Jewishness of the writing in Hasidic English or men's Yiddish for that matter. Instead of "a chassidic mother and wife," in her own words, she became "an enlightened bum." Shpitzle, however, was not a bum, who could not control her lusts and desires. She had become an "enlightened" bum, making reference to the Jewish Enlightenment, whose intellectual ideas had turned her into a woman who treated Hasidic Judaism as a lifestyle rather than a religious truth.

Though Shpitzle used her *haymish* Hasidic English to reject the very community she originally went online to defend, as a woman she was not allowed to continue living a double life for very long. Shpitzle told me that as her blogging got increasingly heretical, her husband contacted his rabbinic adviser, who eventually demanded she give him the laptop she had acquired. Women's access to technology and the ongoing surveillance of their activities (at least potentially) by their husbands and husbands' rabbis, along with their significant domestic duties, all created obstacles to participating in the digital and face-to-face public spaces of the heretical counterpublic, compared to men.

Soon after, Shpitzle divorced and left her community with her young son. Hasidic Rebel was similarly forced out of his community by his rebbe, after he and his wife divorced, something he has written about in his popular memoir.[33] However, Shtreimel remained in his community, living a double life for many years, as have others on the Jblogosphere, such as Katle Kanye. Eventually, while some of the Jblogs have been removed or closed, those that remain available became a resource and a support for the next generation of doubters in their twenties. Even before then, though, the Jblogosphere's networks of friendships spilled over to in-person meet-ups.

Online to In-Person: Meeting Up

While secret doubters discovered online that hundreds if not thousands of other ultra-Orthodox Jews shared their doubts, they could, if they dared, begin to form a whole new life in person, where they could keep their secrets while they explored new ways of being. The heretical counterpublic was formed through online interactions, which moved to include in-person interactions in some sense, confounding what really constituted the ultra-Orthodox pubic sphere.

For example, Shmuel remembered the first time he met the blogger Mis-Nagid ("opposed," a wordplay on Misnagdim, who historically opposed Hasidim). One day, after a year of commenting and more personal emailing, Mis-Nagid wrote, "Why don't we meet? We won't tell each other our real names." They decided to meet on the steps of the New York Public Library. They talked for over an hour, which Shmuel told me was "awesome, great, the coolest thing ever." When they began to talk about their yeshiva experiences, Shmuel suddenly realized he recognized Mis-Nagid because they had coincidentally attended the same yeshiva. "I know you!" said Shmuel. Mis-Nagid turned completely white with fear, Shmuel remembered. He reassured him, and as they began to talk more, they both realized that they had been living parallel lives as questioning, secretly nonconforming teens in yeshiva: Mis-Nagid hacked into computers, and

Shmuel listened to and played heavy metal, both of course, forbidden activities.

It turned out that one of the reasons Mis-Nagid initially invited Shmuel to meet in person was because he was already regularly meeting up with a group of those living double lives who were also heavily involved in blogging. Unusually, the central figure was a woman living a double life, Tamar Klein, someone whom Shmuel affectionately called the "den mother" for those living double lives in the early 2000s.

Tamar was in her early fifties when we were introduced in 2015. She didn't look like some other women I had met who were living double lives. No unusually tight skirts that barely grazed the knee, or headbands instead of a kerchief or hat over a wig, all subtle signs of questioning authority. Tamar was unremarkable on the outside, looking like the Hasidic woman she was—medium brown wig, modest skirt and blouse, thick beige stockings. Inside, however, she told me she had been questioning since she was fourteen or fifteen, though she had never revealed that to anyone, not even her parents.

In the late nineties, before the Jblogs, there were online international forums from Israel and England, especially popular among Hasidim. Tamar had read them avidly, since computers back then were not as reviled as they have become today. She remembered reading a post by a writer who claimed he was an atheist and thinking to herself, "Oh, that's what I am." She got married very young, knowing little about her husband, Eli, except that he was considered "open-minded." She quickly decided to "come out" to her husband in order not "to live a lie." She told him, "I'm an atheist, but I respect your rules." She expected him to pack his bags, she said, but instead he told her, "I don't have a problem with it." Perhaps Eli was more than open-minded or perhaps he liked his wife and just did not want to get divorced, which is so stigmatizing. Regardless, they stayed together and began their family.

When the Jblogs became popular, Tamar read them all, commenting and even occasionally guest posting. She closely followed blogger Not the Gadol HaDor as he blogged about his loss of faith. Tamar told me she thought to herself, "Here is someone going through the same thing I went through years ago, and I get to watch it." There were so many people online, she told me, "It felt like a movement."

She finally initiated a meeting in person despite her fears, what she called her "paranoia." Why, I asked her, would you do something so risky? Tamar said, "I had been living this life for a long time, and I was so sick and frustrated with it." Many bloggers and those writing on forums turned her down. Finally, a blogger she especially admired and somehow trusted, the same Mis-Nagid, agreed to meet after emailing. She described that first meeting:

> My first person that I came out to and exchanged real identities with, that was a powerful moment. I'd been living this double life and nobody knew about it. God, that was . . . I don't know another word for it but delirium. . . . [It was] a revelation. He's normal, He's not disturbed. Not dysfunctional. . . . And once you do that, you realize the sky is not falling.

Communal explanations for religious doubt, as I noted, often included diagnoses of mental illness. Tamar felt vindicated that Mis-Nagid was "normal" despite his disbelief. That meant she was normal too, and so were the many others on the Jblogosphere.

After that initial meeting, Tamar and Mis-Nagid started a small group of four to five people who met every other month at the Second Avenue Deli, a debatably kosher restaurant.[34] Mis-Nagid had recently met Shmuel, and he began bringing him along. When the deli closed for renovation, Tamar suggested meeting at her house. By then, Tamar had made inroads with her husband, who had begun having his own doubts, especially after long conversations with her and a lot of time reading online (she called him "an internet intellectual"). Tamar was unusual in that she, as a woman, eventually succeeded in "flipping" her husband, that is, convincing him that her religious doubts were well founded. All of the others she was meeting online were men, whose wives did not know they were living double lives. As Tamar said, "I was the only one who brought my husband to the other side. He wanted answers and he's a smart man. And slowly he came over . . . you know what helped? The blogs helped."

At first, many of the men Tamar invited were reluctant to come to her house. They told her that exchanging real identities with her was fine, but that they didn't want others to know their names. Tamar, using, as she said, "a woman's persuasion" convinced them that they could all trust each other because they were all "in the same boat." The group began to meet at Tamar's house, and it grew. She said, "We moved from my kitchen, which seats ten to the living room, which seats twenty and sometimes there was overflow." Most men were in their late twenties or early thirties, married with children, and the visits became a time to share the difficulties of living a double life and provide support to each other. As Tamar said, "These were established people who had a lot to lose. . . . it was a support group." They talked, for example, about how hard it was to review homework with one's kids, all the while feeling they were learning "fairy tales." Or to see their children struggle with *gemora* (Talmud study), when they could be learning something useful like chemistry or English. They also talked about ideas, historical change, theology, science, and critiqued rabbinical leadership and their school systems.

Eventually, over the years, Tamar and many of the others became less afraid of being exposed as their social lives expanded. Tamar told me, "I started to become very selective about who I made my friendships with because I had alternatives." She felt safer because "there's others like me. And there's strength in numbers." Sometimes those living double lives crossed paths in the context of their official ultra-Orthodox lives. For example, the blogger Shtreimel was one of the early members of the group, and Tamar realized that she had once rented his apartment. Perhaps those overlaps encouraged those living double lives because, hey, you never knew if your neighbor or landlord might just be a secret heretic, like you.

Many of those friends continued to meet and go out, meaning that they have maintained secret friendships for at least fifteen years or so. For example, at a recent book launch of Shulem Deen's memoir of leaving his Hasidic community, Tamar, Shmuel, and about ten others (including me) all went out for a postevent drink in a nearby Brooklyn bar. Now in their later thirties or early forties, rabbis sometimes called this network of Jbloggers the "lost generation." They had come of age before rabbinic leadership realized the grave dangers posed by the internet and had had fewer filters and religious edicts controlling access than those in their twenties do today. The lost generation's experiences on the frontier of the crisis of authority made them an important resource for the next generation living double lives, offering advice and experiences about child custody, divorce, and therapy virtually, on the phone, and in person. This became increasingly important as rabbis and other leaders began to name the internet as the *nisoyen ha-dor*, the challenge of the generation.

Learning to See Signs of Secret Doubt

By 2008–2009, rabbinic leadership, rabbis, rebbes, *askonim* (self-appointed activists), and educators increasingly made connections between internet use and the loss of faith in their public written and spoken addresses. The Jbloggers, those secret heretics, were frequently portrayed as intent on destroying ultra-Orthodox Judaism. Rabbi Frank, a public figure and the editor of *Ami Magazine*, called bloggers "Nazis," saying in a talk radio program in 2013, "The bloggers, they have become so powerful.

They have such a tremendous *hashpoa* [influence]. They're joining the anti-Orthodox chorus." I actually first heard this recorded comment when it was mockingly posted on Failed Messiah's blog.

Some leaders connected the mockery of leadership on the Jblogs to what they saw as the biased press's coverage of the ultra-Orthodox sexual abuse scandals. They suggested that both secular journalists and the Jbloggers were intent on discrediting contemporary ultra-Orthodoxy by taking down respected rabbinic leaders (the *gedolim*). For example, during the 2012 anti-internet rally at Citi Field (see chapter 3), one speaker emphasized the special damage caused to the "stature of rabbis and Jewish scholars" from the blog posts, in which rabbinic leaders were criticized for their silence and inaction on those charged with sexually abusing children.[35]

As anxiety over those living double lives grew, ultra-Orthodox leadership reached back to historical parallels and familiar Jewish enemies. For example, on his blog Shmuel posted an audio recording of an anti-internet rally in 2006 in Monsey, New York, one of the first of what would be many such rallies, where a speaker called the Jblogosphere a *moyshev letsonim*, a biblical reference to a gathering of those who mock authority (Psalms 1). Similarly, in 2013 an editor of *Matzav*, an online Orthodox English site, warned of ultra-Orthodox Jews who sent rabbinic correspondence to Jbloggers as fodder for their mockery:

> The bloggers may be *tinokos shenishbu* or lost souls. Who knows. But those living in our very midst, who send their kids to our children's schools, who behind our backs are assisting the anti-*frum* [religion] haters out there in the online world, may just be a lot worse. . . . we must beware of those among us—in our very own communities—who are constantly stabbing us in the back. Much, if not most, of the information and details reported on by anti-*frum* bloggers originates from the *frum* community itself . . . to those who derive the greatest pleasure from mocking us.[36]

The story of Zalman's expulsion from his Hasidic community in Brooklyn encapsulates the increasingly aggressive rabbinic response to those living double lives, the search for familiar tropes to blame, and the influence of the Jblogs. Zalman was a confident, charismatic man, who met me for the first time in neat jeans, loafers, and a bare head at a Greenwich Village café, where he ordered bacon and eggs (bacon is, of course, not kosher). He had been forced out of his community just a few months prior, after living a double life for a few years.

Zalman came from a "special" family, a prestigious, well-liked Hasidic family. He was a popular guy, a real *makher* (mover and shaker), Toby, a friend of his, told me; people listened to him, and he enjoyed his life, loved his wife and four children. However, despite being a respected Torah scholar and family man, Zalman had had doubts and questions for years. After trying to get answers from many different rabbis, he eventually told his wife that he had lost his belief. She was appalled, sought divorce, and Zalman was officially ejected from his community.

A few months after Zalman's ejection, his rebbe was preparing his annual pre-Yom Kippur communal address (*drosha*), designed to highlight a special challenge for the year. Zalman told me that the rebbe called Zalman's close friends, telling them to cut all contact. Zalman continued, "He [the rebbe] wanted to hear from my friends that it was the internet that got me, and they said no, he actually used to sit a lot in the library, and he used to read a lot. He [the rebbe] didn't like that, and he just went with the internet."

The rebbe's address that year was different from prior ones. It wasn't about cancer or some more general external threat to Jewish life. The rebbe that year spoke, cried, and yelled about Zalman. Someone recorded his speech and sent it to Zalman, who described it to me:

> Reb ▮▮▮ started crying. He talked about *yingelayt* [young married men], a scholar, respected people, who through the internet, hooked up with groups of other people and eventually became *apikorsim* [heretics]. He screamed, "*shtraymel* and *bekishe* [Hasidic men's garb] *apikorsim*" . . . it was shocking. . . . Maybe that speech brought it [i.e., double life] into the open or maybe my leaving.

The Yiddish Yom Kippur address was then printed, as it was every year, as an editorial in one of the official Hasidic newspapers, which Zalman described as a declaration of war:

> A declaration against the *letsonim* [those who mock] and those who *makhn khoyzek fin rebbes* [make fun of rebbes]; the *ofgeklerte* and the *apikorsim*, who think they are *maskilim*, but are not even at that level.

The rebbe's editorial, Zalman said, declared that Hasidim should no longer tolerate anyone who mocked a rabbinic authority because it was a sign of a "deeper cynicism." He warned his Hasidim to be on the lookout for new signs of doubt. These included ways of speaking and writing, which had been pioneered on the Jblogosphere, and which, in their mockery, echoed another historical time of religious upheaval and challenge, the Jewish Enlightenment.

As another rabbi similarly said, "What I need to stress is that we must curb the urge to opinionate, because opinionating . . . means poor judgment, unfair comments and unwise *khinukh* [moral education]." Anonymous, yet public written expression of individual opinions, especially in familiar Jewish languages, styles, and genres, was dangerous; in contrast, contemporary rabbinic leadership began to emphasize that Jews needed to embrace *emuna peshuta*, simple faith, the faith that asks no questions.

Authority, Media, and Laughter

Religious studies scholar Birgit Meyer describes how specific media at historical moments might authorize experiences of the divine, making certain relationships or ways of being a possibility.[37] This is not to suggest that the medium itself creates certain persons, but rather that a newly introduced medium may legitimate particular feelings and experiences, including different possibilities for social interaction, written and spoken.[38] The Jblogs and the wider heretical counterpublic legitimated the emotional and intellectual experience of life-changing doubt, at least for men. The Jblogs allowed double lifers to express their emerging feelings and ideas, to write new desires into being, and to create real relationships with fellow travelers. The internet, with its speed, its unfettered access to knowledge and interlocutors, and especially its anonymity, did, in fact, create a new kind of counterpublic all within the span of a decade.

The material affordances of a new medium, as anthropologists Faye Ginsburg, Lila Abu-Lughod, and Brian Larkin write, foster particular relations to the body and perceptions of time and space.[39] For example, double-life women with less access to computers and almost no unsurveilled free time had fewer opportunities to explore other ways of feeling and being with like-minded others. Still, for anyone with access to the heretical counterpublic, conceptions of ultra-Orthodox public space could change. The person standing next to you in synagogue praying so fervently or looking so modest might just be one of the Jbloggers who had written scathing critiques of their very own rebbe or the system. Who knew? Where ultra-Orthodox leadership and the faithful might increasingly worry about "imposters among them," those with life-changing doubt were encouraged that there might be hidden kindred spirits instead.

For both Jbloggers and rabbinic leadership, the new medium of blogging invoked the shared historical memory of another medium that had spread heretical ideas, another internal threat from within: the writings and publications of Jewish Enlighteners. In twenty-first century New York and beyond, the European Jewish Enlightenment became the grounds for struggles over mediation, men's literacy, and true Jewish Orthodoxy. The double-life Jbloggers claimed that they were, in fact, not merely lazy or lustful, but rather sincere intellectuals saving Jewish Orthodoxy from extremism, just as they imagined Jewish Enlighteners had in prewar Europe. Aligning themselves with a morally superior generation of critics, contemporary Enlighteners wrote into being a different model of the self: a critical-thinking ultra-Orthodox Jew, an autonomous, independent person with desires and thoughts that were antithetical to much of ultra-Orthodoxy. The medium of the blog, we might say, authorized expressions of individual life-changing doubt, legitimated through comparisons to a more moral past when intellectual giants still lived.

Heretical ideas and questions on and beyond the Jblogosphere were expressed in the currency of ultra-Orthodox authority: Jewish men's scholarship, their literacy, and their networks of friends and relatives. The synergy of the new technology mobilized through the culture of male Orthodox reading and writing created a counterpublic that provided safe, but also authoritative space to mock and parody those in power. As philosopher Hannah Arendt wrote of authority, "The greatest enemy of authority is contempt, and the surest way to undermine it is laughter."[40] As the heretical counterpublic went beyond screens to in-person meet-ups, the threat to ultra-Orthodox authority included time spent together in secret yet public spaces, like homes and not-quite-kosher-enough restaurants.

Blogospheres in other parts of the world from the same time period share similarities to and differences from the Jblogs, raising questions about the mediation of religious authority and language choice in a new communicative technology. For example, communications scholars Anabelle Sreberny and Gholam Khiabany analyze the Iranian blogosphere, "The Blogistan," as a public tool, one which provided a diversity of critiques against the Islamic Republic. They emphasize the importance of considering the medium, the technology, and the mediated content, including language, in its social and historical context. They write, "While a poet *might* just be a poet in England, a poet in Persian is most probably writing between the lines, evading the censor and pushing the boundaries of publicly acceptable expression." They call blogging on poetry or fashion, for example, "politics by other means inside and outside of the country."[41] In multilingual contexts, choice of language, style, and genre on a new technology is often part of that effort to challenge other ways of being and communicating.

Ultra-Orthodox Jews, of course, did not have one all-powerful leader issuing unified religious policy like an ayatollah, and no one was sent to state prison or tortured for expressing heresy or doubts on blogs or anywhere else.[42] However, Jbloggers living double lives did risk expulsion, which could be traumatizing for cutting off social existence, their very humanity, as they knew it. As "Anonymous" posted on a friend's blog only slightly ironically:

> We want to keep the status quo. We don't want our kids thrown out of yeshiva, we don't want to lose our jobs, we don't want you to pressure our spouses to divorce us, and most of all, we want to continue speaking loshon hora with you "Bain Gavra" in shul! [men's relaxed chatting and gossip just after Torah reading in synagogue]

Those living double lives like Zalman, who were exposed or confessed, could be forced out of their family and community into an alien and alienating wider society. Leaving a totalizing community like ultra-Orthodoxy, which structures a person's life from birth to death, economically, socially, politically, morally, and spiritually, could be truly devastating. In this sense Jblogging was similar to the Mormon online discussions anthropologist Jon Bialecki describes, "the Bloggernacle."[43] Occurring during the same period as the Jblogs, the Bloggernacle was a growing series of "Mormon-centered" conversations online, which some activists used to organize calls for change to Mormon orthodoxy, such as, for example, demands for ordaining women. There were real consequences for those who went too far, too publicly on the Bloggernacle, with some prominent activists who used their real names formally excommunicated.

For ultra-Orthodox authorities—rabbis, activists, rebbes, and educators—the Jblogosphere was evidence that the medium of the internet was more dangerous to *emuna* than they had originally perceived in the nineties. For them, the medium was increasingly the message of heresy. It was also, perhaps, a convenient scapegoat for deflecting attention from ongoing scandals and political struggles for power. As social media replaced blogging beginning around 2009, leaders began to develop strategies to protect the faithful from life-changing doubt, which they increasingly blamed on the outside contaminating medium of the internet, the medium that "burned Jewish souls."

3

Ultra-Orthodox Rabbis
versus the Internet

One June day in 2015, Sheyndie received a message from her children's school on her answering machine, which she shared with me on Whats-App. The Yiddish message invited all mothers to a *"froyen* [women's] phone drive," held in a Hasidic-owned hotel in Brooklyn the following Sunday. At the event, organized by the Hasidic *vaad taharayni* (the Committee for Our Purity) and sponsored by Geder (Gate), one of two Hasidic-approved internet-filtering companies, women had two options: (1) They could sell back their smartphones at half price and receive a certified "kosher phone," also called a "basic" phone, that is, a flip phone that only made calls and texted; (2) They could choose from a variety of filtering options for their smartphones that Geder would install and maintain for a $15 monthly fee. The recording for the women's phone exchange in typical fire-and-brimstone language begged women not to let the "spiritual awakening" (*hisoyrerus*) from an earlier women's anti-internet rally dissipate, "Dear righteous women, ensure the future for the coming generations!" (Tayere nushim tsidkonies, farzikhern dem used fun inzere kimedike doyres!)

Of course, I had to go. That Sunday found me on the subway to Brooklyn in one of my old fieldwork outfits of a modest long skirt, hat, stockings, and blouse. I did not know anyone at the phone exchange, but I screwed up my courage and introduced myself to a group of women in their twenties and thirties out in front of the hotel, who turned out to be five Hasidic sisters, chatting in Yiddish about baby clothes as they leaned over their top-of-the-line strollers. When I asked, one of the women explained why they were there, "They said we have to install the filter to protect our kids, and if we want them to go to our schools, we are required to have it. That's the rules. Men need the phones for work, but we don't." Another sister compared the internet to television. "They [rabbis and activists] controlled it back then," she explained, "And it's the same thing with the internet now." The first sister spoke up again, saying firmly, "It's an addiction, and that's why kids go off. . . . That's why there are so many at risk now. It's the internet."

Concerns over digital media—its content, addictive qualities, and negative cognitive effects—are shared across all kinds of communities, in all kinds of places, especially by anxious parents, including me. Ultra-Orthodox rabbinic leadership had these concerns too, but they were projected through a metaphysical lens: they blamed the internet for religious doubt, which threatened to undermine their entire way of life. For double lifers, digital media had created a vibrant, heretical counterpublic, a place they could express their doubts—religious, social, and political—with like-minded others. For them, the internet was a lifeline. However, for ultra-Orthodox leadership, the internet was a dangerous outside medium that exposed Jews to Gentile contamination. This exterior threat corrupted innately pure Jewish souls, infecting them with invisible doubt that blurred the very moral distinction between Jews and Gentiles.

From roughly 2009 on rabbinic leadership tried to protect ultra-Orthodox Jews from religious doubt by increasingly controlling access to the internet. Double lifers frequently railed against "the rabbis," "*askonim*" (self-appointed activists), or "the system," vague categories of powerful men, who despite their religious differences and disagreements, claimed to be the moral voice of their ultra-Orthodox publics. Rabbinic leaders could have various communal positions. They could be interpreters of Jewish law (a *rov*), heads of prominent yeshivas (a *rosh yeshiva*), or closely aligned with a Hasidic leader, a rebbe.[1] These men all spoke out on issues of the day and set religious precedent. I learned about rabbinic leadership's anti-internet activities from double lifers, especially those on my WhatsAppville Yinglish group. They tipped me off to public anti-internet rallies, shared websites, posted snapshots of edicts (*takunos*) hanging in synagogues, on street lampposts, or sent around to parents of schoolchildren.

Religious rulings about the internet were ultimately enforced through the school systems, the *mosdos.* Affiliated with specific rabbinic leaders, schools could threaten to expel any student whose parents did not comply with its religious standards, for example, in dress, behavior, or nowadays, possession of an unfiltered smartphone. Ultra-Orthodox schools were unusually powerful because they were more than simply educational institutions; not getting into the "right" schools or getting expelled affected the reputation of entire extended families. This had serious consequences later when marriages were arranged, making schools critical for the reproduction of families.[2]

Hasidic rabbis, in particular, turned to Hasidic women for enforcement of their emerging internet policies after their initial efforts with Hasidic men were less successful. Through emotional appeals, Hasidic rabbis, activists, and rebbes charged women with protecting their homes from outside influence, connecting Jews across time and space to ensure continuity, and showing the way forward for their husbands and children. As Shmuel wrote in a post on Facebook in 2015, "Women are the soft belly of the Chasidish community. You can't get men in a room and have their hearts massaged by fifty weeping *dayanim* [rabbinic interpreters of Jewish law], you can't tell them that *tayere* [dear] pure *doros* [generations] are in their hands, you can't tell them they are *nushim tsidkonius* [righteous women]." Women, he meant, were more easily moved to compliance with religious rulings, more easily "emotionally manipulated" than men, he told me. This was because so many women felt a moral responsibility not only for their own families, but for the very future of the Jewish people.

Rabbinic leaders used age-old kosher media and languages—public rallies and printed edicts in both Hasidic Yiddish and Hasidic English—to express diverse ideas of how the internet infected individuals with doubt. Some focused on the digital content, especially pornographic images; later, others focused on the kinds of social interaction that social media facilitated; and still others blamed the very medium itself as contaminating. In their writing and speaking over the course of a decade, rabbis integrated two distinct discursive traditions about the self:[3] they drew on Jewish ethical writings (*mussar*) and North American popular psychology, especially on addictions. Both bodies of knowledge resonated with the sense that the internet disrupted healthy, moral structures of Jewish authority. Increasingly, the goal of some rabbinic anti-internet activism was, as one Modern Orthodox therapist explained to me, "to limit exposure to any literature or media or social contacts which might stimulate doubts about our *mesora* [tradition], or the *mitsvos* [the commandments], or the authority of our communal leaders."[4] Note that all three—tradition, commandments, and communal leaders— were equated as equally authoritative. To protect those who might be tempted away from ultra-Orthodoxy—by pornography, online flirting, secular scholarship, or interactions with other heretics—rabbinic leaders increasingly asserted their moral authority to make decisions about the internet for their followers.

Scholarship on religion and media has focused on the unexpected ways (for secular scholars at least) that religions have adopted new media to facilitate the experience of God and support religious faith.[5] However, just as important is the rejection of a medium because religious community members believe it to block or impede the experience of the divine and faith.[6] Ultra-Orthodox rabbinic leadership was not exactly concerned with the disruptions of the experience of the divine. Rather, they worried that an external medium was corrupting naturally pious Jews, making them susceptible to their own inclinations for evil (*yeytser hora*), which could result in religious doubt. Debates over the internet, then, were actually debates about who had authority over Jewish hearts, minds, and souls; indeed, as anthropologist Patrick Eisenlohr has noted, struggles over a new medium often expose conflicting cultural beliefs about the mediation of authority more broadly.[7]

Rabbinic leadership adapted their tactics from debates over the heretical counterpublic in the mid-2000s. Instead of invoking the European Jewish Enlightenment, they reached back to earlier narratives from the Torah in order to claim that the contemporary ultra-Orthodox system was itself divinely authorized. At the same time, they drew on a modern sense of the self that conflated mental and spiritual health. Rabbinic leaders claimed that traditional protective structures of male religious authority were the only thing standing between the "cancer" of the internet and the destruction of the Jewish people.

The Authority of Addiction:
Internet *Shmuts* (Filth)

In the mid-2000s, before social media became dominant, ultra-Orthodox leaders focused their attention on online pornography, a.k.a. *shmuts* addiction. One of the dangers of the internet, according to rabbinic leadership, was that users relied on their individual judgment regarding exposure to content. Men online and unsupervised were at the mercy of the easy opportunities for privately accessing contaminating images, that is, pornography, which led to the sin of masturbation (spilling seed). This sin was increasingly framed as an addiction, a kind of sickness, which led to doubting and even defection. Its cure was the establishment of new structures of authority, ones which could protect Jews' innately pure souls.

Rabbinic leadership's warnings were embedded in Orthodox elaborations of the person based on the Talmud and ethical writings. The internet might be a medium for pornography, but it was each Jew's innate struggles with themselves that that led to sin. Ethical texts elaborate that within each Jew there are two inherent inclinations, one for good (*yeytser hatov*) and one for evil (*yeytser hora*). These inclinations are locked in perpetual struggle, guiding, tempting, or confounding over the course of people's lives. Jews were distinct from Gentiles in their willingness to exercise their will, *rotsn*, to fight the evil inclination—also known as Satan—and discern a moral pathway to self-growth and sanctification.[8]

However, the Torah says that no Jew should morally struggle alone. Trusted authority figures could and should offer critical guidance, helping the individual with *hashkofa*, ideological outlook or perspective, to continue to fulfill religious law. Eli on WhatsAppville Yinglish shared a quote with me from Rabbi Nehorai, which reminds each Jew of the need for a close outside authority, "Do not rely on your own understanding." Zalman explained that each ultra-Orthodox and Orthodox Jewish male was expected to have their *daas toyre*, a divinely inspired adviser authorized to make decisions on religious and secular issues, someone whom you run everything by.[9] Women, of course, relied on their female teachers, their fathers, and eventually, their husbands.

Porn on the internet, which could be accessed secretly, removed that protective layer of outside authority, a mark of Jewish distinctiveness from less disciplined Gentiles. For example, an anonymous cartoon from 2005 that appeared in a daily circular and then online (where I found it) depicted a young ultra-Orthodox boy, who was left alone by his father in front of a computer. Without the guidance of his father, the young boy explored the computer, at first visibly shocked by what he was seeing, but then gradually enjoying it. We, the readers, watch as he is physically transformed the more he watches. First his yarmulke falls off. Then his *peyos* (side curls) are gone, along with his modest button-down shirt. A snout emerges, then long horns, a lolling tongue and a spiky back. The sin of masturbation transformed an innocent religious Jewish boy into a literal

monster. The heading of the cartoon read in Yiddish, "Der oysval iz klor!" (The outcome is clear).

Of course, not only ultra-Orthodox Jews are worried about the effects of unsupervised online pornography. There are thriving psychological practices, books, and organizations in the secular world that offer advice on treating online sexual addictions for all kinds of people. Ultra-Orthodox leadership, however, had other motives than secular parents or anxious spouses. They drew on the therapeutic language of addiction so prevalent in the contemporary United States in part because it removed the blame from Jewish individuals.[10] Addiction was a disease, not an ethical failing. Their treatment for porn and internet addiction was to find ways to ensure ever-watchful Jewish authorities, even for the man or boy alone in front of his computer with the door closed.

A good example of these efforts is the website to treat porn addictions, Guard Your Eyes (https://guardyoureyes.com/). The website dedicated to "maintaining moral purity in today's world" was founded in Israel in 2007 by an American Yeshivish rabbi. GYE offered help to those to who were trying to "break free from pornography, internet addiction, sexual obsessions and masturbation."[11] The English-language site deployed metaphors of disease, natural disaster, and war—all external threats to interior integrity—to warn of the "havoc wreaked" on families and individuals from the internet "scourge."

The site made explicit connection between the "*kedusha* [holiness] crisis" (porn addiction) and other social ills among the ultra-Orthodox. Porn was merely the "tip of the iceberg." An image of an actual iceberg was on the GYE website enumerating these dangers. The visible tip of the iceberg listed, "sexual abuse, broken marriages, off-the-*derech* [path], child abuse and lost jobs." Just below the surface of the icy-blue water were others: "adultery, kids at risk, living a double life, marriages on the brink, pedophilia, sexual harassment, and jobs at risk." And submerged in the deep were "hundreds of thousands at-risk." The creation of addictive categories that spanned sexuality, marriage, economy, and religious doubt implied a domino theory of ultra-Orthodoxy, what so many warned was a "slippery slope." One person's struggle with masturbation could affect the existence of the entire *Klal Yisroel* (Jewish people).

Presenting vague scientific data, the site described addiction as a disease that affected the brain's structure. The cure was to put in place healthy ultra-Orthodox Jews, who could offer surveillance to support the individual's struggle to defeat his inclination for evil. For example, a user could sign up for daily *khizuk* (strengthening) emails, forums, or anonymous partner programs, where a sponsor would be sent an alert if inappropriate content was accessed. There was also information on internet filtering, references for therapists and self-guided diagnoses and goals (e.g., "Stay clean for 90 days"). "Addiction," writes anthropologist Don Seeman, "is a religious problem . . . in part because it is perceived as an external agency or compulsion set up over and against the sovereignty of God."[12] By putting in place human authorities, the cycle of addiction could be broken and ultra-Orthodox Jewish addicts could get cured.

Those living double lives, in contrast, used blogs and then social media to publicly challenge rabbis' efforts to blame internet addiction, especially pornography addiction, for religious doubt. On WhatsApp, for example, Maylech, someone who had been living a double life, parodied the way rabbinic leaders ignored serious problems in the ultra-Orthodox world, such as the expense of Jewish schooling, to focus on pornography. He posed the question:

> What is one of the biggest challenges facing *klal yisroel* [the Jewish people]? Is it faltering community coffers leading to the inability for parents to pay tuition at Jewish private schools? The increasingly obvious fact that *frum* Jews are not better than everyone else? . . . Of course it's none of these; it's porn addiction. Duh.

Someone like Yisroel, whom we met in the introduction, described how he was "diagnosed" by a rabbi as having an internet addiction after he revealed his life-changing doubt. He told me how he had tried to explain the difference between addiction and doubt to the "very nice" Rabbi Klein, to whom he had been sent to study Talmud in the hopes of regaining his faith. Some years back, Yisroel said, he had had a friend who was an alcoholic. Yisroel had been involved with his treatment, going to therapists with him and reading up on addiction. He told me:

> I explained to Rabbi Klein, addiction is something your brain gets, you know. So you're right, if you keep an addict away from whatever it is, even by force, by a hundred days this guy will be able to make his own decision and stay healthy if nothing triggers him. But for me, it is not an addiction. . . . If I'm the type of questioning everything, skeptical, there's nothing, nothing, nothing that can convince me. You can try to manipulate me . . . I'm not smart at all. I'm a very normal guy. But eventually, what happens is I start questioning. I blame God about this, and then I start doing research, and no matter how much you're going to block me, I'm going to find it . . . Nothing triggers me. It's not like my brain needs this endorphin.

Those living double lives and those who tried to protect the faithful struggled to explain life-changing doubt, in part because contemporary ultra-Orthodox Judaism was based on the assertion of an innate superiority of the Jewish people: only Jews have a *neshoma* (a God-given soul). Why would any Jew brought up in a *frum* (religious) community, exposed to what so many described as "the beauty" of Judaism, have life-changing doubt or even leave? In their efforts to answer that question, the faithful and those living double lives debated how to understand the medium of the internet itself. For rabbinic leadership and their followers, the internet offered a ready-made explanation that blamed a non-Jewish, addictive medium that carried polluting content. In contrast, those living double lives, especially men, were invested in claiming that their doubting came from real intellectual questions, not just some new technology. Many were eager to tell me that they had consulted books for answers to their questions long before they had gone online. They all acknowledged, though, that online access to all kinds of knowledge had influenced them, as had finding others with similar questions and creating social networks. Over the course of a decade, rabbinic leadership would come to the very same conclusions, which led them to take serious steps to control internet access.

The Authority of Other Heretics: The Men's
Citi Field Anti-Internet *Asifa* (Rally)

The emergence of social media on smartphones in the wake of the Jblogs shook up rabbinic leaders, some of whom began to suspect that online social interaction with other heretics provoked a more dangerous, more contagious doubt than individual porn addictions. Social media allowed for kinds of interactions, especially between men and women, which in its immodesty actually blurred the line between Jews and Gentiles. Perhaps even more significantly, rabbinic leadership in the United States had closely followed Israeli ultra-Orthodox rabbis' public resolutions from 2003–2005, published in their communal newspapers, restricting usage of smartphones and demanding that cellphone companies offer exclusively kosher filtered phones. As communications scholar Tsuriel Rashi recounts, the Israeli rabbis were successful in presenting obedience to them as a "fundamental, legitimate *halakhic* [legal] obligation that was essential for the future of the community."[13] There had been an attempt by American rabbis to emulate the Israeli model soon after, which had not been successful. In part, they failed because American rabbis did not control the press as Israeli rabbis did. Hasidic and Yeshivish leaders decided it was time to try again.

By 2006 Yeshivish rabbis, who had had more experience with social media than Hasidic leaders, had already formed an anti-internet organization, Ichud HaKehillos LeTohar HaMachane (Union of communities for the purity of the camp). In 2011, that group, which had ties to Guard Your Eyes and the new filtering organization the Technology Awareness Group (TAG), set up a meeting for six hundred Hasidic and Yeshivish rabbinical leaders. There they planned an unprecedented rally (*asifa*) for the following year at Citi Field sports stadium in Queens, New York, to announce their new policies: The internet would be banned from all homes, and anyone who had to use it for their livelihood had to filter all devices with a communally approved kosher filter. At first, the organizers had planned to have those filters for sale at the rally, but grumblings about money-making schemes soon ended that plan, attesting to the ambivalence about the economic component of these new policies (see below).[14]

The Citi Field anti-internet rally that took place in 2012 transformed the secular space of the sports stadium into a public, political display of ultra-Orthodox unity at a historical moment when that unity was contested. The set-up that day was visually impressive. Rows and rows of internationally prominent rabbis and rebbes sat at long tables in the front of the stadium.

The scoreboard was silent, but the jumbotron was alive with close-ups of speakers' faces as they gave impassioned warnings, sobbing and yelling against the internet, with English subtitles for Yiddish speeches. Forty-four thousand men and boys dressed in black and white packed the stadium's bleachers (attendance was required by yeshivas). The event was covered extensively by mainstream and Jewish media. As a woman I couldn't attend, but later that evening I went to a screening of the recorded rally for women, one of a number of designated viewing sites throughout Brooklyn and upstate New York. Officially, at least, the Citi Field rally was not streamed; however, some attendees used their smartphones and uploaded the entire event to YouTube, where I watched it. The *Times of Israel* reported that many "skeptics" also tweeted throughout the event, ironically causing the hashtag *#asifa* to trend high that day on Twitter's topics list.[15]

The show of ultra-Orthodox unity was disrupted, just across the street from the Citi Field rally, by a noisy counterrally organized by Zaakah, a group of formerly ultra-Orthodox Jews, who hoped to raise awareness about the cover-up of sexual abuse charges by rabbis. The few hundred protesters, including some double lifers, chanted and held signs that said, "The internet is not the problem." Passersby on their way to the rally heckled them, though a few stopped to see what they had to say.

Inside Citi Field, many speakers described internet addiction and the effort to fight the inclination for evil. However, Rabbi Wachs, a Yeshivish rabbi from Monsey, New York, warned about a more subtle danger, one that more and more would begin speaking against with time: the invisible destruction of Jewish souls from the kinds of social interactions fostered by social media.[16] With his long white beard, Rabbi Wachs took to the podium, thundering:

> *Rabbosay* [Gentlemen], the internet is no longer a tool or a device. The problems are no longer that it's an easier or a quicker way for someone to access inappropriate material. Today, the internet is a culture. It's a psychology. It's a way of life. *Rakhmuna litslon!* [God, merciful one, save us]. *Toyzente* [thousands] . . . *haymishe* [ultra-Orthodox] young Jewish men and wives, who are actively involved in social media, which is the technological equivalent of the *dor ha-mabul* [the generation of the biblical Flood].

Rather than an addictive medium for sexualized images, participation in social media transformed its users through their participation in ways of thinking and bodies of knowledge, "psychology" and "culture," with their own secular forms of authority. The rabbi's code-switch into the talmudic Aramaic, *rakhmuna litslon*, introduced his comparison of the digital age to the biblical generation, who with the exception of Noah and his family, merited destruction by God for their degeneracy. The digital age had its own equivalent in the "lost generation," those men and women defined by their unsupervised access to the internet before protections had been decreed by rabbinic authorities.

Rabbi Wachs claimed that social media invisibly transformed users' interiors, that is, their hearts, souls, and minds. He said, "[The internet] is reprogramming our way of thinking, our emotions, our relationships, our *hashkafas* [Jewish outlooks]. Our very life." These changes were dangerous to the still faithful because they were not immediately apparent. He explained that people on social media might look the same on the outside, but on the inside, he used a talmudic expression, "It's *srefes ha-neshoma ve-guf kayem* [immolation of the soul with the body intact]."

Pounding the podium, Rabbi Wachs warned the faithful to remain vigilant for subtle, new signs that souls had been destroyed, some of the same verbal and embodied signs that rabbis and others had warned about for the Jbloggers:

> You can see it [destroyed souls] in the ebbing of the light and the vacant eyes of the *yungelayt* [young married men], of the jittery inattentiveness of our children, in the flippant and callous language and attitudes. The cynicism, the *leytsones* [mockery], and the unbelievable, unbelievable breaches of *tsnius* [modesty, i.e., sexting] in the most *haymishe* [observant] of *yiddishe* [Jewish] neighborhoods. People are changing. They've become someone else. They're entering a different world.

So much of this rhetoric resonates with people everywhere concerned with the profound effects of digital media on our concentration, civility, inability to connect with others, and easily accessed exploitative sex. But for ultra-Orthodox rabbinic leadership the changes wrought by the internet were so worrying for metaphysical reasons, not only social ones. I remember Hasidic women telling me that Jewish distinction from Gentiles was always visible in innate Jewish refinement, in ways of talking, feeling, and being. Social media, by destroying Jewish souls, threatened to erase these very physical, embodied signs of the distinction between Jews and Gentiles. And that distinction, with its promise of reward in the coming of the messiah, was what the entire ultra-Orthodox world was built on.

Unsurprisingly, those living double lives were not impressed by the Citi Field rally. When I asked Toby, a thoughtful Hasidic woman living a double life, what her friends and family thought about it, she said with a snort of mocking laughter, "My husband was so impressed. My online pals [i.e., double life friends], not so much." Like those protestors at the counter-rally, a number posted on Facebook that the Citi Field rally had been a waste of time, a distraction from the real problems of sexual abuse and corrupt leadership.

Later that evening, at the screening of the entire Citi Field rally held for women and girls in a packed Brooklyn wedding hall, women shushed each other, actively paying attention despite no access to the English subtitles for the Yiddish. Many had their phones out (this was before the filtering), and when a prominent rabbi entered the stadium, women excitedly pointed him out. Some took pictures of the screen, and others seemed overcome by emotion, wiping their eyes. This was when I realized that some women took the bans against the internet and phones quite seriously, perhaps more seriously than their husbands did.

The Authority of Hasidic Women

The 2012 Citi Field rally did not result in across-the-board compliance among Hasidic men, many of whom refused to give up or filter their smartphones. As a result, in the next few years Hasidic leadership turned their attention to women. In rallies and publications, rabbis appealed to women's moral responsibility for protecting their homes, their children, and future generations of Jews.[17] This was not that unusual given that Hasidic women often took it upon themselves to anonymously enforce rabbinic edicts, especially around other women's breaches of modesty. For example, a number of women living double lives told me that they had had anonymous letters from female neighbors slipped under their front doors, warning them that their boundary-pushing clothing had not gone unnoticed. In one such note posted on WhatsAppville Yinglish in Hasidic English and duly mocked, the writer anonymously warned her neighbor that she had seen her at a wedding, where her top was "a bit too wide by the neck," that is, did not fully cover her collarbones as it should (my translations):

> Dear neighbor, I am writing to you this letter just to make you aware on a ענין of צניות
> [an *inyen* of *tsnius*, an issue of modesty]. . . . Don't forget you are hashem's [God's]
> chosen princess and therefore we must fit our position. May we all be zoycheh
> [merit] an abundance of brachos [blessings]. Your dear friend

The anti-internet rallies for Hasidic women were unusual in that Hasidic and Yeshivish rabbis deputized women not just to protect the sanctity of their homes. They also deputized them to circumvent their husbands if necessary and to turn to other trusted male authorities. The cultural logic for this break in the male hierarchy of authority across home and synagogue—husband/father to rabbi—became clear in an anti-internet rally in Brooklyn in 2014 that I attended. There various rabbinic speakers also made the causal argument that the internet created religious doubt, and they made a temporal argument for the special role of women since biblical Egypt in protecting their families from assaults on Jewish survival.[18]

I went to the rally with double lifer, Toby, whose daughter's school had organized the event. She was expected to attend anyway, and I invited myself along. Toby told me that her teenage daughter, Leyeh, had emphatically told her she would not be sitting with us. Her daughter said that she wanted to listen and maybe even get spiritually moved to give up the internet. Who knew? But, she told her mother, if she sat with us she knew that wouldn't happen, since she had long ago figured out that her mother's faith might not be all it should be.

We walked into the huge wedding hall where rows and rows of white folding chairs had been set up, fifteen thousand to be exact. Workers were still erecting the one-way piece of glass (for modesty) in front of a long table on a stage, so the men speakers couldn't see the women, but the women could see them. A bilingual Yiddish-English booklet in a mix of Hebrew and English orthography on each chair was entitled, "כה תאמר Kinus N'shei [Thus We Say, Women's Assembly] ▮▮▮▮, 28 Sivan, 5774, Let's Save Ourselves and Our Generations." The anonymous author rallied the readers on the English side: "Hashem [God] awaits the efforts of our Mamas. Our future generations are pleading with our Mamas. We can. We must. We will not let down our children and the Ribono Shel Olam [the Master of the Universe, i.e., God]!"

On the Yiddish side of the pamphlet was a series of images that built a temporal argument, which compared the sacrifices of prior generations of women to other threats to the Jewish people's existence. The pamphlet reminded women and girls that "כלל ישראל דארף אונזער ערליכקייטן" (klal yisroel darf inzer erlikhkaytn; the Jewish people need our piety). The pamphlet showed four snapshots: Egyptian pyramids, a street in Madrid, the Krakow ghetto, and a streetscape in Brooklyn. The text on the right described the martyrdom of Jewish women when they were slaves in Egypt, during the Spanish Inquisition, and the Holocaust. According to the text, women in those frightening times had to make sacrifices for their families with their lives. Women these days merely have to "live with holiness, with purity" and to be the *veyg vayzers* (those who show the way) forward for their children and husbands.

The very first speaker, one of the organizers of the event, Rabbi Landau, was emotional, practically crying, reminding women that throughout history they have held the *goldene keyt* (golden chain) connecting Jews across time and space. This time, though, he explained, there was a new danger: invisible doubt and technology were today's "Amalek," the spiritual threat to Jewish existence. He thundered, "We know after Citi Field that this is a very different *Klal Yisroel* [Jewish people]. . . . There are more and more who look the same on the outside but are *laydik* [empty] on the inside." Rabbi Landau concluded that only Jewish mothers, *yiddishe mamas*, with their *yiddishe gefil* (Jewish sensibilities) could protect future generations.

Next, a well-known Hasidic rebbe was ushered onto the stage by an assistant holding his hand. The rebbe was very old and very tiny, and it was difficult for me to hear or understand his Yiddish, so inflected was it with Hebrew/Aramaic. He whispered a statement, and one of his chaperones repeated it. Toby explained to me that he was blessing the assembled women and "empowering" them to fight the challenge of our times, *keylim* (digital devices). Meanwhile Toby was busy on her phone. As the rebbe finished speaking, she showed me her Facebook post to a closed group in English: "█████ Rebbe in da house with Ayala Fader," tagging me. As I laughed, watching her post get many likes from her OTD and double-life friends, it occurred to me that this was exactly what rabbinic leadership was worried about. Those, like Toby, who looked and acted *frum* on the outside, but who were secretly mocking authority from the inside. I felt guiltily complicit for my own laughter, which did not seem very professional, so I turned to the woman on the other side of me to get another perspective. I asked her if she had understood the rebbe's blessing, and she told me, "For a rebbe you don't have to understand. Just put the words in your heart."[19]

Toby was not the only one with wandering attention; women chatted through much of the four-hour rally and were often shushed by the emcee, who also told them repeatedly to turn off their phones. However, the final two speakers got everyone's attention and the huge room grew silent. Rabbi Feldstein went to the podium, reminding the audience of the Technology Awareness Group (TAG), which had recently opened a new Brooklyn branch, installing filters on smartphones for free. Making an explicit comparison between a physical illness, the structure of authority for decision-making and the danger of the internet, he said, "When you have to call *Hatzalah* [the private Orthodox emergency response corps], you don't hesitate. You dial the number. . . . don't take the risk, *khalila* [God forbid] and be sorry later on." The physical threat of bodily harm, requiring an emergency call, was compared to the "unhealthy" and equally dangerous threats posed by the internet. The speaker then gave women the authority to use their own judgment when their husbands were too in thrall to their own phones, to turn to other ratified male authorities, such as ultra-Orthodox technology professionals at TAG. In effect, this speaker leveraged women's own sense of moral responsibility, putting the internet into the purview of established male hierarchies of authority, even if it excluded their husbands.

Rabbinic authority to dictate everyday life for others from internet filters to birth control was exactly what many of those living double lives agitated against. For example, double lifer Moishy wrote me a sarcastic text mocking the belief that individual Jews should never rely solely on their own judgment, but should seek out a mentor to consult with on everyday decisions:

> With the onslaught of technology, we can't follow these things constantly, that's why we organized a group of "experts" [i.e., TAG] who will make sure our devices are kosher and only what they approve can be used. We can't be trusted or left to our own devices.

The final speaker, Rabbi Cohen, was a well-known Yeshivish anti-internet activist, who explained exactly how social media caused religious doubt, integrating secular research on cognition with God's design for each Jew. First, as many inspirational speakers do, he drew on secular psychological research with its own authority, while deprecatingly noting that even Gentiles worried about the internet's effects. Rabbi Cohen, for example, quoted journalist Nicholas Carr's book on the negative cognitive effects of internet use to appeal to every Hasidic mother's fears. Carr described the internet's disruption of individual concentration and memory, something that Rabbi Cohen pointed out was the bedrock of boys' Torah and Talmud study. Disrupting Torah study, Rabbi Cohen told the women, is a bigger threat to Jewish holiness than all the porn (*shmuts*) out there on the internet.

Rabbi Cohen also invoked Jewish theological notions of the self and struggles with good and evil. He explained that the medium of the internet itself, not only its content, was dangerous, code-switching between

English and Yiddish, "We are talking about a harmful medium. We are talking about a *shtik yeytser hora* [part of the evil inclination]." That is, the internet was more than a conveyer for things in Satan's bag of tricks to lure well-meaning Jews into doing the wrong thing. The medium *itself* threatened belief because it created contexts for social interactions, which disrupted God's design to protect each person's struggles with the inclination for evil: feelings of shame that came with private, individual reflection.

Anybody, Rabbi Cohen explained, can be assailed by lust or the inclination for evil, or God forbid, a romantic connection. Good people, he said, can have bad thoughts. However, God created the world, so that when a person thinks a bad thought he does it alone, and "he is ashamed of that thought. He thinks he is the only crazy person in the world." (Er sheymt zikh fin dem. Er meynt az er iz der eyntsiker meshigener af der velt.) However, on social media that person can explore impulsively and find others with the same "inappropriate *makhshoves* [thoughts]," who assure him he is not crazy at all, that he is "normal," a common ultra-Orthodox term for someone who "fits in" and does what is expected. And in fact, Rabbi Cohen was exactly right. Many people living double lives told me that the internet had allowed them to find others like them, "normal" people as Tamar said. And this made them suspect that they might just not be crazy after all; in fact, maybe they were right.

Rabbi Cohen defined social media using a term from psalms (26:5), *kinus reshoyim*, an assembly of evildoers, invoking an age-old threat: the erasure of the moral distinction between Jews and Gentiles. This was evident in the feelings Jews had for technology, especially smartphones, which were becoming the most dangerous of all. For example, Rabbi Cohen concluded:

> Too many of us walk around feeling just like a *goy*, that technology is a blessing. It's a wonderful thing. People love their iPhones. If they weren't embarrassed they would kiss them. The main thing is to change that feeling in our heart. We have to recognize that this is something which is out to destroy us.

One rabbi had even begun calling smartphones "*shmad*phones," conversion phones, a pun with the Yiddish verb *shmadn* (baptize), implying a forced conversion; the phone itself could turn a Jew into a Gentile, effectively annihilating them.

Ultra-Orthodox women's challenge, what rabbis were asking of them, was to recognize that technology was part of the inclination for evil, part of Satan's endless effort to inflict harm on them and their families. Once women recognized the threat, they had to exert their will, their *rotsn*, "to submit to the rule of Torah," as a rabbi at another anti-internet rally for Hasidic women that I listened to on DVD emphasized. He concluded:

> We prayed *bashefer* [creator]. You created an inclination for evil, but also ways to defeat it. . . . Help us God. Help us raise our families with piety. . . . we can compete with this inclination for evil. With a strong will, we will beat it.

For women living double lives, the decision to target women in the fight against the internet resonated. Suri posted on a closed Facebook group, "I do see them succeeding with women on this. They are idealizing the spiri-tuality of the technology free life aside from kashrus [the laws of keeping kosher]. And preaching that even in the goyishe world they unplug every night to be with their families." Controlling smartphones, however, proved to be very complicated, since they had become integral to ultra-Orthodox livelihoods and lifestyles for men and women. Rabbis and activists leaned on the schools to enforce the new rules, while some ultra-Orthodox en-trepreneurs began turning phone filtering into its own business.

Institutional Authority and the Business of Kosher Phones

Ultra-Orthodox schools as institutions wielded a great deal of authority beyond their own walls, especially in comparison to New York city public schools. Affiliated with particular rabbinic leadership, ultra-Orthodox schools not only educated children in Jewish and (some) secular studies. They simultaneously, through continuity across home and school, social-ized students into a whole way of life. Students learned, for example, the "right" way to dress modestly, eat kosher, celebrate Jewish holidays, and, by 2017, that smartphones had to be filtered. What students learned in school was generally reinforced at home. Families and schools worked together to provide children and teens with a coherent view of the world and their place within it.

The schools were also critical sources of information in the final years of high school when it came time for parents to arrange marriages for their children. Working with matchmakers, parents sought not only to find God's predestined soulmate for their child, (their *bashert*), but simultane-ously to strengthen and build their extended families. The goal was to make a match with a "top-tier" family if they could, defined by a combina-tion of wealth, lineage, personality, compatibility, attractiveness (mainly for girls), and reputation for Torah study (for boys). Parents and match-makers called up and quizzed teachers and high-school friends to find out what kind of student, person, and friend the intended really was. Choice of school itself provided information about prospective families. In this sense, the schools were like colleges or high schools for many other New Yorkers, which offer clues to a person's social class, abilities, and political orientation. Except the ultra-Orthodox were interested in different markers of prestige.[20]

In their effort to enforce rabbinic rulings over smartphones, the schools began working with kosher filtering organizations. This implicated the school system in the business of filtering, which expanded demand for ultra-Orthodox and Orthodox technicians capable of filtering phones and monitoring those who had complied. For owners of the filtering companies, school rules about filters potentially promised an unending revenue stream. As Sheyndie cynically posted on WhatsApp in response to the new filtering requirements, "Ver zits beim shisel, varem zich" (those who sit by the bowl warm themselves; meaning, those in power control the cash flow).

The fight against the internet and smartphones had not been, at least publicly, about financial opportunity. There are hints that this has begun to change, though my data is relatively scant. Initially, anti-internet rallies and internet-filtering services were funded by charitable donations from wealthy individuals and Orthodox Jewish businesses. For example, at that Hasidic women's anti-internet rally I went to in 2014, each seat had a complementary swag bag containing bottled water, a pastry, and a program. The sponsoring kosher vitamin company's name graced the front of the bag.

Once rabbis and schools began requiring filters, the filters themselves, their installation, and continuous phone monitoring were all integrated into the diversity of distinct rabbinic and school policies that regulated everyday life, which included rulings on modesty, *kashrus* (kosher food), and access to secular knowledge. Different filters became associated with particular rabbinic stances on internet access. Some filters blocked certain words, images, or pages within sites that were allowed. Some systems had a "white list" for kosher sites and a "blacklist" for banned sites, that included porn, social media, some news sites, and video sharing sites. For most ultra-Orthodox filters, Google was the only search engine allowed, but even the results of Google searches were filtered.[21]

Smartphones were in the process of becoming like other media or objects whose content had been made kosher (e.g., women's magazines, sushi, popular music) and that sustained rabbinic structures of authority, economically, religiously, and socially. Take the Hasidic women's phone exchange I went to, for example, where each woman there was required to fill out a Geder filter application form, which asked for personal contact information and a credit card number. There was a ten-dollar set-up charge and then a fifteen-dollar monthly fee for the filtering service after that. Hasidic women attendees were positioned at long tables collecting applications, and behind them was a ceiling-to-floor black velvet curtain. I couldn't resist peeking behind it: modestly concealed from view were about a seventy-five Hasidic men in shirtsleeves, all lined up busily installing filters. The women's phone exchange not only offered women access to kosher phones, but it simultaneously employed many Hasidic men and provided an ongoing revenue flow for others.

To extend their markets, different ultra-Orthodox groups allied themselves with certain brands of filters. For example, by 2014, Satmar Hasidim, led as they were by two different rebbes, each had their own brand of filters, Geder or Meshimer, along with their own butchers, synagogues, and schools. These brands created and sustained their own economic markets, since followers of each were required to buy only products and services endorsed by their rebbe.

Some on my WhatsApp group were especially angry that these two filtering companies had begun to try to expand their markets by mobilizing their influence on the schools. For example, a Meshimer representative had recently contacted Mendy, he told us on WhatsAppville Yinglish, to warn him that his file was still open, that is, he was not completely approved, because his Hasidic boss at work did not use Meshimer. He used a different filter because he was affiliated with a different Hasidic community. The Meshimer representative warned Mendy that his children could be expelled if he did not convince his boss to switch to Meshimer.

Over the course of a few years, the school systems gradually were able to exert more pressure over parents to filter their phones. Moishy, for example, a successful employee in a finance company, told me about the evening in 2015 that a school representative knocked on his door and confronted him, in front of his wife and five children, for having an unfiltered phone, demanding he get one by the following week. In a text to me (not on our WhatsApp group), he told me why he hadn't complied:

I don't want them to have access to my phone, for good reason, I don't want them to see what's going on, because I know that they CAN. I would be extremely uncomfortable with them having access, besides the fact it [the filter] pretty much renders the phone useless as this phone just really sucks, and then they're also forcing you to pay 15/month to do all that, right?

Moishy ignored the deadline, suggesting to me that the school was not really prepared to expel his children for not having a filter. Indeed, a few weeks later he wrote to me, "To update you. Deadline came and went and kids were not expelled." When I asked if he had talked to others—parents or those living double lives—he said no. "If I do, then people start talking, that I was threatened, and then it gets back to them [the school], and then I become a target, so the best way to do this is to just do your thing and keep quiet." Perhaps his financial success also allowed him more leeway in complying with the school's rules.

However, in 2017 the same school had a plan in place and the authority to take action in cases of noncompliance, at least perhaps for some families. For example, Leyzer posted a note in Yiddish to WhatsAppville Yinglish that he had received from his children's school, warning him to filter his smartphone (translation by Rose Waldman):

> Since we've been informed by the *Vaad Mishmeres* [Meshimer Committee] that after many reminders, you still haven't abided by the *tekunes* [rules] of the *mosdos* [schools] in regards to your technological devices, we are letting you know that if you don't get all your devices completely in order—yours and your wife's—by next Thursday *tetsaveh*, 6 p.m., your children will be sent home from our *mosdos* one of these days without any arguments from you. For your own good, get in touch with Meshimer filter at ███████. . . . Signed, *Hanhallah* [Board] of the Yeshiva P.S. Attached is your signature confirming that we can send your children home from the *mosdos* if you don't comply.

Leyzer had apparently, as all parents do in Hasidic private schools, signed a contract agreeing to the school's conditions if the family did not comply with its standards. This included no visits to the public library and no unfiltered smartphones at home. Note that the filtering company had their own committee (*vaad*), which seemed to be working closely with the school authorities.

Leyzer ignored that letter at first, but then he got a call from the school. His children had all been pulled out of their classes and were sitting in the principal's office about to be sent home. In a private chat on WhatsApp I began later that day, he told me that his wife was being "dramatic" since now "they're playing hard ball and playing with the kids. She doesn't care if I have a filter or not, other than doing whatever it takes to keep the kids in school." He got the filter quickly, telling me, "So far I'm tagging along with the filter and no second phone. Kids are just upset since they used to watch YouTube on my phone."

For those living double lives, social media remained an important space to safely and anonymously vent about these increasingly stringent measures toward smartphones, as well as to get information on policy making. For example, Zisi posted on a closed Facebook group, *Eyd*, to express her anger that rabbis had been focusing their attention on women in particular, comparing, as many did, the extremism of certain forms of Islam with their own form of Judaism:

> Wondering about the Geder phone *hechsher* [a rabbinic seal of certification]. Where else is this being pushed besides ▊▊▊▊▊? They are closing in on enforcing it for real. I especially hate how some men say that women go first. After all they [women] do not need it for business!! Ready to punch one of 'em. Steer clear of me today. (And everyday). I feel like I've been deported to Kabul.

As the thread continued, Suri responded, "And until now you felt you were in America?" Others suggested that the only solution was to have two phones, one that was filtered and another one that wasn't.

Rabbinic leadership soon tried to go further, to change the very feelings that smartphones inspired. They aimed their efforts at the generation they had the most control over: young people. For those with grown children, rabbinic edicts had had less influence. Sheyndie told me, for example, that her Hasidic women friends who were in their early forties all had iPhones or Androids that they were not planning on giving up or even getting filtered. Note that most of their children were already married, so they were less reliant on the schools or worried about their reputations. Once school filtering policies were firmly in place, some rabbis tried to further influence children and teens, those who had not yet experienced owning smartphones. They tried to make them afraid of smartphones' contaminating potential. Ultimately and unexpectedly, their efforts created a generational conflict between parental and rabbinic/school authority.

Generational Authority and Smartphones

With filtering policies in place in schools, some rabbis began to try to change how the next generation felt about smartphones in the wider context of mediation, that is, they tried to change cultural and religious meanings, the media ideologies, of smartphones. A number of rabbis began classifying smartphones in a category of material objects that should be avoided owing to their inherently polluting qualities. They subjected smartphones, even filtered ones, to rules for other immodest objects or those which are *muktsa* (forbidden to touch on the Sabbath), which can inspire feelings of disgust. In this way, smartphones as contaminating objects might similarly evoke disgust, but primarily for the young.

I learned about these efforts to change the media ideology of smartphones from WhatsAppville Yinglish, whose members were personally invested in analyzing changing tactics by leadership. Some members, for example, described a strategy to make smartphone owners feel ashamed to display their devices in public. They posted snapshots of official signs posted in their Brooklyn synagogues asking members not to take out their smartphone in the building during prayer and to keep their smartphones hidden in their pockets, so as not to offend or influence anyone nearby.

Then, some synagogues went further. Zalman shared a sign, originally posted in Israel in a Hasidic synagogue, that was making the rounds on many WhatsApp groups. It stated that the devices of others, their impurity, was polluting the environment and, as he translated the sign from Yiddish, "It's justified for the secondhand inhaler to get rid of someone else's device, even on Shabbes, to save oneself from danger." The sign compared cancer-causing secondhand cigarette smoke to proximity to a smartphone. The very air around a smartphone could be deadly. The implication was that those without smartphones had the authority to physically remove the contaminating device in order to save their own lives, even if it violated the Sabbath, or, for that matter, the prohibition against stealing. Shloymie shared another similar sign, reposted from a picture someone had taken in a Hasidic town upstate. He translated the Yiddish and gave his analysis:

> It says that a businessman who must have a smartphone or a tablet, must first of all use the Geder filter. But then it adds the interesting part: he should have a SECOND kosher phone [a phone that just makes calls]. This way people won't see the smartphone as much. They're trying to roll back the normalization of seeing and being seen with smartphones.[22]

The effort to, as Shloymie called it, "roll back the normalization" of having smartphones in the ultra-Orthodox religious public sphere led some in schools to teach their students that smartphones, even with filters, were still immodest and dangerous. For example, Leyzer told the WhatsAppville Yinglish group about his fifth-grade daughter's Hasidic principal who gave a modesty (*tsnius*) lecture to the whole school, which extended the concept of guarding one's eyes (*shmires eynayim*) to looking at a smartphone. Leyzer reported that his daughter quoted the principal, "You have to watch your eyes. And watching your eyes means that you can't look at a smartphone. It doesn't matter if it has a filter or if it doesn't." (Me miz hitn di oygn, in hitn di oygn maynt az men tor nisht kikn af a smartphone, nisht kayn khilik tsi es hot a filter oder nisht.)

This strategy eventually backfired, though. Teaching children one thing in school, when their parents did another at home, disrupted the moral hierarchy of authority: parents passing on *mesoyra* (tradition) to their children. Some children learned in school to be afraid to even touch a smartphone from its potential pollution or infection. This could imply that a parent, who might need that filtered smartphone for work, was suddenly on a lower moral level than their own children.

This problem was evident in Leyzer's next post, where he told us about a friend's son's moral dilemma: how to respect his smartphone-using father:

His 14-year-old פרומע [*frume*, religious] son started studying הילכות כיבוד אב ואם [*hilkhos kibud av v'em*, the laws of respecting one's father and mother] because he struggles how to respect his father, given that he has a smartphone with a filter. Said friend goes to mikvah [men's ritual bath] before lighting Chanukah ליכט [*likht*, candles], so you get an idea of the type of person [i.e., very pious]. Insanity!

In this incident the pious teenager felt he had to strengthen his faith by going back to one of the most basic commandments in the Torah, respect for one's parents. This was despite the fact that his own father was so religiously stringent that he went to the *mikva* before a minor holiday when most didn't. Nevertheless, because the teen's father had a filtered smartphone, the teen felt he was unable to completely fulfill that most basic commandment of parental respect.

The sense that smartphones had become contaminating, forbidden objects was aimed at teens and children and originated in schools. However, the disgust for and fear of being seen publicly with a phone eventually filtered down (no pun intended) to other adult contexts. For example, Sheyndie posted in 2017 that at a cousin's wedding she had her phone out and was recording some of the festivities because her sister was the emcee on the women's side of the celebration. A friend glanced at her and said, "Yoysh, how do you dare?" Sheyndie told her, "It's not my crowd, so I can."

Nevertheless, the schools' policies had the most emotional and social impact on children. For example, Leyzer posted this to WhatsAppville Yinglish in September 2017 (my translation):

Yesterday I took along my 7-year-old nephew to the park with my kids, as I often do. While driving, he noticed my phone and yelled out, "Yoy! a smartfone! M'tur nisht!" [Wow! A smartphone. That's not allowed!]. The kid was in a panic. My kids assured him that it wasn't a smartphone, only an iPhone [making them complicit actually]. The campaign is working. There's a generation of kids growing up with the knowledge that a smartphone is evil. Insanity.

That same year an anonymous activist began manufacturing *shomrim kartlakh*—"Guardian" trading cards, which detailed smartphones' dangers. *Shomrim* (guardians) are the private ultra-Orthodox emergency responders, so the cards played on their heroic image, suggesting the cards were similarly providing a protective service to the ultra-Orthodox. A few boys' schools in Brooklyn even distributed the cards for free, I heard, and some children began to collect them. When I called a Brooklyn store to see if they carried them, they said they were sold out.

Images of the cards were, of course, posted on WhatsAppville Yinglish and made fun of. They were stylistically diverse. Some cards had cartoon images, such as an anthropomorphized, human-sized smartphone laughing, holding an ultra-Orthodox Jew by the nose, asking in Yiddish, "Who has whom by the nose, heh, heh, heh?" (i.e., who's in control?). In another, a smartphone is depicted as the historical figure of Haman, the villain in the Purim story; only the ultra-Orthodox Jews do not bow down before the Haman/smartphone. Other cards had Yid-

dish and Hebrew text instructing children on how to know if a phone was "clean" (*rayn*) and how to judge if a Jew was pious (*erlikh*) from his phone use. Some had images of ultra-Orthodox parents distracted by their phones, with children longing for their attention or even put into harm's way, for example, a stroller pushed into oncoming traffic with a distracted mother on her phone. There were also cards that depicted the dangerous effects of cellphone use, such as an ultra-Orthodox Jew, disheveled and deformed from phone use, with flies buzzing around him, rotten to the core.

Eventually, I heard on WhatsAppville Yinglish that some parents had gotten fed up with the cards because they "disrupted *mesoyra* [tradition]," where parents had the moral authority to educate their children, not vice versa. Someone posted an incident to YouTube where a Hasidic man kicked over a table set up with Shomrim Cards for distribution on one of the main avenues in Borough Park, Brooklyn, accusing the purveyor of teaching kids to be *khitspedik* (willfully defiant of authority, chutzpah).[23] Someone else even posted an anti-Shomrim Card: it showed an ultra-Orthodox Jew refusing to accept the Torah from God (displaying the fifth commandment, "Honor your father and your mother"), because he was too busy delivering a box of . . . Shomrim Cards! Indeed, right before Pass-

over in 2016, when all the leavening is swept out of houses and publicly burned, someone posted a picture of a bonfire, with Shomrim Cards tucked into the sides of the metal trashcan ablaze.

Religious Authority vs. Individual Autonomy

Despite the pitfalls of the Shomrim Cards, a few years later they made a comeback, and children began to collect them again. More important, smartphones really did begin to inspire disgust in some of the younger generation. While schools realized they could not disrupt parental authority, the voluntary rejection of smartphones gradually became an additional stringency that anyone could choose to take on in order to reach a higher level of piety. In 2016 someone on WhatsAppville Yinglish reported overhearing teachers in a girls' school saying that their daughters had decided not to touch smartphones altogether, although this created the inevitable moral dilemma over what to do if an older person asked them to pass them their smartphone. Should they obey the older person as they were obligated to by the Jewish commandments, or potentially endanger themselves? Even in matchmaking fact-finding missions, girls were asked if they had a smartphone to see how *erlikh* (pious) they were, along with other questions about themselves. A few months later, I heard that Leyeh, Toby's daughter, had actually been so moved by her school's anti-Internet rally that she traded in her smartphone for a kosher all-talk "basic" flip phone with its certified sticker. At the end of that year she was awarded a prize by her principal for never having texted in high school.

Rabbinic leadership continued their efforts to protect the faithful from the internet's corruption by shoring up their own authority. They used their voices, landlines, and print, the most kosher media of all, to assert that only they were the rightful custodians of Jewish truth. When men refused to give up the internet altogether, leadership adapted their strategies over time. In their speeches and their edicts, they invoked not the Jewish Enlightenment as they had years earlier, but the more ancient temporality of the Torah. They compared social media users, for example, to the generation of the Flood or smartphones to Amalek, the archenemy of the Jews. The invocation of biblical characters and narratives mediated contemporary challenges in New York, casting its own prophetic authority.

Leaders interpreted the internet's threat to individual faith by drawing on ideas of the self both from Jewish ethical writings and from popular psychology, which was becoming increasingly accepted. The internet could be part of the evil inclination, which had to be struggled against, but it could also be an external source of addiction, which was beyond individual will or control, requiring another Jew's supervision. Over time that message evolved to associate smartphones with mental health problems. For example, in 2019, a public speaker, whose lecture circulated on WhatsApp groups, described ultra-Orthodox Jews who used smartphones as *tsefrasket* (צופראסקעט), a new Yiddish term implying, as Zalman wrote, "A personal failure in society, probably coming from a dysfunctional family and a difficult childhood."[24] The speaker also called anyone who used a smartphone a *rakhmunes* (someone to pity, a loser), as Zalman put it, a "basket case." Rabbinic leadership increasingly conflated psychological health and Jewish ethics with the willingness to submit to authority.

Ultimately, this most recent threat to Jewish Orthodox existence could only be fought by reinforcing existing male hierarchies of religious authority; the individual should not, could not, be trusted to decide for themselves how to use the internet, just as no one should decide alone if a piece of meat was kosher or a skirt was modest enough. There were experts for those decisions, (in a way) divine mediators, men who had the scholarly knowledge and experience to make ethical judgments. Hasidic women and sometimes youth could be effective allies in supporting those male hierarchies who were ratified to make decisions about a new medium. Zalman predicted on WhatsAppville Yinglish, only half-jokingly, that there would soon be legal religious publications on the issue of smartphones in ultra-Orthodox life, and Leyzer agreed that sooner or later there would be.

Those living double lives contested rabbinic authority. They claimed the right to make their own ethical judgments because they no longer accepted that rabbinic authorities were actually divine mediators of the truth. The alternative moral systems that they developed, however, put them in direct conflict with their still-religious spouses and families. In order to live their new morality with its own individual authority, they had to paradoxically keep secrets from and lie to those closest to them.

PART II

4

The Morality of a
Married Double Life

Facebook Messenger, a Sabbath afternoon:

Pinny: Hi git shabbos! 😊

Ayala: .. . . We had so many mutual friends I friended you- do we know each other? I am an anthropologist working on a book about double lifers, the Internet and those who try to build emineh [*emuna*, faith]. Just to let you know.

Pinny: Oh great! I'm a double lifer myself. I'm chasidish living in ▮▮▮ originally from ▮▮▮▮▮▮▮▮.

Ayala: . . . I'm especially interested in the family dynamics when one person is double life

Pinny: My wife is frum [religious] she didn't know about my status for a while but then after opening her mind a bit I felt I can trust her and I told her that I'm agnostic. And that I don't keep anything [i.e., religious laws]

Ayala: Was your wife ok with your agnosticism? She didn't want to divorce?

Pinny: No, she didn't go for divorce because I didn't tell her anything before I felt comfortable enough that she will take it with a open mind. Even though I wasn't so scared of divorce because I couldn't live this double life in my own home anymore

Ayala: It was too difficult the double life at home? How did you open her mind?

Pinny: Well it took me years of therapy and loads of money, convinced her to start reading, slowly started watching movies with her (it's a big no no in her upbringing) and from here on its a very long story how I worked like the biggest engineer to talk to her about open minded stuff but she shouldn't connect it to me. But after 5 years of non stop therapy a bit from everything worked something

Ayala: Complicated. would you ever meet me for an interview?

Pinny: Why not? I see we share a lot of friends so I assume you understand how secret is has to be because I have everything to lose. But I would love to meet with you

I did meet with Pinny soon after, and as with so many others I met, I heard about the difficulties of keeping secrets in intimate domestic spaces. Living a double life often included lying to, hiding from, and sometimes betraying a spouse. This made everyday life rife with ethical choices. Those living double lives had to navigate murky moral dilemmas in their marriages. For still-religious spouses who discovered a husband or wife's life-changing doubt, their worlds turned upside down. The uniqueness of each double lifer's marriage tells us more broadly about the diversity of life-changing doubt over time.

Sociologist Georg Simmel long ago defined secrets as knowledge kept by some and away from others, creating insiders and outsiders, those who know and those who know they don't know. Secrets themselves are never inherently moral or immoral; rather, they are generative, creating boundaries between people who struggle with the tension between revelation and secret keeping.[1] For those living double lives that tension between revelation and secret keeping meant choosing between self-fulfillment and comfortable familiarity, individual truth and protection of their family. Under the very noses of their still-religious spouses, double lifers secretly began violating the religious laws and obligations upon which their marriages were built, all the while appearing as ultra-Orthodox men and women to friends, family, and their communities. These kinds of moral compromises were the price those living double lives paid for their reluctance to leave the security of the known. They made what they saw as the most ethical, responsible decision of all: to shield their families from pain by keeping their life-changing doubt a secret.

Anthropologist Tanya Luhrmann, writing about secrecy among contemporary witches in England, noted, "To hold a secret is to assert some control over your private life, to choose what you make public."[2] When those living double lives rejected ultra-Orthodox morality and its obligations, they often developed an alternative moral system, one inflected by North American liberal ideas about the individual's right to autonomy, their personal authority to make ethical judgments, along with other liberal values like tolerance and pluralism.[3] Their emerging liberal ideas about the person contrasted to ultra-Orthodox notions, which emphasized each Jew's moral responsibility to use their individual autonomy to submit to religious authority to fulfill the destiny of the Jewish people. Double lifers, in contrast, often redefined *yiddishkayt* (Jewishness) as "a lifestyle" or as "cultural" rather than a divinely revealed truth. With shifting morality, their priorities also changed to include personal fulfillment (over religious adherence), romantic love, and an ambivalent desire to fit in with or at least participate some in the secular world.

Men and women, of course, had different resources for living double lives. Men with intellectual doubts had a deep Jewish history of heresy (*apikorsus*) to draw on, which in some ways legitimated their struggles as intellectuals. Living a double life required independence, mobility and time, which were all in short supply for many ultra-Orthodox women, especially mothers. "You don't think it is more difficult for a woman to release herself than it is for a man?" posted a woman on the comment thread on a blog about Orthopraxy, "Men get respect, a woman who does this will be dragged through the mud."

Not only did women have fewer opportunities for keeping secrets and less support when they did, they also had much more to lose if their secrets were discovered. On that same comment thread, someone remarked on the potential loss of child custody in cases of divorce, "A woman would have her children ripped away from her, potentially forever." Divorce in ultra-Orthodox families was at the discretion of the husband, who had to present his wife with a written *get* (a divorce document) in order for the divorce to be legal according to Jewish law. When custody for the children could not be resolved in the Jewish Orthodox court system (*beys din*) couples went to civil family court, which was costly and time-consuming. I have heard that extended families on both sides often sided with the still-religious spouse (male or female) if that spouse wanted the children, offering financial and emotional support with the goal of keeping the children religious at all costs. Women generally had fewer financial resources than men, since so many of them stayed home with their children. In one of the most public divorce cases, for example, Tsippy described to me how her own parents had testified against her retaining custody in favor of her husband since she had gone OTD (off the path) and her ex-husband had remarried a religious woman and had a religious home. The fear of divorce, which was stigmatizing to entire families for generations, kept many double lifers, but especially women, in the heretical closet.[4]

Anthropologists have long been interested in moral norms, codes and institutions of societies, going back to French sociologist Émile Durkheim in the late nineteenth century. More recently, though, in works that build on Aristotle's ethics and the later work of philosopher Michel Foucault, a number of anthropologists have focused on what individuals actively choose to do in their efforts to become certain kinds of virtuous people.[5] Anthropologist Didier Fassin argues, however, that the opposition between obligation and virtue, between either following the moral rules of a society or ethically working on individual virtue, does not adequately account for the "the evaluation of the consequences" of what a person does or does not do. That is, a person's evaluation of the emotional and practical consequences of their actions will depend on how that person is positioned in their society. For example, women and men in ultra-Orthodox Judaism have different possibilities for their individual strivings to be ethical, just as they have different moral norms and obligations to follow in ultra-Orthodoxy as husbands and wives. Not to consider these social differences erases politics from the study of ethics and morality.

In real life, Fassin notes, people in different positions "simultaneously take into account moral norms, practice ethical reflection, and consider the emotional and social consequences of their acts."[6] Those living double lives juggled competing moral systems even within their own marriages, ethically torn between their gendered obligations and their newfound desires and ideas. This included constantly evaluating the emotional consequences of secrecy and revelation in their families. Double lifers kept up religious practices in the privacy of their own homes, intent on deceiving their spouse in order to protect their families. Betrayal was the only way to live an ethical double life, unless, like Pinny, one was lucky enough to "flip" a husband or wife and go on that journey together (see chapter 7 for children of double lifers).

Some flirted with confession by living what anthropologist Michael Taussig called a "public secret," the secret everyone knows not to know.[7] They made small changes to their dress, head-coverings, or beards over time to assert their own authority, to fit in more with their perception of secular life, to try to feel more comfortable in their own skins. They slowly let their spouse and families get used to the knowledge that they were changing, all in the name of doing the right thing, of making an ethical, emotional judgment. As Leyzer said one day on WhatsAppville Yinglish: "Am I afraid of the cold world out there? Sure, but I'd take the plunge if I weren't afraid of hurting my family and breaking my parents' hearts."

Double-Life Men

Along with many of their *frum* peers, as teens many men had secretly experimented with the forbidden, broken minor religious laws, or were just not that emotionally invested in being pious. Shmuel told me, for example, how he and some friends in their stringent upstate yeshiva cleverly recorded heavy metal over inspirational lectures on audiocassettes. When a rabbi would pass through their dorm and ask to see what a *bokher* (student) was listening to on his headphones, he could innocently show him the cassette labeled with a prominent rabbi speaking words of Torah. Others described clandestinely watching movies or television, or playing basketball. Zalman told me that as a teen he would go to a Manhattan hospital every week to donate blood, just so he could watch television there. He had the track marks to prove it too.

Most remembered that as boys they had had theological and philosophical questions, which they tried to answer themselves. Gavriel for example, who came from a very prominent Hasidic family, began to independently read a lot of the *kiruv* (outreach) literature for newly religious Jews, which was more open to questioning. Others similarly "looked into *sforim* [religious books]" on their own to try to resolve theological or intellectual contradictions. In many cases, their efforts to find answers led them down paths to forbidden texts (for Hasidic Jews), such as Maimonides's *Guide for the Perplexed* or the writings of the more contemporary Rabbi Avigdor Miller or Rabbi Natan Slifkin. Very few ever asked their questions to a rabbi or a family member, though. Pinny explained his own unresolved questioning, "You can't tell anyone. You're not going to have any *shiddukh*s [matches]. Your life is [would be] over. . . . But always you think about it."

By twenty most were married in arranged matches. For some the lead-up to the marriage was a time to start over, to try to get more serious about *emuna* and repress doubt. Before his wedding, Gavriel made a pilgrimage to the graves of his family in Poland and Hungary. Over the grave of an ancestor who was a prominent rabbi he made a promise, "I won't delve into philosophical books. . . . I have to make a new life." He would try to embrace *emuna peshuta* (simple faith). However, the relative freedom that many experienced as newly married young men, accountable to no one but their new wives and growing families, created time and space for old questions and doubts to resurface. This time, the internet facilitated their search for knowledge and for social approbation, and this time, though they remained in the closet, many of them dramatically changed their understanding of their worlds and their places within it. Life-changing religious doubt was never just an intellectual dilemma (though some men liked to frame it that way). Life-changing doubt might be rooted in theological questions, but it was shaped by temperament, social standing, and the intimacy of familial relationships.

Yitsy: Enlightenment and Moral Autonomy

I met Yitsy for the first time in a café in Brooklyn, where he stood out among the tattooed hipsters, despite the ubiquity of full beards and hats. As a teen known to be *ofgeklert* (enlightened) he had long had doubts about "Hasidic beliefs, like with the rebbe. . . . I couldn't reconcile my beliefs . . . with the Hasidic belief system." He was sent to a yeshiva in Israel to study, where he dipped into forbidden books that tried to reconcile biblical criticism with religious sources. But even then, he told me, he was not a *koyfer* (heretic), "I didn't touch the question of God or *toyre min ha-shamayim* [Torah from heaven, i.e., divine revelation at Mount Sinai]." He did, though, eventually begin to explore what he called "theological issues," and two particularly bothered him. First, how was the Torah's command to kill Amalek (Jews' mortal enemy) moral? That is, how could God command a Jew to kill anyone, even their mortal enemy? And second, if we no longer have direct contact with God as they supposedly had in the Torah, why should he have to do what any old rebbe told him, just because "he learned a few more folios [sections] in *gemora* [Talmud]?" This was a direct challenge to a rebbe's authority; Yitsy felt his rebbe did not have any greater connection to God than he did, refuting the kind of divine authority as mediators that some rebbes claim.

Soon after, Yitsy entered matchmaking. Despite his reputation as someone who was "a little different," he was still a good learner from a "nice" family. In matchmaking the prospective groom is expected to be a learned Torah scholar, or at least competent. Being a nonconformist thinker, Yitsy said, wouldn't bother people as much as someone who shaved his beard, for example, or who went with short *peyos*, neither of which he was doing. He told me that at that time, while he was questioning the authority of the sages (*khazal*), he still "believed strongly in *halokha* [religious law]." A good match was swiftly proposed; he got happily married. As Yitsy summed it up, "We love each other."

As a married man, he learned with a *khevrusa* (partner) in *kollel* (yeshivas for married men), which provided a stipend and had flexible hours. With his newfound free time, he began to question the idea that there was only one way to be ultra-Orthodox. He increasingly relied on his own individual authority to make decisions about belief and practice. Describing his present-day agnosticism, he said:

> I'm actually convinced that Torah wasn't given at Mt. Sinai the way it's perceived, and I also don't think that's the only way that one

could keep the Torah. The Torah could be like Reconstructionist Judaism, that keeps *mitsves* [commandments] because it is their culture and that's believing in the Torah as well. Why isn't that Orthodoxy? Who decides what Orthodox is?

Yitsy emphasized his autonomy to make his own judgment about religious practice; he told me he was keeping "most" of the *mitsves* "out of a choice." Ironically, Yitsy loved learning more now that he no longer had to believe everything he read was true. When he used to learn he found the inconsistencies in the texts and the attempts to explain them away deeply troubling. He told me that by using a historical perspective, he understood the texts as providing insight into "our history, what they [historical figures] said and thought about." The inconsistencies no longer had to be reconciled because he no longer believed the words to be God's.

At first, Yitsy shared his new ideas with his wife. He told his wife that his conviction in his own ethical judgment was so strong that "if I would encounter Amalek, that I wouldn't kill, even if God said to kill him I wouldn't. And I wouldn't feel guilty about it either." That is, Yitsy told his wife that he would disobey a direct order from God because he, as an individual, disagreed with it. Yitsy's wife was not thrilled that he was increasingly becoming what he called an "outlier" in the community, but she also did not question him too closely. Yitsy's priority and hers was staying together. Yitsy said, "I didn't make a commitment to tell her the truth, but I won't lie to her. I'm pragmatic." He said, "She knows I'm very skeptical, and I don't believe things that deeply, but she doesn't go there most of the time. She doesn't ask me and just assumes I probably believe, and after all I'm Orthodox. I keep everything."

Yitsy and his wife shared his secret, enabled by silence, avoidance, and gendered authority. His wife did not even protest when on vacation, Yitsy dressed, as he described it, like a tuna baygel (i.e., a bum in shorts, a T-shirt, and tucked-up side curls under a baseball hat).[8] His wife was economically, socially, and emotionally dependent on him and had been taught her entire life that he should be the leader of their spiritual life together. As a psychiatrist who had worked with a number of double lifers explained it, "Women are trained to be facilitators and help-mates since conception, pre-conception."

In a twist on the Hasidic male role of being his wife's guide in spiritual matters (*rukhnius*), Yitsy enjoyed explaining to his wife how the text had developed historically, hoping to make her feel more relaxed about her religious stringencies, especially around sex. Sometimes this backfired, though, like the time that she told him, "You're so persuasive, you're going to brain-wash me." He responded, "*Khas ve-sholom!*" (God forbid!) He told me that he did not try to influence her much anymore because he knew personally how "it can be torture to try to change your beliefs." Instead, his decision to keep silent was a way to both protect her faith and his own secrets.

For self-defined *ofgeklerte* men like Yitsy, living according to his own moral framework did not preclude continuing to be the authority of his household, even as he explored knowledge facilitated by new media. For example, Yitsy had started reading and writing on the Yiddish online forum, *Kave Shtibl*, with other open-minded men. After learning in the mornings, he spent many afternoons hanging out with a few other *of-geklerte* newly married Hasidic men in a Brooklyn café, where they discussed books, gossiped, debated, and dreamed.

Wives in marriages like Yitsy's were often willing to overlook their husbands' lack of *varemkayt* (warmth, fervor) in religious matters, if they continued to keep up their outside appearances and religious practices in ultra-Orthodox public and private spaces. And even mockery (*leytsones*) could be a cover for heresy rather than revealing it. For example, Tamar's husband (chapter 2), who actually had become a complete atheist over time, was never kicked out of his synagogue, despite sometimes yelling the Arabic phrase *Allahu akbar* (God is great) at the conclusion of *daven-ing* (prayers). Those around him laughed, assuming that he was joking. After all, there he was like everyone else, sitting in *shul* on a Sabbath morning, with his long beard and side curls, and striped prayer shawl (*tallis*) draped over his shoulders. What or who he believed he was praying to, or even whether he had tucked some other reading into his prayer book and wasn't praying at all, was less important.

Boruch: "Flexible Morals" to Make Life Bearable

Boruch, who was also Hasidic, agreed to meet me in my office one autumn afternoon. His reddish beard wasn't that long and his *peyos* were rolled up and tucked behind his ears, almost out of sight. On top of his white button-down shirt, he was wearing a cardigan, not a long black coat, and he was only wearing a big black velvet yarmulke, not the hat on top that most Hasidic men wear. He was a businessman, who had became very success-ful. When I asked him how he defined himself, suggesting perhaps *of-geklert*, he quickly responded, "I'm way past that. I was *ofgeklert* when I was twenty, and now I'm thirty-six. I've settled past that."

Boruch had been very curious as a teen, but he kept his questions to himself. He knew that asking too many questions would hurt his reputation. He did, however, regularly sneak into public libraries with his study partner, where they read whatever they wanted. His study partner stayed a believer. Boruch did not. A brilliant student, teenage Boruch was sent to a yeshiva in Israel, where he continued his habit of visiting forbidden libraries. He remembered an experience in the library of Hebrew University that was transformative:

> I walk in to this big study hall. It was the middle of the summer, and I see this *khevrisa* [study partnership]. The woman was barely dressed. It was hot, and her partner was a guy in shorts and a tank top. They were learning *gemora*, they had the regular *gemora*, the one I use, same *sforim* [religious texts] and they were sitting there and arguing loudly, a man and a woman. . . . I remember this "aha" moment then. To me, it's like, "Wow!" You are always taught in yeshiva that the only way to learn is how we learn. . . . But these people looked like they were even more lively on the subjects than I would be.

Watching that study partnership in Israel made Boruch wonder what other things he had been taught as essential truths that were not so.

Upon his return to New York he got married as expected, but he quickly realized that he and his wife had very little in common, except they were both opinionated, strong-willed people. He began to explore the city, as well as socialize with non-Jews at his job. He quietly went to lectures at Yeshiva University, where he formed a friendship with a Modern Orthodox rabbi, something that was really not acceptable to the ultra-Orthodox. They had long discussions together, and Boruch made the independent assessment, a judgment, that what he had been raised with as religious law (*halokha*) was, in fact, merely interpretation. Like Yitsy had, Boruch was making a historical critique of contemporary ultra-Orthodox authority. He asserted his right to choose the less religiously stringent path, arguing that leniency was not a violation of religious law.

At home, Boruch kept up the pretense that he was fulfilling the expected male daily ritual practices, but in fact over time he did less and less. Initially, he felt he could live a Modern Orthodox life, but as he began to read "these online forums" he started "not seeing the point." Soon he had stopped observing all Jewish laws in private, away from communal and familial eyes. When I met him, he described how every morning he left his house early as if he were going to *daven*. Instead, he walked around the block and got a cup of coffee. Sometimes he told his wife he would *daven* at work. "It's nerve-racking," he said, "But I've been doing it for so long that I'm used to it." Because he no longer believed in the truth of ultra-Orthodoxy, he did not feel guilt at the religious transgressions themselves. Boruch's strategy was to "fly below the radar." He elaborated, "I keep to myself. I don't make a lot of noise."

However, the secrets Boruch kept from his wife and his children did make him feel guilty. His wife, he said, didn't know even "20 percent" of what he believed and what he did. At one point he had tried to share some of his changing ideas with her, but she had gotten upset. "She wasn't ready for that," Boruch said. Instead, he soon began to see other women, meeting many on the dating app Tinder. When I asked about it on WhatsApp, he explained, "I sometimes do feel guilty on my marriage state. I feel much more guilty about my kids and that is what drives me to not to dissolve my marriage. (It should drive me to better keep my marriage vows 😔 and sometimes it does)."

Boruch's changing morality made him prioritize his marriage and self-actualization above religion. This was something his wife refused to agree with, which was how he justified seeing other women. He wrote, "I tried to drag my spouse to therapy, so she puts my marriage first and tries to understand me and my struggles and live with them. Rather she puts religion and perception [i.e., reputation] ahead of the marriage." And as a result, he wrote, "I possibly put myself and my survival ahead of my marriage too." At the end of the day, though, Boruch concluded, "Justifications and rationalizations don't make any of it right. They are just excuses and cop-outs, but enough to numb the guilt (unfortunately)."

Boruch ended up living in a state of what he called "flexible morals," meaning that in order to survive and stay with his family, he had to engage in—according to him—some ethically questionable activities, like having affairs and lying to his wife. Boruch's wife, like Yitsy's, rarely confronted him, except for occasionally threatening to ask family members or rabbis to talk to him. Those threats fell flat though when Boruch told her he would welcome them. He surmised that she would have been humiliated to have her family or any rabbi know the truth about him. Boruch's wife relied on her husband, and she was in no position to "rock the boat," fearing as she did, the effects of divorce on their children.

Boruch and Yitsy were both well-positioned men: financially stable and good learners from "good families" (i.e., well respected). Their intellectual questioning led both to redefine Judaism as a cultural tradition, a historical legacy, rather than a revealed religious truth. This, in turn, legitimated their claims to individual authority to make ethical judgments, undermining the authority of their rabbis and even the Torah. Their different marriage situations, though, had implications for how they lived their life-changing doubt.

Still, their newfound autonomy was often exercised at the expense of their wives, who were unable to create the kind of Jewish homes they might have wished for, where husbands and fathers were the leaders in spiritual matters. There were some men who were able to convince their wives over time to change and become more open-minded. Pinny, whose Facebook message opened this chapter, described, for example, how over a period of ten years he persuaded his wife to distinguish between her obligation to follow *halokha* and religious *khumra* (stringency). He said, "She didn't break anything, but she's gotten less . . . guilty about everything." A wife's willingness to keep her double-life husband's secrets could be one of the only ways for her to maintain intimacy with her husband, as well as respectability, protecting her children and assuring her own reward in the world to come.

Motti: Tormented by the Anxiety of Secret Doubt

One of the private Facebook groups for those living double lives used to be called "Double the Life, Double the Fun." There were, however, plenty of men with life-changing doubt who were deeply frustrated, unhappy, guilty, and stuck. There were some who were so conflicted keeping secrets and living double lives, that they attempted to abandon their double lives altogether. Pinny told me on Facebook, "They go back, become *frum* again. They started thinking, maybe there is something to it [religious belief]. Why should I take the chance?" They were, he told me, brought up with such a fear "that they can't help but worry that it might be true."

Motti, for example, found the stress of living a double life unbearable for a time. Short, with a long blond beard and perfect *peyos*, he had a vulnerable, slightly startled air, like a deer caught in headlights. He was from a comfortable Hasidic family. His slide into life-changing doubt followed that of many other men: he had a quick intellect, was dissatisfied with the answers he had been given, and was a huge reader of all kinds of books and blogs and social media. Little by little he began to question his own beliefs and the system. All of this happened while he got married, had four children, and began working for a tech company.

As he began to question, his double life expanded. He soon found other Hasidic men with doubts, becoming especially friendly with Yitsy, Yonah and Gavriel, with whom he regularly hung out. He got on WhatsApp and Facebook and went to some of the double-life get-togethers. Then he enrolled in Brooklyn College. I was impressed by his broad-ranging curiosity. When he came to meet me at Fordham for an interview once, he asked me to arrange for him to talk to a priest, just for curiosity's sake. He was an artistic soul in a community that he described as not valuing art. Whenever we met, he asked me about my own views on feminism, Israel, the nature of language. We had long arguments about the meaning of life, making me feel like an angsty teen all over again. Temperamentally, though, Motti was high-strung, and he struggled with anxiety. Living a double life had only made him more anxious. When I asked how he was doing another time, he taught me a new Yiddish word, *ungetsoygen* (stressed out). One day, he suddenly disappeared from social media. When I asked, Yitsy told me that Motti had "gone back." Unsure if I was intruding, I wrote to Motti on WhatsApp, but he barely answered, and we stopped corresponding. I missed his voice over the year.

Then, just as suddenly, a year later he reappeared on WhatsApp, where he posted a rant called "Ruined by Facebook," which he gave me permission to print here:

> I've always believed that the Internet has made my life easier. On the Internet, I found answers to many pressing questions that were on my mind, and I have made most of my closest friends on social media and internet forums.
>
> However, I've come to realize that the internet has in many ways been a disaster for me. It alienated me from my community and family, it made me lose my faith and thereby turned me into an impostor. It increased my anxieties tenfold and now I don't even have a God to turn to in my distress. I am wondering if the internet is, indeed, as dangerous as the charedim [ultra-Orthodox Jews] claim it is . . .
>
> I now often wish I could unlearn the things I've discovered on the internet but it is too late. The terror of modernism is already part and parcel of my identity and I feel unable to extirpate it. Or perhaps it's just me and my endless pessimism that sees the negative aspects of anything and everything.

Motti blamed the internet for everything, especially life-changing doubt that turned him into an "imposter." He was even deprived of the comfort of God because he no longer believed. At the same time, at the very end of his screed, he acknowledged that his own pessimistic outlook must have been to blame as well.

I wrote to him on WhatsApp to try to understand, asking him what had made him "go back in." Motti responded, "I didn't exactly went [*sic*] back in. I mean I've always been in, and I still am." He explained more:

> Well, for over a year I lived an extremely isolated life. Hardly spoke to anyone at all. So it's not as much as I went back in. What I would say is that I've come to a certain acceptance of the place I live in. That it isn't gonna change. And I try to take the best of both worlds.

Lately Motti seems more at peace, at least on social media, where we keep in touch. So far, his wife has kept his secrets, as far as she knows them, from their families. In fact, Motti told me that despite having revealed to his wife that he had many questions and that he rarely prayed, she had decided there was no real problem. She explained to him that despite his doubts, she still thought his level of spirituality (*rukhnius*) was much higher than hers because he knew so much more Torah. In this way, Motti's wife used his knowledge of Torah, rather than his actual belief system, to legitimize his continuation as head of the household, as it should be.

Double-Life Women

Jewish studies scholar Naomi Seidman remembers growing up ultra-Orthodox in Brooklyn, aware that what she really wanted to become just didn't exist for girls. She wrote, "A boy might conceivably become an *apikoyres*, but transgression in a girl could only mean something sexual. . . . I myself aspired to something more dignified, something that signaled intellectual force rather than bodily weakness. I was a philosopher, I hoped, not a whore."[9] Ultra-Orthodox women and girls did not have the option, the privilege of being intellectuals, even when they became heretics. Those who were too smart, too eccentric, or even too pious were often labeled immodest because they called attention to themselves. Girls like Esty, who wanted to "study like a boy," or Sheyndie, who told her mother when she was thirteen that she didn't want to get married, troubled God-given gender roles, a sure sign that something was wrong with them, religiously or psychologically.

Men who doubted were often preoccupied with truth claims. Some men swapped out *emuna* for atheism, trading one essentialized truth for another. Women who experienced life-changing doubt had intellectual questions about truth(s) too, of course. However, their doubts were less often rooted in consistency of theological texts, since as girls they had had limited exposure to those texts at all. Instead, women with life-changing doubt were often angry that they had sacrificed their dreams by submitting to the patriarchal authority of the system that they no longer believed was true.

Like their male counterparts, teenage girls surreptitiously experimented and did things they were not supposed to. Suri described how she would secretly iron her clothes on Shabbes. Blimi snuck into the bathroom to listen to talk radio. Some girls had same-sex relationships, which, given gender segregation and the fact that meeting boys could destroy a girl's reputation, were easier to manage. But despite youthful questioning or not fitting in, all the women I spoke with remembered that they were excited to get engaged, hopeful that they would be happy and fulfilled at last.

For many, marriage was a disappointing experience, one that reawakened teenage doubts in the system. In part this was structural. In contrast to men, whose marriages often brought a newfound freedom, marriage for women, especially once they had children, made their time and their bodies even less their own. Married women's fertile bodies were constantly surveilled by their husbands, along with nosy neighbors and relatives. Any change in clothing or headcovering was cause for concern, raising suspicions about immodesty. Even a woman's menstrual cycle, which regulates a couple's sex life, was a communal affair: if a wife had any doubts that her cycle had finished for the month, she would consult her husband, who consulted his rabbi, which sometimes required that both men examine the staining on a woman's underwear.

Unlike men, married women could not simply go out at night to be with friends in public spaces. They were expected to be home with children, and if they weren't, their husbands asked why. Women were even forbidden from driving in some communities, so they had very little mobility, which was especially isolating outside of New York City. In fact, when Saudi Arabia decided to allow women to drive in 2017, WhatsAppville Yinglish commentators emphasized the irony that many Hasidic women in New York still couldn't. And, as I noted in chapters 2 and 3, women had less access to technology and media, and the access they had was at the discretion of their husbands. As Shpitzle wrote to me in an email, "I see so many men who live very vibrant double lives, but much fewer women. Men have a lot of freedom, and that's what matters."

Over time, though, I did meet ultra-Orthodox women living double lives, women who mostly knew of each other, perhaps because they were few. Like their male counterparts, they kept secrets from their husbands about what they did and what they thought. And they also made judgments about how to live ethical lives despite the necessity of lying, betrayals, and sneaking around. In contrast to men, women who doubted often had fewer resources and were more dependent. Their husbands could require that they consult communal experts, such as outreach rabbis or bride teachers, and threaten them with divorce. Even small changes that women with life-changing doubt made to their clothing or head-covering drew concerned attention. When Sheyndie began wearing a sparkling barrette in her wig, her husband found it both attractive and upsetting. Was she flirting with men? Was she having an affair? Only a very few were able to fly "under the radar," as Boruch or Yitsy did; and those lucky few often came from well-off families with good reputations.

Esty: A Frustrated Intellectual

Shmuel introduced me to Esty, and we met one day for lunch in a kosher restaurant. Esty was a no-nonsense Hasidic woman in her twenties, wearing a hat on her wig and seamed beige stockings. She told me, "My crisis of faith really was a crisis for me." She described herself as a fervently pious girl, who dreamed of studying like a boy. She wanted to wear a *tallis,* to learn *gemora,* to become a *posek,* a rabbi who makes religious judgments. She, like some other women I met, also never wanted children. Girls couldn't become *poseks,* though, and, in fact, her unusual desires worried her family and teachers. They told her she had *yiras shemayim* (awe of heaven) problems for wanting what seemed to them unnatural. A person who felt proper awe of God would never question the natural order of things, where boys and girls had different lives. Nevertheless, Esty was never a girl at risk. She told me she always wanted to be a "good girl," which was especially important in matchmaking for families like Esty's, who were not very rich or especially learned.

In the early years of her marriage, she told me, she worked hard to "connect" with her husband to make the marriage work, and they quickly had four kids. Esty's crisis of faith was triggered by online reading at her office job. She remembered reading from a collection of responsa (rabbinic rulings on religious questions). She came across the familiar prohibition against teaching girls Torah, which she had learned in school would be "bad" for her. (In fact, that interpretation posits that teaching girls Torah makes them promiscuous.) However, juxtaposed on the same page were a number of different rabbinic interpretations of that text, several of which did permit girls' Torah study. She realized at that moment that what she had heard all her life as the truth was actually a minority opinion in a much wider, more diverse body of Orthodox Jewish scholarship. The discovery was not liberating, though; it was devastating. She felt, she told me, that she had been "betrayed" by the system, denied access to interpretations of Jewish text that would have given her desire to study Torah legitimacy. She kept her disillusioned doubting a secret from everybody for years, keeping most of the *mitsves* despite continuing to read widely on the internet, including the Jblogs. As she read Hasidic Rebel, first she felt shocked, "How does this guy know exactly what I'm thinking?" Then she felt relieved, "I'm not the only one." Over time she became agnostic, but with no money of her own and four children she felt desperately stuck. Initially, she was suicidal, she told me. Eventually she decided that the only way to save herself was get an education and control her own body. Her husband checked with his *rov* (a rabbinic adviser) to get approval for her to use birth control for a few years. This request was not that unusual, and their rabbi agreed. She also enrolled in an online college course, hoping to work toward her bachelors degree.

Esty "came out" when her husband walked in on her in the bathroom surreptitiously using her phone on the Sabbath. Her husband was appalled. How can you be that kind of person, he wondered, you seem so "normal"? What he meant, Esty told me, was that she did not seem "sick" or "crazy" or like a "drug addict." However, something must be wrong, Esty's husband decided, so they each consulted with ultra-Orthodox authorities considered "professionals": rabbis, Jewish life coaches, a bride teacher/adviser, and therapists. Esty initially sought out the advice of a well-known *kalla* (bride) teacher. When they talked, Esty focused exclusively on her feelings of being trapped, not her *emuna* issues, which she felt were simply not acceptable. The *kalla* teacher soon recommended a licensed *frum* therapist, whom Esty saw several times. They too spoke about her frustrations, but when she touched on her religious doubts, the therapist told her she had to go "work on her *emuna*" with a *rov*, not with her (see chapter 5). Esty's intellectual doubting in this therapeutic context was silenced, treated as a separate issue from her emotional dissatisfactions.

Frustrated, Esty decided to go speak to an outreach (*kiruv*) rabbi. *Kiruv krovim* (outreach to those born religious) rabbis used techniques developed in outreach to secular Jews with those born into ultra-Orthodoxy. *Kiruv* rabbis were believed to be adept at answering all kinds of questions, not easily shocked, and used to argumentation because of their experiences with secular Jews. Esty met with Rabbi Hirschberg, and his assessment was that her education had been too religiously stringent, which had given her emotional problems, which had led her to doubt. The rabbi told

Esty that her desire to get an education was merely a bid for attention. If she were shown more love, he promised her, she would no longer need school. By that point Esty was completely disillusioned with the system. She was also angry, so when her husband suggested she try yet another *kiruv* rabbi to get answers to her questions, she told him that she no longer had any.

At that point, Esty's husband was advised by an *askn* to consider divorce, which frightened her. However, together they decided, for their family's sake, to try to make the marriage work. Esty told her husband she was willing to compromise on religious practice. She would not break the Sabbath anymore, even with her phone, to satisfy him. But Esty also decided that she would remain on birth control indefinitely. She told me, "It's my body," and she gave herself exclusive authority over it. Indeed, in the years that I continued to meet up with her, I noticed she slowly began to change her clothing and head covering. She told me on WhatsApp that these changes made her "feel different," that she felt she had the authority to make an independent decision to "fit in" a little more with the secular world around her. In a way, her audience changed:

> I wear thin beige tights with seams [instead of the thick beige seamed stockings her extended family all wore]. Because I made the decision. And if I don't fit in with the goyim [Gentiles], at least I fit in slightly more with other chassidish people and maybe I'm not pegged immediately [as one Hasidic group]. And not wearing a hat on a sheytel [wig] is a little like a chusid [a Hasidic man] wearing a baseball cap. Does he still look like a chusid? Yes. But a tad less noticeable from a mile way than with his large black yarmulke.

In fact, I had noticed at a wedding we both attended a few years later that Esty had since moved on to wearing gray seamed stockings. As we watched her dancing with her friends, I wondered about her stockings. Her friend, Yidis, hypothesized that Esty was showing her world she was changing, but just a little bit. She said, "She's still wearing seams. A color is one thing. It's a continuum. Seams are either there or not." Ironically, despite their sexiness in some secular circles, among Hasidic Jews seams on stockings are considered a religious stringency, since their presence makes clear that a woman is actually wearing stockings.

It would be easy to say that Hasidic women who were intellectually unfulfilled and frustrated were vulnerable to doubt, that they were searching for something else because they were intellectually and emotionally dissatisfied. This position assumes, though, that *emuna* is the normative ultra-Orthodox state for healthy people. That is, if a person is healthy and emotionally satisfied, they will trust in God, even if they have questions, and continue to practice Orthodoxy. Esty's experience shows otherwise. She completely participated in ultra-Orthodox life. She was willing to submit to a system that forbade her from religiously expressing herself as she wished, but she was only willing when she thought the system was true. Once she decided it was not, the legitimation for her own sacrifices crumbled. Then, like Boruch, she gave herself the authority to prioritize her own needs and desires, especially for intellectual exploration and control over her body.

Of course, there were also differences among women living double lives in terms of resources and opportunities, financial and social. For example, Toby was able to go to college and maintain a network of many friends unbeknownst to her husband and children because her mother paid her tuition and watched her children. In contrast, another woman living a double life, Malky, told me her husband was using her college tuition bill as a bargaining chip in her marriage, forever dangling it as an incentive to cooperate and conform and stop making trouble for the family.

Blimi: Having It All

Blimi was a mother of seven in her late thirties. She wore a daringly thin diamond-studded headband on top of her shoulder-length blond wig; her sisters, in contrast, all covered their wigs completely with kerchiefs. She always dressed modestly—she told me she had never tried on a pair of jeans—but her clothes were glamorous, form fitting, and sexy. As a girl growing up in a well-off Hasidic family, Blimi had been quite pious, however, she was eccentric and certain expectations of the system had always irked her. Why should she have to shave under her wig as a married woman, she wondered, when biblical women never shaved? She was sent to Israel for her last two years of high school, itself a marker of trouble for girls. But she came back all grown up, ready to enter matchmaking in earnest, eager to please her parents. She married a very *erlikh* (sincerely pious) man. He was, however, rather ascetic, and though she tried hard to connect, Blimi was disappointed in their romantic life. Years later she would meet someone else; however, that did not happen, she said, until she really started questioning the truth of ultra-Orthodoxy.

One of the first chinks in Blimi's belief came when she enrolled in college. Readings in the humanities made her wonder if all religions were really the same, and as she met all kinds of students, she began to question whether Jews were actually so special. She went from thinking that Jews were the chosen people to thinking that "we are all the same," a core tenet of pluralism. Confused and upset by these intellectual doubts, she turned to a rabbi, a family friend, for advice, something she had been taught to do. That relationship ultimately took a romantic turn, though I am unclear exactly what happened. She told me she quickly cut ties with him. Soon after, Blimi got an administrative job in a Manhattan office, with internet access, and there she began to read and then comment on the Jblogosphere. She met some of the bloggers in person and began long-term friendships. As her social circle expanded, she and her new friends would read together and intensely debate their changing beliefs, touching on topics like evolution, biblical criticism, and the afterlife.

In contrast to Esty's husband, Blimi's husband never confronted her. She conjectured that her husband was in denial because he just did not want to "rock the boat." In addition, Blimi was less reliant on her husband financially and socially. Her husband was often suspicious or protested when she went out, Blimi told me, but he knew she had friends from her office job, so his suspicions remained just that. A few years ago, a distant relative, another double lifer, set her up with a married Hasidic man, who had been living a double life for years, Moishy, who worked in finance in Manhattan. They have been in a relationship for over four years and are deeply involved in each other's lives, including sharing decisions about child-rearing.

Having jobs in Manhattan has allowed Blimi and Moishy to claim a certain amount of independence. Moishy told me, "We've taken crazy risks together, an insane amount of risks, but you live once. We walk together in the streets. I pick her up from her house." They also go to movies, out to nonkosher restaurants (so they don't meet anyone they know), to plays. They even colluded to both attend a Shabbes at a kosher hotel with their families in tow, where Blimi managed to sneak into Moishy's room a few times when he pretended to be ill.

Blimi distinguished between lying and hypocrisy. Living a double life was a lie, she told me, but not hypocritical. It would be hypocritical if she told her children to *daven* (pray) when she herself did not. However, she explained, "Hiding the real you is not being a hypocrite. It's a lie, and liars are not as bad as hypocrites in my book." In a way, Blimi redefined the morality of living a double life: she was not telling her children to do things she herself did not do. Rather, she was simply not revealing all that she was, all that she believed, and all that she did outside of the home.

Blimi also lived in two parallel moral systems with different standards for her husband and for her lover. For example, she still continued to go to the *mikva* (the ritual bath for purification after menstruation) every month. She said, "It sounds a little ridiculous, but um—because my husband—if he would know, I mean, and why would I? I think it would be very wrong of me [i.e., not to go] . . . I don't go crazy with it, you know, but I go." Despite not believing in this basic religious practice for women, Blimi decided it would be unethical to deceive her husband in this case, since it would have had huge religious ramifications for him. However, with Moishy she did not practice the laws of family purity, which dictated when they could have sex, since neither of them believed. In fact, Moishy told me, chuckling, that the first time they slept together, she told him, "You just fucked a *nida* [a woman who was "impure" owing to her period]!"

Betrayal for Blimi was complicated. She would never cheat on Moishy, she told me, even though she had been cheating on her husband for years. At the same time, despite being deeply in love with Moishy, Blimi was reluctant to break up her family, and she never considered going OTD. Indeed, she told me repeatedly that those who went OTD often had "emotional" troubles to begin with. Blimi claimed that she had found a way to both fulfill her responsibilities as a Jewish wife and mother and find romantic happiness with her lover. Blimi felt she had it all, saying, with a wink and a smile, "I even look way hotter in my *sheytel* than most women look in their real hair!"

Zisi: Isolated and Stuck

Zisi lived in an ultra-Orthodox community in Queens. We had seen each other's posts on a closed Facebook group, and I had private messaged her asking to talk. At first, she assumed I was "one of us on this closed group where we talk our secrets." After Googling to check me out and realizing I was an anthropologist, she decided she was still willing to speak. We talked on the phone because it was too complicated to meet in person. She called me one evening while she was doing her daily "power" walk, so no one would listen in.

In contrast to Esty or Blimi, Zisi was unable to make any real changes to her everyday life despite her dramatically changing interior world. At thirty-three years old, she had seven young children, a limited income, as well as an authoritative husband who was a "conformist." She was, she said, very lonely. However, in the past few years Zisi had gotten onto social media, Facebook and WhatsApp. This enabled her to lead a double life that was almost exclusively split between the continuity of her everyday family life and her forbidden online expression and exploration with others.

Growing up, Zisi said, she had always been different, "contrarian-thinking, and romantic." She had been allowed to read widely and had a sense, she said, "for the outside world." However, deep-thinking kind of people here, she told me, fall by the wayside. While Zisi always yearned for a more "sophisticated" life than she had, she also tried very hard to be "good." Married young to a local boy, she quickly had a bunch of children.

Her real doubts began, she explained, when she developed a platonic, intellectual crush on her husband's friend, someone whose wife eventually divorced him for heresy and who was subsequently kicked out of his community. They had never met in person, only talking a little on the phone or online, but Zisi suggested that this man had "opened up everything inside." Zisi had always had internet access because she had a business selling vitamins. However, she had never read the Jblogs or gone online to find other answers until her interactions with her husband's friend. It seemed to me that it was the idea of a relationship with a man, outside of her marriage, someone who also had had dissatisfactions and questions, that was so exciting, rather than the reality of the friendship.

Soon enough, Zisi set up her own "fake Facebook account." In her everyday life Zisi could never tell anyone about her growing doubts. And while she told me that she could rarely meet other double lifers, she began to interact with them on Facebook, especially in the safety of closed groups. There she posted her poetry, observations, questions, and reviews of books.

However, despite her digital world, its growing networks, and her own expressivity on it, when she attempted to make some changes in her family life, she was quickly shut down. When, for example, she grew out her hair (under her wig), even two inches, her mother noticed and said, "What's this?" When she tried to convince her husband that growing her hair out a little might be romantic, he unplugged her modem. The internet, he said, was giving her all kinds of ideas, again linking nonconformism with dangerous female sexuality. Eventually, Zisi convinced her husband that the internet was not the problem. She was, she told him, unhappy in the marriage, a complaint taken seriously by rabbis, so they went to a Hasidic marriage counselor, which she told me, "helped him to take me seriously." She never revealed her "loss of belief" to her husband, though. She felt that if she ever fully revealed her doubt, her husband would just "send me back to my parents." At the point I talked to her she told me she still believed in God, that she was a spiritual person who enjoyed prayer. I can't be defiant, she told me, but things just don't make sense to me.

Like men, women's opportunities for making changes to their lives after their life-changing doubts depended on their marriages, and even more, their extended families, their own new desires for love or education, and the communities they found themselves in. Esty, Blimi, and Zisi all lost their belief in the system, but not necessarily in God or some spiritual being. What they shared was the constraint of being women with children, already imbricated in a system that offered them little independence to change their lives.

The Still-Religious Spouses

The exercise of a double lifer's newfound autonomy directly compromised their still-religious spouse. These spouses were forced into ethical dilemmas that were not of their own choosing, dilemmas that could lead to gendered shifts in authority at home and in the street. They were also required to keep secrets if they wanted or needed to remain in the marriage, secrets that they found morally repugnant because they required lying to innocent others.

Just as gendered authority structured life-changing doubt for the person living a double life, it also structured possibilities for the still-religious spouse. Newfound opportunities for religious authority for women, for example, were often unwelcomed by women themselves because they violated the moral order. Having attended an ultra-Orthodox class for brides years ago as part of fieldwork, I knew that wives were not supposed to be their husband's *mashgiakh* (religious supervisor) at home. Your husband, said the *kalla* (bride) teacher, should always be the leader in *rukhnius* (spirituality). When a husband's or a wife's doubts and transgressions were discovered by the still-religious spouse, gendered relationships were often thrown into disarray.

Social media was the arena where dilemmas over religious authority and doubt were often played out for still-religious spouses, just as it was for double lifers. Some spouses, influenced by rabbinic campaigns against the internet, blamed social media for their spouses' doubts and transgressions. Facebook, WhatsApp, Instagram, or Snapchat were threatening secret spaces where spouses met immoral others and developed dangerous addictive behaviors. For some others, though, especially still-religious wives with no other recourse, social media offered a way to ease isolation, to safely and anonymously ask for advice about humiliating betrayals, or even to create new forms of religious authority.

Aron and Tsiri: Unable to Control His Wife

I was introduced to Aron, a Hasidic man in his late twenties, through a mutual acquaintance. Aron knew I had spent time with his wife, Tsiri, and he told me he wanted the chance to tell his side of the story, what it was like to be the *frum* husband of a wife living a double life. Aron arrived at my office in full Hasidic *levush* (dress), with a long brown beard and fly-away *peyos*. He began by telling me that though he had initially "pinned" a lot of his marital problems on religion, it had become clear to him, after talking with many therapists, marriage counsellors, his brother, and his rabbi, that his wife actually had a personality disorder. This was, he said, the real problem between them, something that her religious issues merely exacerbated. His explanation, blaming religious doubt on mental illness, was one echoed by many mental health professionals and rabbis in their dealings with those living double lives, especially women (see chapter 5).

Tsiri and Aron had never had a good marriage. They agreed on that. Even after they had a daughter whom they both adored, they fought over everything. Tsiri had told me that after a rebellious adolescence she had gone into the marriage committed to living a *frum* life, certain it would bring her happiness, as a beloved high school mentor had promised. However, when it didn't, many of her adolescent doubts returned, and she felt betrayed by the system. Once Tsiri lost her faith in God (one day, reading through Maimonides's Thirteen Principles of Faith and realizing they meant nothing to her), she began to change in ways that affected Aron too, at home and in public. Her secret interior changes became increasingly public and visible first just to Aron and then to others.

Tsiri's initial changes were a growing leniency with Jewish law at home. Aron told me that he tried to be understanding. He considered himself "open-minded" about religious stringency, although he was always a believer. He said nothing, for example, when she went out and bought herself a Blackberry even after the big Citi Field anti-internet *asifa* (rally) of 2012. He actually got himself a tablet soon after. Then they bought a television, though they kept it a secret from their families. The main problem began, he said, when she made changes that were public, where others could witness her transformation. He said, "She was going from taking off her beige stockings to (putting on) black stockings. And then she took her hat off of her wig." These changes had been humiliating for him. He remembered saying angrily to Tsiri, "I'm a dead person at home. But this dead person wants a little bit respect in the street. The people don't know I'm a dead fish. Don't put me out there."

The problem, one might argue, with Tsiri's changes was that she made them too quickly, in contrast to Esty, who took years to go from hat on her wig to a band on her wig, and who always wore seamed stockings even though the color had changed. Even more disturbing for Aron, Tsiri had relied on her own authority to make all these rapid changes. This was something that no Hasidic woman (or man) had the right to do, since these were family and community decisions. Even men who wanted to change their hats had to consult with their rabbinic authorities and abide by their decisions. Everyone knew there was a clear line of men in Tsiri's life, from her husband and father all the way to the rebbe, that had to be consulted before she even thought about changing something like her stockings.

I asked Tsiri why she even bothered with such small changes. Why make waves, I wondered, over stockings? Tsiri told me that back then, she needed to feel "more comfortable" if she was going to stay in her marriage and community. She wanted her exterior to represent how she was feeling on the inside. Not only that. Tsiri wanted her non-Jewish coworkers at her job to know that she wasn't just like every other Hasidic woman in the neighborhood, that she had gotten more politically progressive. She even felt like she wanted to "blend in" on the subway more, to look more like other New Yorkers. Perhaps she was also conducting an experiment. How far could she go before her child got kicked out of her private Hasidic school? Before her husband filed for divorce? Before neighbors started coming up to her to offer their support just because she had taken her hat off of her wig, and they assumed something was wrong? Actually, she told me with a sad smile, a neighbor had just approached her the day before asking if she needed help.

Indeed, soon after Tsiri's changes to communal modesty standards, Aron's younger brother confronted him, "What's going on with your wife?" People had noticed her hat and stockings, and they were also saying she had joined some kind of Facebook group, that she was even going to Footsteps, the organization that supports questioning ultra-Orthodox Jews. Aron did not know how his brother knew this, but it turned out that, indeed, Tsiri had gotten on Facebook and joined a closed group for those in a "(religiously) mixed marriage" and used her real name. Perhaps a *frum* troll had recognized her—I heard there were many—and had told the family. Ironically, Aron then got on Facebook, too, just to be able to see what she was up to. He followed her for about two months, sure that she was eating *treyf* (nonkosher) and going out, maybe even with men.

Tsiri eventually confessed her secret to Aron, that she had completely "crossed over," meaning she no longer felt obligated by the prohibitions and commandments of Jewish Orthodoxy. She had even tried McDonald's, she told her husband. Aron felt he had to protect himself from the on-slaught of new ideas Tsiri tried to discuss with him. He told me, "Regard-less of what science and data she's going to bring me, I'm still going to believe, because I grew up in a house where . . . *emuna* is simple, accepted as fact." Aron acknowledged that he had not always lived up to God's ex-pectations for him because he felt "in a certain pressured, psychological, emotional complicated place." And as Tsiri grew bolder, bringing unac-ceptable food into their home, Aron felt more awkward fulfilling his own religious obligations. He told me that a condescending look from his wife as he began to pray "drove him crazy." With a flash of self-insight, he con-cluded that "her disorder plays into my weakness or at least that's my ra-tionalization for my failure of compliance [i.e., not praying or watching television]."

Eventually Aron and Tsiri separated, and when I met with Aron they were in the process of hammering out a custody arrangement with an Or-thodox Jewish mediator. Aron told me that his family had been advising him to try to gain sole custody of their child. However, he knew he could never manage as a single parent even with his family's support. Tsiri was relieved when he told her he would not fight her for custody, a fear that had stopped her from moving on. In fact, they were able to figure out an equitable shared custody arrangement in Jewish religious court (*beys din*) that involved compromises on all sides to benefit their child.

Aron told me he was hoping to get remarried in the future, declaring that he would willingly relinquish "certain freedoms" (e.g., Facebook or television) for a relationship and a *frum* home. He dreamed of regularly going to *shul* and sponsoring a *kiddush* (a reception after prayers), of hosting the Shabbes meal at his home every week. Actually, he told me with a resigned laugh, his rabbi had told him that a lot of good marriage prospects were waiting in the wings, but he just "had to lose a little weight first."

Dovid and Shoshana: Unwelcome Authority for a Religious Wife

The 2011 *Ami Magazine* article "Imposters among Us" (see chapter 2) pop-ularized the concept of Orthopraxy, where despite life-changing doubt a person continues to observe all the commandments. One of the central figures in that article, which upset many readers who wrote in to complain about its publication, was an Orthoprax *posek*, a respected rabbi respon-sible for religious rulings, who had become a secret atheist. A mutual friend introduced me to him, Dovid, a Yeshivish (non-Hasidic) double lifer. He was a shy, awkward man, with a short beard and side curls tucked behind his ears, common for many Yeshivish. Dovid's story was similar to many other Hasidic Jews with life-changing doubt, but his wife Shoshana's response was distinctive from the Hasidic wives I heard about, given that she herself had more access to media and education.

Like many others, Dovid had always had unanswered questions. When he got married he tried to repress his doubts, to start again. But as his marriage eventually foundered under the stress of having six young children in six years, and his own growing depression, his doubts resurfaced. After a few years of online reading, which was less restricted in Yeshivish communities than Hasidic ones, he attended a Richard Dawkins lecture at the New York Society for Ethical Culture. There he realized, with growing despair, that atheism was the only philosophy that finally answered all of his questions.

Dovid's wife, Shoshana, who was also Yeshivish, was completely devastated when Dovid finally confessed his secret, but then she took an unusual step, a very public step, that a Hasidic woman might not have taken. She wrote a letter to the editors of *Ami Magazine*, calling herself the "wife of the *posek*" in the Orthoprax article they had published. Below is an excerpt with my translations in brackets:

> To the Editor:
>
> It was this past Tisha B'Av [a holiday that commemorates the destruction of the Temple] that my husband informed me that he was no longer a believer. At least the timing was perfect. Of course, I noticed the telltale signs. . . . I inwardly cringed as books, radio, Internet replaced the Talmud, Chumash [Bible], sefarim [religious texts]. I remained silent as the warning of my mechanchot [teachers] echoed in my ear, "Do not be your husband's mashgiach" [religious adviser].
>
> I would love to kick and scream, but I know as a religious person that life is a test. The spiritual future of my family lies in my hands. . . . I feel that I am being personally summoned by Heaven to work on my emunah [faith]. It is my hope that sometime in the future I will look into the mirror and smile at the person I have become, that I will hold my frum [religious] grandchildren close and think . . . it was all worth it. I would love to be in touch with those who are living through a similar situation. You can email me at *husbandoffderech @aol.com*.

Shoshana then posted the published letter all over the web, on blogs and on the Orthodox forum ImaMother, where it made a "quite a splash," she told me proudly, while I was visiting one afternoon. She explained why she had written the letter in the first place, "I was just curious to know the profile. Are there other men like that?" She had talked to about twenty women on the phone after the letter, mostly Hasidic and a few Yeshivish. Surprising to her was that most of those wayward husbands did not have "psychological problems" or bad marriages. In fact, many had "beautiful marriages" (unlike her own). What she learned was that none of those husbands ever regained his faith.

Unusually, Shoshana used her own independent research to make some decisions about her life, in direct contrast to what rabbinic advisers suggested. A charitable neighbor who knew Shoshana's case bought her a round trip ticket to Israel so that she could consult some important Yeshivish rabbis about divorce. However, she was unimpressed by their understanding of her situation, especially when they told her that if she worked on her marriage and took responsibility for maintaining the level of piety in their home, Dovid's *emuna* would return. Shoshana explained to me that she knew their advice was unrealistic. If she tried to maintain their level of piety at home, her marriage would fall apart. She decided to focus on her marriage, so that her children could grow up in a "healthy and happy home." Shoshana grew less stringent about the family's religious standards, though it pained her. Her son was allowed to watch television on a tablet with his father, and holidays and Shabbes were more "chilled out," only "sweetness," no obligation or stress for Dovid.

Shoshana shared her knowledge with other women in similar positions. When women called her for advice (word had gotten around), she told them their husbands were never going to change, so they had to work on compromising on different levels of religiosity in the home. One woman complained, for example, that her Orthoprax husband was always chewing nonkosher gum at home because he claimed it had more flavor. Shoshana advised, "Let him." At the same time, she told another wife whose husband listened to non-Jewish music at home, "He doesn't have to flaunt it. Like put on headphones when he wants to listen to music." She told me that no wife would tell her husband that he had to believe, but they should be able to agree on how to respect the religiosity at home, to "keep up the level of the home" for the sake of the children.

An ethical conundrum continued to haunt Shoshana, though. She was keeping Dovid's secrets. That is, she was implicated in Dovid's Orthopraxy because in order for him to remain in the community, she had to lie for him. She explained:

> It comes up all the time. Like when I was in the hospital [giving birth], people are like, oh should we send someone over in the morning, so your husband could get to shul? With like at night, or tutoring, or picking up, carpool, your husband is probably in shul. I'm always lying. I'm always lying. Because this is a tight-knit community and everyone thinks they know you.

Perhaps the most disturbing thing for Shoshana was that lying eventually got routine. She said, "I got used to it. First, I was, like, gagging. Now I'm like, yeah, whatever."

The Morality of Secrets

The morality of a double life was lived through men and women's distinctive emotional experiences and responsibilities. Women who lost their faith were more often angry than desolate, something many men described. This is unsurprising, given that women felt they had made individual sacrifices to remain faithful. When they lost faith, they were angry that they had been duped in a sense to be second-class citizens, that they had willingly given up some of their dreams for what they no longer believed was true. Men who lost faith in the system or God, in contrast, described feeling bereft. They had lost faith in a system that authorized them to be the moral leaders not only in their families, but in the wider world where they could claim to be God's chosen people. Ultra-Orthodox men's moral legitimacy, their sense that they, as observant Jewish men, had a direct mandate from God, came tumbling down once they came to doubt its premise. In response to this loss, some men living double lives made a distinction between ultra-Orthodox Judaism as a "lifestyle" (not a true religion) that they appreciated and their continuous belief in some God. For example, "Anonymous" commented on Shtreimel's blog in 2005:

> I feel quite comfortable with the Jewish religion (even without proof to its veracity) so it will be in this context that I will try to worship the almighty. I have no feeling and don't believe at all in Hasidism as part of the religion rather it is only a cultural lifestyle that I got to despise for obvious reasons. In a way I made peace with myself to continue living a Hasidic life and still pursue my dreams. I happen to successfully combine a Hasidic lifestyle and a more open-minded and worldly culture. For that's the true meaning of freedom.

Though he continued to believe in God, Anonymous had lost his faith in Hasidic Judaism. This meant that freedom for Anonymous was not about becoming secular at all, but about an individual's access to "pursuing their dreams," whatever and wherever they might be.

However, even this version of ultra-Orthodox freedom was shaped by ultra-Orthodox social and political factors. Sometimes a person from a prestigious, well-known, wealthy family had more responsibilities for publicly conforming. More often, being part of a good family allowed a little more leeway in terms of conforming to gendered religious expectations. For example, Boruch made a comfortable living, so he relied less on family or the community. Similarly, Blimi relied less on her husband because she worked and also came from a well-off family. Tsiri's troubled family background gave her fewer marriage options and fewer options for staying and living a double life. Maybe that's why she is in the process of trying to leave. Ultimately, those without access to independence, money, and good social standing had fewer options for living double lives.

Gender also shaped opportunities and limitations for still-religious spouses. Still-religious wives, in my experience, had less authority to make demands on their doubting husbands, and rabbis rarely advised them to divorce. Men were more often authorized to divorce their wives when they became too blatantly rebellious, and there seemed no hope for religious return. For those men, families and the wider community often offered moral and financial support, something women were less likely to get.

Both men and women living double lives secretly developed another moral system, one more closely affiliated with North American liberal values, with an emphasis on personal fulfillment, individual moral autonomy, rights, and freedoms of many sorts. This alternative morality developed at the same time that keeping Jewish laws became increasingly onerous, physically uncomfortable, boring and meaningless. Once the discipline of Jewish commandments was no longer tied to truth, the myriad rules and obligations shaping everyday life were a yoke to be thrown off rather than embraced. Shimon, for example, told me that when he was still a believer he had been willing to focus on his five lovely children and his respected position as a rabbinic consultant in his community. He was able to feel that the sacrifice of his unhappy marriage was an ethical compromise he made for playing his part in ensuring ultra-Orthodox continuity. After all, everyone makes compromises in their lives based on a hierarchy of values and virtues. Once Shimon no longer believed in the system, though, he could not discount his need, maybe his right, to a loving relationship. Despite being unwilling to abandon his family or his job, he felt legitimate in having secret affairs outside his marriage in order to fulfill a part of himself, since he was sacrificing living the life he wished for.

Secrets between family members, as anthropologist Hugh Gusterson writes, create "a disciplinary distance," that is, a kind of self-surveillance to avoid disrupting everyday life.[10] For example, the nuclear weapons scientists whom Gusterson worked with were obligated by their laboratories and the federal government to keep their public work lives secret, so they did not talk much about their work at home. Their spouses knew not to ask, to avoid the topic, to opt for silence. Together, scientists and their spouses chose to keep a public secret even at home.

Ultra-Orthodox double lifers similarly had to keep all kinds of secrets from their spouses. They hid their secret lives or pretended to participate in religious activities, keeping up the illusion that things were fine. However, unlike Gusterson's nuclear weapons scientists, whose work was valorized by the public sphere, double lifers' secrets were anathema to the ultra-Orthodox religious world. The pressure for double lifers to keep secrets both in the ultra-Orthodox public sphere and at home could be incredibly stressful. Perhaps this was why so many living double lives, even over the few years I knew them, eventually "came out," as they described it, to their spouses. However, confessing or being outed at home did not always bring relief. Once a double lifer's secret was revealed to or discovered by a still-religious spouse, a range of authorities and new experts were brought in to help cure their life-changing doubt.

5

The Treatment of Doubt

In December 2012, *Hamodia*, the daily newspaper of "Torah Jewry," published the following in their regular advice column, hosted by a prominent rabbi/psychiatrist, Rabbi Tessler (translations are mine):

> Q: I am a 19-year-old yeshiva bachur [unmarried student]. For some time I have been having thoughts doubting my emunah [faith]. I've read seforim [religious books] on emunah but this does not relieve my doubts. I wonder if there might be a psychological block that prevents me from having firm emunah and if so, what can I do about it? This is really tormenting me.

> A: There are primarily two reasons for questioning one's emunah. One is the yetzer hara [inclination for evil], which can be unrelenting. The sifrei mussar [Jewish philosophy books] say that the yetzer hara does not accept restrictions. It wants a person to be free to do whatever he or she desires. Believing in Hashem [God] requires one to adhere to the restrictions dictated by the Torah, therefore, the yetzer hara tries to weaken a person's emunah so that he will be free to do whatever he wishes. This is a struggle that is dealt with in most of the sifrei mussar.... It is also important to discuss this with talmidei chachamim [learned Torah sages] who can give you chizuk [strengthening] in emunah. You must also consider another possibility. Repetitive annoying thoughts may be due to a form of OCD [obsessive-compulsive disorder]. This condition has been referred to as the "doubting disease" because it does not allow one to accept some things with certainty. If this is the problem, you can benefit from psychiatric/psychologic treatment. I suggest that you consult a mental health

professional for an evaluation to determine whether you have this type of OCD.

Rabbi Tessler did not blame the internet for this young man's doubts, as many rabbis did (see chapter 3). Instead, he offered an explanation that drew on two textual bodies of authority on interiority: Jewish theology and the "bible" of American psychology, the Diagnostic and Statistical Manual of Mental Disorders (the DSM-5). Religious doubt was either the influence of Satan or a mental illness, and those who should treat it were either rabbis or therapists.

There was an ongoing struggle for moral authority between those living double lives and those who ministered to them. Double lifers told me they often feared for their own sanity, stalked as many were by confusion, depression, and anxiety, the common companions of life-changing doubt. When they sought help or were forced to by a terrified parent or a spouse, there was a diverse therapeutic landscape waiting. One might first consult semiprofessionals, such as outreach (*kiruv*) rabbis, activists, or Jewish Orthodox life coaches, who offered emotional support, philosophical debates, and frequently made informal diagnoses. At the same time, many consulted with religious (*frum*) therapists, both men and women, whose training ran the gamut. Some had been formally trained in universities and licensed by the state, while others merely had a "feeling" (*khush*) for listening. Religious therapists, licensed or not, and other informal experts provided treatment for life-changing doubt, often in conversation with a client's rabbi and family, effectively triangulating their care.

Most therapeutic professionals rejected the common rabbinic explanation in circulation for the contemporary crisis of faith—the internet. Instead, they drew on the authority of therapeutic discourse, prevalent in the United States, to argue that it was emotional and interpersonal dynamics that obstructed *emuna* (faith). That is, emotional health formed the foundation for strong faith, and emotional problems were often blamed for life-changing doubt. In a few unusually egregious cases, religious doubt was pathologized, that is, was framed as an illness, one that required medical treatment.

The embrace of the therapeutic framework more generally was a recent phenomenon among the ultra-Orthodox. Until the late nineties, especially among Hasidim, the fields of psychology and social work were "anti-Toyre [Torah], the Devil," explained Nosson, a social worker living a double life. Very few ultra-Orthodox people would admit to going to therapy back then. Medication for mental illness was grounds for divorce and hidden in matchmaking proceedings. By the twenty-first century, however, therapeutic treatment had become less stigmatized, and as a result religious therapy and other helping professions grew for all kinds of issues. Yeshivish, Hasidic, and Modern Orthodox therapists, life coaches, and rabbis formed working alliances, crossing denominational and occupational boundaries. The field of religious therapy, in contrast to Jewish life coaches or rabbis, found its practitioners increasingly grappling with ethical dilemmas. In their international organization Ruach, many reflexively debated their own biases and responsibilities as both observant Jews and professionals, balancing on the fine line they had drawn between religion and science.

Those living double lives had a wide range of experiences with those who tried to help them. In the worst cases, there were misdiagnoses, overmedication, and violations of patient-client confidentiality. This mobilized some living double lives to become resources for others with life-changing doubt. They increasingly shared information on the phone or online about therapists who were too invested in a client staying religious or who were not licensed to diagnose or write prescriptions for medication. They also recommended therapists or rabbis who had truly helped them. Some felt their sanity, even their humanity, was vindicated when they found a good therapist who could provide a neutral space to communicate better with their spouses or help them make healthy decisions for themselves and their families.

Psychology since Freud has often been described as a replacement for religion.[1] However, the social upheavals of the 1960s in the United States, which ushered in the psychotherapeutic revolution, influenced American religions as well, particularly Evangelical Christianity. Tanya Luhrmann, for example, explains that in the context of the self-help movements of the seventies and later, the recovery movements of the 1980s and 1990s (e.g., Alcoholics Anonymous), Evangelical communities in the United States began to adapt psychological frameworks, so that mental health and spiritual health became equivalencies.[2] Evangelical therapeutic frameworks translated the language of sin into the language of addiction and illness, as Tanya Erzen describes, for example, in reparative or conversion therapy in the "ex-gay movement." The goal was to "reintegrate the self" in order to bring about religious and sexual conversion, that is, religious health and sexual health depended on each other.[3]

The ultra-Orthodox adaptation of the therapeutic was subtly different. Rabbis remained experts in theology and ethics, and a new group of therapeutic experts attended to mental and emotional health. Like Evangelical adaptions, ultra-Orthodox Jewish engagement of the therapeutic also drew on the language of addiction rather than sin, and the normative, healthy Jew was understood to be religious. However, in contrast to the Evangelicals described by Luhrmann or Erzen, ultra-Orthodox psychotherapeutic knowledge had to engage with another set of perspectives on human nature, which originated in centuries-old Jewish ethical texts (*mussar*). So, while rabbis remained the authorities in matters of religious law, those troubled by the emotional effects of life-changing doubt were sent to the first line of defense: Orthodox Jewish life coaches, *askonim* (activists), and outreach rabbis. If those semiexperts failed, religious therapy was the second line of defense. Ultra-Orthodox and Orthodox Jews adapted the therapeutic, Shmuel clarified, "Not necessarily to pull one over on the rabbis, but because they themselves were pious Jews and needed a framework for seeing therapy as not heresy, and also a way to see it as rooted in psychological insights of the great sages [*tsaddikim*]." The authoritative knowledge of the therapeutic could legitimate religious therapists' own career choices by staking out their particular expertise and methods, which would not challenge the authority of religious sources.

In my earlier work I argued for moving beyond exclusively formal religious doctrine and practice in studies of religion. The same could be said for the study of life-changing religious doubt, which was almost never exclusively a theological disagreement or rejection of certain religious texts. The emotional component of doubting—the upheaval, loneliness, fear, pain, and the moral confusion—became the realm of therapeutic professionals, leaving intellectual or theological problems to rabbinic advisers. Following the twists and turns of the "social life of therapy" shows the therapeutic gaining authority for some as an explanation and cure for religious doubt, as long as it did not challenge the authority of the rabbis to make ethical judgments, or the system itself.[4] Double lifers and other religious therapists, however, challenged that structure of care, arguing that the therapeutic encounter should offer a neutral space to give doubting clients the individual authority they needed to make their own decisions.

The First Line of Defense: Outreach Rabbis, Activists, and Orthodox Life Coaches

When Dovid, the Orthoprax *posek* I described in chapter 4, decided after years of exploration and an epiphany at a Richard Dawkins lecture at the Society for Ethical Culture that only atheism made sense to him, he was desolate. Like many other men who had lost faith in the divine revelation, he described feeling almost suicidal. "Tormented" or "agony" are words a lot of men used. After weeks of lying in bed in a deep depression, "totally at sea," he began to seek out rabbis and self-appointed activists (*askonim*) who specialized in helping those with doubts. He hoped they could convince him that his theological questions indeed had answers.

The rabbis that Dovid turned to were part of a group of semiprofessionals, the first line of defense for those with doubts, which included Orthodox Jewish life coaches, along with rabbis and self-appointed community activists. These experts generally employed two distinctive strategies. First, they tried to answer a doubter's intellectual questions using argumentation drawn from historical and theological texts. Second, if that was unsuccessful, they suggested that the doubts were symptomatic of an underlying and undiagnosed emotional problem. That is, either the doubter did not know enough yet or the doubter was using their intellect to cover up emotional problems that needed to be addressed, which usually resulted in a referral to a religious therapist. The implication of their strategies was that a normal, healthy person should be able to deal with doubt or uncertainty and still continue to practice Jewish Orthodoxy. Doubt that actually made it impossible to continue religious practice, even secretly, was pathological.

The rabbis Dovid consulted were a specific kind of outreach rabbi, those who ministered to doubting ultra-Orthodox and Modern Orthodox Jews. The *kiruv* (outreach) movement began in the sixties and seventies in the United States to bring nonobservant Jews back into the fold. Those who worked in *kiruv*, Shmuel explained to me, offered an "energy boost" or a kind of spiritual revival for Jews who were not observant. In the mid-nineties, however, a number of ultra-Orthodox and Orthodox *kiruv* rabbis decided to use their outreach approaches to those who were *frum* from birth, known as the "FFB." Rabbi Morris, one such prominent rabbi, explained in a recorded lecture that I purchased from his organization how he began to work with Orthodox Jews with life-changing doubt (my translations):

> In the late nineties, I started to receive phone calls from *frum* people, usually the mothers. That had never happened before. But suddenly mothers figured, if Rabbi Morris could work with, you know, Christophers and Christinas, maybe he could work with Shmuleys and Suris. So . . . I just decided to shift my life from *kiruv rekhokim* [the "far": secular Jews] to *kiruv krovim* (the "near": religious Jews, the FFB).

Rabbi Morris subsequently founded an organization, one of many that used outreach approaches for helping at-risk religious teens and adults.

When Dovid reached out to *kiruv* rabbis for answers, he got what has become a familiar repertoire of responses to his life-changing doubt. One rabbi told him, for example, that his questioning was evidence that he just couldn't control his desires/lusts. Another introduced the Kuzari proof, an argument first articulated in the eleventh century by poet and philosopher Yehuda Halevi. The Kuzari argues that 600,000 Jewish men and women were eyewitnesses to the divine revelation at Sinai. Each subsequent generation told their children about this revelation, leaving no doubt as to its veracity because there had been witnesses. Nevertheless, Dovid's doubts based on his own readings in biblical criticism and archeology were not assuaged.

The next *kiruv* rabbi he went to switched tactics, blaming emotional issues for his disbelief. He told Dovid that he knew he and his wife had an unhappy marriage, so it was natural that he would want to go OTD (off the *derekh*, the path). He had stopped being a *mentsh* (in the sense of a whole person). Once he became happy with himself and his life, he would "just become a normal person again." The last *kiruv* rabbi that Dovid saw before he gave up on them entirely was very different. He told Dovid, "Why do I believe? I believe. I want to believe. I'm sorry, but I don't have any way to help you, and I don't think you will ever get your belief back."

Women with life-changing doubt, in contrast, did not have their own *rov*, rabbinic adviser. When a woman grew cool to Judaism, *kalt tse yiddishkayt*, she did not generally seek out rabbis herself, though she might turn to a female bride teacher or a life coach as Esty did (chapter 4). In fact, in bride classes young women were explicitly taught that they should ask their husbands any religious questions, who in turn should consult with their own rabbis. When a husband found his wife using her phone on Shabbes, like Miriam's husband did one long Saturday afternoon, he might ask or demand she talk to a *kiruv* rabbi too.

Miriam, a quick thinker and a fast talker, told me that when she got married as a young Hasidic woman, she was even more fervently pious than her husband. However, studying at a community college and going online with others eventually led her to reject divine revelation completely. She became a hard-core rationalist, devoted to science and math. Miriam agreed go to the *kiruv* rabbi because, she told me, she "got something really good from it": her husband let her go on a trip abroad by herself. Bargaining with an at-risk adult to stay religious was not at all unusual, though it was criticized by more professional religious therapists.

Tsippy, who eventually left her Yeshivish community, told me she earned at least $2,000 going to different rabbis, all paid for by concerned community members whom she did not know. Paying someone to keep the commandments speaks to the belief that the discipline of religious practice (regardless of intention) can bring the right feelings to unruly interiors.

Miriam's phone call with the *kiruv* rabbi, Rabbi Morris, was very similar to Dovid's. She told me that first Rabbi Morris presented a more flexible Orthodoxy than what she had grown up with, denying any incompatibility between being *frum* and exploring the secular world. Then he offered what Miriam described as a "Pascal's Wager" kind of argument: he told her she had little to lose by believing and a lot to gain, such as not burning in hell if divine revelation turned out to be true. He offered other arguments, based on Jewish exceptionalism, all of which Miriam rebutted.

Then he asked her about her marriage. She explained to me, "I saw he is digging for an emotional reason. That's what they do. They try to find a hook that they can latch on to." She told him that she and her husband had little in common. A few days later, Miriam's husband confronted her, very hurt. Rabbi Morris had called him unbeknownst to her, blaming their bad marriage for Miriam's uncontrollable attraction to the secular world. Rabbi Morris had told Miriam's husband that he would be unable to speak further with her because she, like most Hasidim, was just too argumentative.

It seemed important to get the *kiruv* perspective on those living double lives, but when I contacted a number of *kiruv* rabbis, including Rabbi Morris, they just did not want to talk with me. One of the deciding factors was that I was not Orthodox, so they were unsure where my loyalties lay. Life coaches felt the same way. One explained by email that she would love to help me with the research, but she felt it was too much responsibility for her in case what I wrote was not a *kiddush hashem*, a sanctification of God's name, so she "respectfully declined to participate." Rabbi Morris told me on the phone, "We've all been burned by different people with different agendas. Not all perspectives are wholesome." I took this to mean that not all perspectives prioritized the interests of ultra-Orthodox communities, certainly an accurate assessment. But patience in ethnography usually pays off; through connections I eventually found a few life coaches willing to meet with me, and popular *kiruv* rabbis produced printed lectures and recordings of their public lectures for a small fee.

Jewish life coaching has grown increasingly popular since the early 2000s among the ultra-Orthodox as a less stigmatized form of support than therapy, but perhaps a little more professionalized than a *kiruv* rabbi or an activist. Some life coaches had certification, though there was little oversight by any professional organization. Both life coaches and activists tended to interpret intellectual questioning as a symptom of emotional problems, but unlike *kiruv* rabbis, they rarely engaged in intellectual theological argumentation or proofs. Most were not shy about their own agenda, which was trying to help those with doubts find their way to staying with their families. This often involved working out moral compromises regarding Jewish law and interpersonal honesty, an ethical flexibility for a greater good. Given the diversity of interpretation of shared religious texts, life coaches and activists could semilegitimately encourage double lifers to settle for the most religiously lenient interpretation of their obligations, no matter what their communities chose. Ironically, ethical flexibility around religious practice often highlighted that religious truths could, in fact, be merely cultural interpretation.

One snowy morning, for example, I visited Chaya Klein, a Lubavitcher *mashpia* (informal spiritual mentor), who also had some life coach training.[5] Lubavitcher Hasidim are often considered eccentric by other Hasidic Jews for their emphasis on outreach to secular Jews and belief among some that their previous rebbe was the messiah. However, Mrs. Klein told me that she regularly had referrals from Satmar Hasidic married women and men who were struggling with doubts and living double lives. In these encounters she saw her role as helping clarify what a doubter "really wanted," while showing them how they could continue to live a religious life even if they did not really believe. In this way she hoped to encourage them to stay in their families and to free them from guilt.

Mrs. Klein remembered telling an atheist living a double life, for example, that she did not need to feel the guilt of hypocrisy. She said, "There's no such thing as hypocrisy with God. You're not fooling God." When I couldn't help but point out that she actually was "fooling" all of those around her, she told me, "There is no reason to disclose everything. It's how you present yourself. What goes on in your own mind and heart is private." Mrs. Klein aimed at easing the ethical conundrums of a double life. An honest relationship with an all-knowing God was private and need not be disclosed to anyone else. In fact, the emphasis on a private relationship with God might be a uniquely Lubavitch theology, much less elaborated in other Hasidic groups. However, when other Hasidic theologies might be less forgiving, the Lubavitcher approach was considered therapeutic. Even if, Mrs. Klein told double lifers, you don't believe in keeping kosher, just keep doing it because "the reality is, it's a *mitsva* [fulfilling a commandment]."

Mrs. Klein's counsel included distinguishing "lifestyle choices" from "religious choices." She told me that a few years ago she had worked with a couple in a "mixed marriage," where the husband was no longer obser-vant. According to Jewish law, the husband was not allowed to make kid-dush (the blessings men make over wine) for his family on the Sabbath anymore, which presented a conundrum for his still-religious wife. Mrs. Klein counselled that treating each other with mutual respect especially in front of their seven children was more important than social expecta-tions of religious practice. She recommended that their mother tell them, "*Tatty* [Daddy] and I have decided I am going to make kiddush from now on. We know it's very difficult for you, but that's what we decided." In that case, the family remained intact and respectful, and the children and their *frum* mother continued to observe Shabbes according to reli-gious law.[6]

Life coach Levine, in contrast to Mrs. Klein, who was relaxed and flex-ible up to a point, was like a triage doctor. He worked all hours of the day and night in emergency mode, fielding calls from desperate parents of kids at risk. In fact, he called me to talk at 10:00 p.m. one evening, telling me he had heard from other coaches and rabbis that I wanted to speak to a *frum* life coach and that it would be fine if I took notes while we spoke. Coach Levine, who was Modern Orthodox and a self-described "kosher coach," told me that he modelled healthy relationships for his clients that he gleaned from Torah sources. His approach included criticism of certain strains of ultra-Orthodoxy as unnecessarily stringent and potentially sti-fling for the formation of healthy men and women.

Contemporary rabbinic efforts to control the internet, he suggested, were a distraction from the sexual abuse cover-ups, which were a symp-tom of overly stringent piety. No one ever went off the *derekh* because of technology, he told me. Rather, addictive behaviors, including rejecting religion and drug abuse, were a form of self-medication for pain, whose cure was unconditional love, just like what God had for Jews. This was part of a wider critique by some Yeshivish and Modern Orthodox of Hasidic stringencies, particularly in schools. They felt that religious doubt was an effect of the stifling atmosphere in Hasidic schools and homes, where con-formity and discipline were emphasized over individual expression. Coach Levine assured me that a person who had developmentally matured and led a fulfilling emotional life would not be asking *emuna* questions.

The underlying assumption among some life coaches and *kiruv* rabbis was that there had to be a traumatic reason why someone who seemed fine on the outside would suddenly decide to stop praying or putting on tefillin or even stop believing that God gave the Jews the Torah at Mount Sinai. As the ultra-Orthodox world since the mid-2000s slowly acknowledged that sexual abuse and molestation could actually have long-lasting psychological effects, that soon became an explanation for religious doubt. A number of those who led double lives or had left told me their parents had confronted them, some even years later, and asked if they had been abused, which they had not. Mrs. Klein, the *mashpia*, told me the families of those with doubts frequently wondered: "If you're ok, then why wouldn't you be keeping kosher? Why would you do this? There must be something that happened to you." She acknowledged, in fact, that sometimes we just cannot know why some people stop believing. Nevertheless, when life coaches and *kiruv* rabbis detected depression, anxiety, or simply ongoing nonconformity, they often made referrals to a religious therapist.

The Second Line of Defense for Life-Changing Doubt: Religious Therapy

Frum therapy was rooted in the complementary integration of Jewish religious texts and popular psychology. A key architect, writes historian Andrew Heinze, was Rabbi Abraham Joshua Twersky, who was trained as both a rabbi and a psychiatrist. In the nineties, he developed what he saw as a connection between Jewish ethical philosophy (*mussar*) and twelve-step programs, with their emphasis on self-esteem and growth. *Mussar* notions of human nature were often severe and pessimistic, with some believing that only fear of God's punishment kept observant Jews from sin. *Mussar* located emotions in the heart (*lev*) and emphasized the importance of the will (*rotsn*) in self-improvement, particularly in struggles with the inclination for evil (*yeytser hora*). In the *mussar* model of the person, those with problems, including religious doubt, were blamed for their weak will in fighting their inclination for evil. Mental health problems were framed as individual moral failings.[7]

In contrast, Twersky and a growing number of others emphasized that emotions were found in the brain, so that the will could not always help those with psychological illnesses. This led to the development, as Heinze suggests, of "a more nuanced and empathetic" treatment of human addictions and other psychological problems.[8] In this schema, religious doubters were no longer conceptualized as undisciplined or insane. Unrelenting intellectual or theological doubts were understood as symptomatic of underlying emotional issues. Therapy, in these cases, should work toward ameliorating what doubting often dragged along with it—depression, anxiety, conflicted marriages—with the hope, for some at least, that faith would then return. Rabbi Simcha Feuerman a religious therapist and former president of Ruach, who held a master's degree in social work told me, "I happen to personally believe that if they [the person with doubts] have healthy attachments [i.e., social relationships], their relationship to the religion is going to change for the positive for the most part. . . . Because I think it's a very warm, wonderful experience."

As religious therapy became a viable profession for the ultra-Orthodox, it came to include a diversity of approaches, with attendant training and levels of professionalism. Not all who claimed to be religious or "Torah" therapists actually had training or licensing. This was especially the case with Hasidic men, some of whom did not finish yeshiva with a high school degree or, as I noted, proficiency in English. Pursuing a college education and then a master's degree, with many children and often not much support, could be daunting. Further, Gentile credentials and degrees, in my experience, were not always valued as a metric of effectiveness among the ultra-Orthodox, especially Hasidim. This meant that there were those who claimed to be therapists, but who, in fact, had little actual training and were not licensed by the state. Perhaps the most notorious case of the misuse of unlicensed therapy was that of the rabbi who claimed to be a "Torah therapist." When the parents of an at-risk high school student were told that they had to send their daughter to therapy or she would be expelled, this therapist was recommended. The Torah therapist charged the parents huge sums, while he actually sexually abused their daughter for years. In 2012 his victim, now an adult, sued him in state supreme court, where he was sentenced to 103 years in prison.[9] Even after his sentencing, some of Blimi's Hasidic women friends from high school who were in a WhatsApp group together refused to believe his guilt, suggesting that the courts were antisemitic.

Over the past decade, options for training have continued to expand despite, for some, a conflict between a therapist's adherence to the authority of the Torah or that of the American Psychological Association.[10] A number of programs with state recognition have developed options for ultra-Orthodox Jews. Long Island University and Adelphi both have master's program that are sensitive to Orthodox sensibilities, such as different classes for men and women students. I even heard from one therapist that the program invited a rabbi to speak the same day that the controversial class on Freud and sexuality was taught. An ultra-Orthodox graduate student at Long Island University told me that he decided to attend only after his rabbi said that the program was kosher.

As religious psychological perspectives gained credibility, a division of labor emerged between rabbinic advisers and some *frum* therapists, between ethical judgment and medical diagnosis. Not-for-profit referral services offered rabbis a choice of vetted Jewish professionals, including educating them as to their different qualifications.[11] Economic and religious relationships supported the triangulation of care, reinforcing that ultra-Orthodox faith was "normal" (a common term in the ultra-Orthodox world) and simultaneously reproducing hierarchies of religious authority. At the same time, activists and rabbis often held the key to ensuring a religious therapist's successful practice through their patient referrals, so that each relied on the other. Rabbis tended to encourage treatments with measurable and swift outcomes, such as cognitive behavioral therapy or prescription medication for depression or anxiety. Fewer advocated treatment with prolonged individual exploration, especially psychoanalysis, whose very founder, Freud, had been a Jewish heretic.[12]

Struggles over the practice and meaning of religious therapy played out in the professional organization for *frum* therapists and rabbis, Ruach International. Founded in 1992, with a membership of over 750, Ruach's objective was, "To bring Orthodox Jewish professionals and rabbis together to address mental health issues." Their stated aim was on their website (my translations):

> To enhance the emotional well-being and achdut [unity] of Klal Yisroel [meaning Orthodox Jewry]. Together we are developing timely and effective approaches that are based on widely accepted mental health principles, within a Torah perspective and halachic [Jewish legal] framework.

I attended the organization's annual conference in 2014, which met in a hotel on Long Island, New York, during the week between Christmas and New Year's, a significant time for everyone except ultra-Orthodox Jews. The conference felt comfortingly familiar at first, reminiscent of countless other academic conferences I had attended. In the lobby, I checked in and got my name tag along with the usual tote bag with publishers' ads. But when I went to hang up my coat, high black *biber* (beaver) hats Hasidic men wear on top of their yarmulkes were quietly lined up on the overhead racks, reminding me that this was a different kind of conference than the American Anthropological Association. The full range of Orthodoxy was on display in the main lobby, from Modern Orthodox (no beards, small crocheted yarmulkes, shorter dresses, and even jeans) to full-on Hasidic dress. There were many panels and posters on "kids at risk" and the "OTD crisis," along with career development, networking, cultural sensitivity training (for Jewish Orthodoxy), and psychological research findings. Most panels offered hours for graduate students working toward accreditation.

The two keynote speeches (recorded and available for purchase) at the conference addressed the working relationship between a rabbi and a *frum* therapist: "When a Rabbi Refers to a Therapist" and "My Therapist Told Me to Go to a Rabbi." The talks were given by two of the rabbinic advisers to the board of Ruach, Rabbi Twersky and Rabbi Cohen, who noted the increasing acceptance of psychology by rabbinic leadership. Rabbi Cohen said:

> In earlier times, they [rabbis] didn't accept what the psychologist had to say, simply because what does he or she know that I don't know? That has changed quite a bit, it took time, but that has changed.

Growing rabbinic acceptance of psychology, however, created the need for psychologists to clarify for rabbis and their Orthodox clients how their ministrations were distinctive. In the full room, which had informally separated into a men's side and a women's side, Rabbi Twersky clarified:

> I believe it's generally safe to say that a therapist should not make decisions and a therapist should not give advice. Our job is to help a person clarify his or her thinking, to get rid of some of the distortions that may be leading the person to making some maladjustments in their life. But to tell them, you should divorce, you shouldn't divorce, that's not our job. We deal with health and illness in terms of emotions, we don't deal with right and wrong. Right and wrong is the area of the *rov* [a rabbinic adviser].

A *rov* and a *frum* therapist had distinctive realms of authority, and by working together, they could share responsibility for the health and continuity of Jewish Orthodoxy.

Rabbi Twersky distinguished between health and ethics. He placed religious doubting and adherence to religious practice in a *rov*'s domain, not a *frum* therapist's, who only dealt with mental health issues. Only a *rov* with *daas toyre* (immersion in Torah) had the authority to make moral judgments and rulings and offer the "euphoria of knowing you did right," suggested Rabbi Twersky. This meant that on the relatively rare occasions, at least according to the therapists and those living double lives I spoke with, when religious doubts did come up in therapy, they were often treated by therapists as a proxy for underlying emotional issues. Rabbi Feuerman told me, when I asked, that questions of faith rarely came up in sessions, but if they did, he would just say, "Look, let's talk about what you really want."

Triangulated care included a religious therapist's own rabbinic adviser at times, in order to clarify where their moral responsibility lay when a patient's actions challenged their own religious ethics. Rabbi Twersky explained to the therapists in the audience:

> In cases where someone is very angry at God and then feels guilt at that anger . . . that anger is not an *apikorsus* [heresy] because it is ok to be angry at God. But you might need to bring in a *rov* to *pasken* that [to determine], that the anger is not heresy. And then the therapist can just deal with the anger, not the guilt.

Guilt, Rabbi Twersky noted, could be a healthy religious emotion, making the person repent for a sin, or it could be a problematic psychological issue when, for example, a person felt guilty for something that was beyond their control.

Only a rabbinic adviser had the authority to make that decision for the therapist, so that the therapist could then help the patient. For example, an ultra-Orthodox PhD student in psychology told me that before he began work with a gay client he consulted with his *rov*, who told him that as long as he was working exclusively on social issues, he as the therapist was not responsible for his client's sexuality, which was considered a sin. He would, however, decline taking on a gay couple for counseling, he told me, because by working with them, he would be condoning their "lifestyle."

Frum therapists' authority came from their qualification to diagnose a problem in medicalized discourse, which gave a rabbi the authority to advise treatment. Rabbi Feuerman told me:

> They [rabbis] see therapy as a medical cure. So I have a few rebbes and rabbis that consult with me, and they always want to know the

diagnosis . . . because if they know the diagnosis, then it's somehow kosher. . . . and they're able to work with it.

While Rabbi Feuerman understood his own therapeutic approach as helping patients form healthy attachments, he made medicalized diagnoses for rabbis. He framed this as a way to get his patients the treatment necessary for their emotional health, or at least what the rabbi and the therapist agreed was necessary. This might include a more lenient ruling from a rabbinic adviser, so that a person could remain in their community, an ethical flexibility similar to Mrs. Klein's strategy. A woman diagnosed by a therapist with postpartum depression, for example, might be granted permission by her husband's *rov* to use birth control for a few years. Similarly, watching pornography might be permissible if it enabled a couple to stay together.

Despite rabbis' increasing acceptance of psychology, the leadership of Ruach continued to do outreach to clarify for rabbinic authorities how therapeutic treatment differed from rabbinic moral directives, often framed in the shared language of Jewish religious texts. For example, in 2015, then-president of Ruach, Rabbi Feuerman, wrote a public letter to "*rabbonim* [rabbis] about psychotherapy" that circulated in English and Hebrew. The English version, which aimed to help "clear up some of the misconceptions that occur between rabbis and therapists," is excerpted below. Rabbi Feuerman began with a quote from Proverbs:

> "Good counsel is a well of deep water in the heart of man,
> and a man of understanding can draw it out."—(20:5).

> Given that rabbis and therapists both engage in matters of the soul, one would think there would be much consonance between rabbinical counseling and psychotherapy. . . . Nevertheless, at times there is conflict between the rabbinic mindset and the psychotherapist's mindset. These conflicts play out particularly in the area of morality and religious rules and standards. Rabbonim [rabbis] may find it difficult to comprehend why a therapist avoids offering moral guidance, particularly if the client seems to be doing something glaringly improper from a religious point of view or even from an ethical point of view. Consequently, the rabbi might feel exasperated and think, "I sent this person to get treatment for this issue. The therapist is religious, the client is religious. If so, why can't the therapist just tell the client this is wrong behavior and start working on him?!"

Coming from a strictly rabbinic perspective, this is a reasonable question. However, if the philosophy and process of psychological treatment was understood better, the therapist's passive stance would no longer be objectionable to a rabbi or seem improper. . . . When it comes to therapy, where powerful repressed thoughts and feelings can come to the surface, it is critical for the therapist to maintain a compassionate, non-judgmental and curious interest in the client's inner life, his wishes, fears and conflicts.

Rabbi Feuerman continued, using Jewish sources to legitimize psychology for a rabbinic audience. For example, he referenced rabbinic sources to explain the notion of the unconscious, in effect showing that this concept was Jewish after all. Rabbi Feuerman even made the case that despite Freud's "heretical, egregious and fantastical" writing on Judaism, it was important to note that his family never actually converted, that Freud and his father knew Hebrew, and that they were, in fact, proud of their Jewish heritage despite their lack of observance. He also briefly outlined some basic ideas of psychoanalysis, noting that even the Lubavitcher Rebbe had sought out a consultation with Freud. By showing that psychotherapy echoed ideas originally articulated by Jewish sages, Rabbi Feuerman urged rabbis to allow therapists to care for their patients in their own way, emphasizing their shared goal for a healthy outcome.

The triangulation of care gave non-Jewish knowledge (*khokhmas b'goyim*, Gentile wisdom) rabbinic approval to help those who were suffering, but it simultaneously tended to reinforce structures of authority. In so-called secular therapies, confidentiality is critical. In the triangulated care of a rabbi and a religious therapist, there was the potential for violation. Some therapists got a call from a rabbi for a referral and the interaction ended there. In other cases, a rabbi and therapist conferred over the diagnosis and the treatment plan, even including a spouse or a parent at times, unbeknownst to the patient. This created opportunities for abuse of the very notion of therapy, which both double lifers and some *frum* therapists were keenly aware of.

Chavi's Treatment of Doubt and Its Discontents

Chavi was a thoughtful Hasidic woman, a deep thinker. Her treatment history highlights the potential danger when rabbis and therapists collaborate to prioritize keeping a client within the fold. At the same time, despite a lot of suffering along the way, Chavi gradually figured out how to get help to clarify some major decisions she needed to make. This included therapy with a non-Orthodox psychiatrist, reading online, and meeting others living double lives, who had lived through very similar experiences.

Some years ago, Chavi found herself wondering, "Why am I not like everyone else? Why don't I like to just stay home and bake *kakush*-cake [a delicious Hungarian "cocoa cake" similar to babka]?" Chavi, in fact, had gotten very depressed at the birth of her fifth child, when she began to feel trapped and hopeless. She said, "You know, the drudgery of having babies and not wanting to be locked in. That's how it started." She described getting increasingly cool to Judaism, despite having always been a very "emotional, spiritual person." This coolness led to inappropriate desires for a Hasidic woman, like telling her husband, who was stringently pious, that she wanted to stop shaving her hair under her wig. She wondered if she had postpartum depression or if she was "crazy," she told me. Over the next three years, as she slowly became an atheist and began living a double life, she would end up seeing a social worker, an activist, psychiatrists (one Orthodox, the other not), and a religious psychologist. She was also misprescribed medication for disorders she did not have.

It all began, as it does for many, when Chavi's husband discovered her breaking the Sabbath with her phone. Very upset, he asked her to see a rabbinic activist, an *askn*, Rabbi Frank. She agreed because in fact, she and husband were at an impasse about more than her phone. Rabbi Frank came over, and they spoke for hours. They began meeting regularly. At first, Rabbi Frank was sympathetic and constructive, helping Chavi and her husband communicate better and encouraging her husband to be less religiously rigid. However, as she started trusting Rabbi Frank, Chavi let her guard down, revealing that her dissatisfaction was not just about her marriage; she had *emuna* questions too, and she felt trapped in her life. Rabbi Frank did an about-face. Wanting to be different, he told her, that wasn't normal for a Jewish woman, a wife and mother. He wondered if she might have a mental illness, and he recommended she go to a Modern Orthodox therapist he knew, who would even meet her right in his office.

Rabbi Frank's initial referral to the Modern Orthodox therapist at first seemed like a good fit. The female therapist was quite sympathetic to Chavi's feeling of being "locked in." Chavi remembered that the therapist said to her, "I get you because when I go to *shul*, I don't have an issue chatting with my husband's male friends, and if you were to tell me I couldn't do that, that would be very stifling for me. So why don't you become Modern Orthodox?" Chavi rolled her eyes, remembering this suggestion that revealed so little understanding of Hasidic hierarchies of authority. She explained to the therapist that making such a decision by herself, as a Hasidic woman, would be impossible, considered a form of going OTD in fact. The therapist then decided that Chavi had other issues and might benefit from medication. She referred Chavi to a psychiatrist, who gave her a diagnosis and a prescription. At that point, Chavi was both terrified and angry, and she threw out the prescription.

Still, she agreed to try talking to another activist her husband's rabbi had recommended, because, as she said, "I was really doubting myself. I was buying it because I also had really depressive episodes." That activist diagnosed her as bipolar, based on her depression and the fact that she had become casually friendly with some guys at her part-time job. Those friendships, he told her, were your manic periods, your sexual expression, because when men and women are friends, they're having sex. You're mentally ill, he concluded, because you're trying to flirt. In fact, Chavi had been doing nothing of the sort, but activists often frame any interaction between unrelated men and women in sexualized terms. He took out the DSM-4 and asked her to read the entry for bipolar disorder. As she read, she broke down in tears, and he said, "See, you're sick." And he sent her to a different psychiatrist, who prescribed a medication for bipolar disorder after talking to her for ten minutes.

Chavi's husband and a family friend who had gotten involved as well both pressured her to take the medication this time. They were really worried about her. The drug was, she told me, mind-altering. It affected her concentration, her memory, and it made her a "zombie." She was on it for eighteen months, but once her body got used to it, its effects weakened. "Guess what I wanted then?" She asked me, "I wanted to extend my hours at work and grow out my hair." Finally, she confided in a trusted uncle, who was visiting from London (where her father's family was from). He called the activist, who told him everything without Chavi's consent or knowledge. Then the psychiatrist decided to increase her dose for another six months, continuing to see her weekly in the activist's office. Even as she was talking to me, the relationship between that *askn*, the psychiatrist, her husband, and her uncle made Chavi really angry. The *askn* didn't have a license, she fumed, and he didn't ask my consent to consult with any of them.

Around the time that Chavi's dosage was raised, she began to doubt in a different way. No longer simply unhappy, she wondered, "Why am I doing all of this? Why am I religious? Do I believe? Is all of this [i.e., the therapists and rabbis] for belief worth it? It was like *mesiras nefesh* [self-sacrifice] for something I don't value." She decided she really didn't know, and she felt isolated and afraid that she was the only person in the world who had those thoughts.

Finally, Chavi decided she could only rely on herself. She began reading about religion and about medication and mental health online. She thought, "I'm not this person they're saying. I shouldn't be on this medication. Enough is enough. This medication is making me somebody else." She told the activist, her uncle, and her husband that she was no longer going to take the medication and that she would only see "an independent doctor who didn't speak to anyone but me." The activist capitulated and recommended psychiatrist Susan Katz, who was on the roster of an Orthodox referral service.

Going to Dr. Katz, Chavi said, changed her life. When Chavi told her the medication she had been on and the diagnosis, Dr. Katz was shocked. That drug, if it's not administered properly, she said, could actually bring on schizophrenia. Dr. Katz also assured Chavi that she was not bipolar; she was probably feeling anxious, and rightly so, because she was in a tough place and had some hard decisions to make. Chavi described how Dr. Katz had her think about the consequences of her actions and acknowledge the challenges inherent in each decision, such as staying or leaving. Let's work on the possibilities, Dr. Katz suggested, and weigh the implications.

With Chavi's permission, I interviewed Dr. Katz, who estimated that she had seen between five and ten people living double lives over the past few years, mostly Satmer Hasidim, but Gur, Bobov, and Pupa Hasidim, too, all referred by a rabbi or activist (with whom she did not have contact after the referral). She felt her double-life clients had been "pathologized in a deeply serious way" and then "medicated up the wazoo." This was not to say that rabbis were trying to "snow them into submission," or simply silence them. Rather, she suggested that the faithful needed to "see the aberration from the cultural norm as psychiatric pathology." That is, psychiatric diagnoses were the acceptable explanation for religious doubt or nonconformity. However, in her professional opinion, a truly mentally ill person would have a difficult time managing a double life. She explained to me:

> A mentally ill person would not be capable of going online and leading a double life and covering their tracks. . . . It's like having an affair basically. It is. It is having an affair with another culture. And you've got to have your wits about you to keep it straight.

Chavi's work with Dr. Katz helped her clarify the conflicts she was experiencing and decide what she wanted going forward. Once she was feeling more like herself, she reached out to someone who she had come to trust online, and this person introduced her to a loose group of seventy people living double lives, part of a closed Facebook group that called themselves "Reverse Marranos" or RMs (see chapter 6). During the Spanish Inquisition, Jews were initially given the choice to be killed or to convert to Catholicism. Those called Marranos converted, but they continued to practice Judaism in secret. RMs in New York inverted the term. They too were forced to embrace a religious doctrine against their will, but in their case they were forced to be Jewishly observant though they secretly explored secular lives. As Chavi began to socialize in that RM group, she realized that many of them had been referred over and over to a small group of religious social workers and psychiatrists by the same rabbis, something that Shmuel called, the "*frum* therapy industrial complex." After one of our interviews, Chavi sent me a list of five therapists' names that had appeared again and again, texting on WhatsApp, "My thought that it is a corrupt system isn't just a thought anymore. This made me so angry." In fact, there have been a number of stories in the popular press making similar accusations of misdiagnoses and overmedication for non-conforming behaviors by religious therapists working closely, maybe too closely, with certain rabbis.[13]

The more Chavi hung out with the RM group, the more she felt she wasn't alone, that she could talk with people who had already, as she said, "hashed out all these questions that I didn't know where to start." She told me that what was so "life changing" was interacting with others who were "normal and bright and talented. And they're ok. They're not crazy, so maybe I'm not crazy either." The heretical counterpublic offered another standard for judging who was a moral, healthy person, a judgment that could include those with religious doubts and heretical beliefs and practices.

There were others with stories like Chavi's, which I heard from a range of sources: a Facebook questionnaire I posted to a closed group, in interviews, and during a talk I gave at Footsteps. Zev, for example, who answered the questionnaire, told me that he had been seeing a religious therapist, whom he later learned was unlicensed. When Zev eventually revealed to him that he was having religious doubts, in addition to the depression he had come in with, the therapist started to yell at him, "Do you think you're smarter than Rashi?"[14] That same therapist kept insisting that he go see a psychiatrist that he worked closely with and no other, hinting at a kernel of truth to Chavi's sense that there were some therapists, rabbis, and psychiatrists who colluded to keep those with doubts in the fold.

However, a good therapist, religious or not, could actually be extremely helpful for those living double lives, easing some of the psychic pain and providing a neutral space for new kinds of talk. For example, Yisroel (see introduction), in addition to all the *frum* therapists and *kiruv* rabbis he and his wife went to, also met with Dr. Katz at Chavi's recommendation. At Yisroel's first session, Dr. Katz remembered, he began posing all of his theological questions, ready to argue or ask her for answers. She told him, "That's not really what we do in here. Let's talk about why you're asking me those questions." In fact, this was the exact same point that the religious therapist Rabbi Feuerman asked his clients when they brought up their theological questions. Similarly, Suri told me that in therapy she learned to appreciate the fact that the world wasn't black and white. "That was huge," she said. Shimon, about whom I'll say more, used couples therapy with his still-religious wife to negotiate how much secular reading material his children could be exposed to, even enlisting the therapist to support his argument that (nonreligious) reading was important for children's intellectual and emotional development. In their networking and socializing, those living double lives often exchanged information about therapists who were too invested in Judaism to be helpful to them; they pushed back on social media against the pathologizing of religious doubt that so many experienced.

Dissenting Voices among Religious Therapists

Dissenting views, often from a generation of therapists around the same age as those living double lives, explicitly debated the tension of being therapists and religious Jews, which was particularly complicated in their treatment of religious doubt. Not all religious therapists were willing to participate in the triangulation of care that Chavi had experienced, and certainly the majority of trained therapists were not invested in keeping those living double lives in the fold at any cost.

However, one Ruach member, a social worker and popular columnist, summed up the potential personal and professional dilemmas of working with a doubting client in an excerpt from one of her monthly columns, "Therapy Corner," in the ultra-Orthodox *Bina Magazine* in 2015:

Today as a therapist, I struggle: Who am I first? A social worker—or a religious, Orthodox Jew? . . . So how do I counsel that teen who is *mechallel* Shabbos [breaking the laws of the Sabbath]? As a therapist I am fully present with her in her pain and do not seek to foist my values on her but rather, am moved to help her discover her own path; but paradoxically, as a religious Jew, it pierces me to my core and I want her to find *Yiddishkeit* [Judaism] again.

The therapist ultimately put her ethical dilemma in the hands of God, concluding, "In truth, the no-brainer is that we do the best we can and the rest is up to Hashem [God]."

One particularly stubborn explanation for religious doubt that continued to haunt religious therapists was the notion of *tayves*, or uncontrollable lusts, as a default explanation for doubt, along with other forbidden behaviors. An earnest, thoughtful therapist like Yehuda Herbst, a licensed social worker, whose card listed his specializations as "existential crises and SSA (Same Sex Attraction),"[15] tried to walk a fine line between giving his patients agency without condoning violation of Jewish law. His role for doubting clients, as he saw it, was "repairing their emotional wounds," so that they could then make a "healthy" decision about "whether or not they wanted to remain religious." Yehuda told me that those who left to go OTD or who had SSA (note these were considered similar maladies) were not necessarily mentally ill; they had just not learned to discipline their desires—"not repress," he emphasized, "but discipline," meaning learn to work through their impulses. He saw therapy not only as "healing wounds," but also as an opportunity for working on impulse control. A gay client might choose to remain in his community by disciplining his inappropriate desires.

For some others, like Dr. Rosenberg, a Modern Orthodox therapist on the board of Ruach, this argument explaining life-changing doubt was simply not true. He wrote to me in an email:

> They [those therapists who talk about *tayves*] are basically saying that a lack of belief in Orthodox Judaism has nothing to do with their actual beliefs and can be much better explained by seeing it as a wish to fulfill one's urges for forbidden pleasures. I think that this is false. . . . There are many reasons someone could choose to go [leave Orthodoxy]. Everyone has "tayves" but they don't all leave Judaism because of them.

According to Dr. Rosenberg, only a minority of religious therapists believed that *tayves* led to doubt, though they were loud on the Ruach listserv I frequented. In his own work, in contrast, Dr. Rosenberg fore-grounded his position as a therapist rather than a religious advocate. On a different occasion he explained to me in an email, "I believe there is no such thing as 'frum therapy.' I'm an Orthodox Jew devoted to the study and observance of Torah. There is no reason that Jewish observance should alter what one does or how one intervenes as a psychotherapist."

Social worker Eitan Goldman, one of the most thoughtful religious therapists I met, had a different approach to religious doubting, one that acknowledged a *frum* therapist's religious identity, but used that to facilitate the therapeutic process. I saw this in action when he allowed me to sit in on a supervision group he ran for eight ultra-Orthodox therapists who had all earned their master's degrees in social work at Long Island University together.

The group met monthly in Eitan's basement office, where he laughingly pointed out to me that he kept his Jewish books on one shelf, his psychology books on another, and his controversial books, like Freud's *Totem and Taboo*, in a locked closet. Group members presented cases they had been working on that month for discussion. Trading fist bumps, quotes from the Talmud in Hebrew ("because it's our language of interacting, it's who we are"), and applause for reports of progress, the group was good-natured, serious, and supportive.

One case that night that a Hasidic therapist, Yonason, presented was a client who had been secretly violating Jewish laws. Yonason told the group that in order to earn his client's trust he had told him, "I work for you, not the *aybershter* [God]." The group questioned him and wondered if this was a case of countertransference, an emotional entanglement between a therapist and their client. Eitan suggested a different strategy that addressed Yonason's visibly Hasidic exterior but gave the client more agency. He told Yonason, "Why not smile and say, 'It must be strange to tell this [violations of Sabbath] to someone who looks like me.'" This put the authority in the hands of the client, not the therapist, which was the very purpose of therapy, Eitan suggested.

Eitan aimed to redefine religious therapy by embracing the shared religious and cultural understanding between client and patient, while he simultaneously hoped to transform the system (not that he was at all living a double life). For example, he told me about a patient he had who had watched pornography in a moment of weakness and felt ashamed. A secular therapist the client had seen minimized the incident as "natural" and "nothing to be ashamed about." He, in contrast, had "sat with the shame, about what it meant to the client" because he, as a religious Jew, understood the moral stakes for his client. He found, he told me, that the overwhelming majority of rabbis that he worked with appreciated the benefits of nonjudgmental, agenda-less therapy. At the same time, he said, we need someone on the inside who can show authority figures how the system is oppressing some, while helping victims rebuild their lives on their own terms. In this version of religious therapy, the autonomy of the client to make their own decisions was not threatening to religious authority; rather, Jewish Orthodoxy itself might change to become more compassionate, more flexible, and ultimately perhaps more moral for those who would not or could not "fit in."

There were other inklings that explanations for religious doubt might be changing in some therapeutic quarters. For example, at the 2015 annual conference of Agudas Yisroel, an umbrella organization for Orthodox Jews, I attended a panel on those who had left Orthodoxy. A prominent Modern Orthodox therapist on the panel told the packed room that he did not know why, but that, "sometimes Orthodoxy just doesn't work for a person." No blame, no reasons, simply an acknowledgement that people were different. Similarly, there were popular family therapists, like the founders of Tangled Parenting, who advocated that parents put their relationships with their children above their religious convictions. Instead of cutting ties, a common response to an OTD child, these therapists claimed that unconditional love was most important, as was keeping families together. Tangled Parenting had even found two ultra-Orthodox rabbis willing to give their approach a *hekhsher* of sorts, rabbinic certification that the approach was kosher.

A Famous Correspondence: Competing Explanations for Life-Changing Doubt

Those living double lives had begun to resist the ways they were often depicted by rabbis, activists, and some religious therapists as either mentally ill or at the mercy of their lusts, that is, either sick or bums. One such effort was a correspondence that Shimon, a prominent Hasidic scholar and father of five who had lived a double life for a decade, had with the rabbi who responded to the troubled teen in the newspaper column cited at the opening of this chapter. Many others living double lives had proudly told me about the exchange, which had circulated on the heretical counterpublic. The personal correspondence was an effort to push back on a prominent rabbi-psychiatrist's explanations for life-changing doubt, showing they were inaccurate and harmful.

Shimon told me he was surprised and upset when he read the response to the troubled boy in *Hamodia*. Rabbi Tessler had told that Yeshiva boy with *emuna* questions that there were two possible explanations for his religious doubt: either his evil inclination was getting the upper hand and he needed to consult a rabbi for support, or he had OCD and needed to see a therapist. Shimon was so upset, in fact, that he wrote a long letter to Rabbi Tessler. Here is part of Shimon's first letter, where he introduced himself (my translations):

Dear Rabbi Dr.,

Although I was born and bred in the Chareidi [ultra-Orthodox] community by my dear Chareidi parents, and although the Yeshivas I attended were considered crème de la crème, I do not identify as a religious man. . . . My current keeping of Mitzvos [commandments] is limited to the extent that I need to maintain my dignity, or the dignity of others associated with me—family, friends, etc. The reason for my lack of religion may sound foreign to you, but it has no connection to any major life event, neither is it related to any taavo [lust], which as a matter of fact I have no access to more than my typical Chareidi cohorts. I simply discovered what IMO is the truth. Or rather what is not the truth. I discovered the fallacy of much that I have been taught, and after sitting in libraries and combing through every book that I thought will satisfy my intellectual curiosity, I was left very much a "doubting" individual . . .

I was going through a severe crisis in rebuilding my understanding of moral responsibilities with the lack of God. . . . The people I spoke to in the community, some of them actually knowledgeable and *Chushive* [important] people, were not helpful in the least bit. They only reinforced the self-doubts about my own sanity rather than validate any of the questioning or other resolutions to questions that I considered more valid at that point. And here came along the internet. The internet saved my life. It gave me validation and more information. . . . It allowed for some social connection with like-minded people.

But living a double life started to have terrible effects on me that have been steadily worsening for the past 10 years. Unfortunately, with my spouse being a firm believer, there is no exit-option without my children being removed from me as from a leper. The agony of being unable to live your true self compounded with the pain that came with understanding that my staying in the community and raising my children religious is perpetuating the cycle and possibly getting them into the same mess, this pain is so harsh that many a therapist can make a good living off me.

The agony and pain I am describing is not very unique to me. Over the years I have come to know more people in similar situations trapped in the community as Orthoprax, or as they would call themselves, Marranos. And please don't take that term lightly. We are constantly hounded by the possibility of an inquisition, and some of us have indeed been subjected to trials by their peers over their lack of Emunah [faith]. We have been labeled Reshaim [wicked ones], Apikorsim [heretics], selfish, and mentally ill. We are forever living on the edge.

While our situation is really terrible, there is one place that we do feel trust in, and that is the secular therapist's room. We understand the concept of therapist-client confidentiality, and we understand the concepts of Psychology relatively well. It is in Psychology that we trust. It is for the psychologist to confirm for us and ourselves that we are human. We may have lost God, but we have not lost humanity.

It is with this background that I challenge your recent Q&A article that appeared in the Hamodia. After reading this article in the paper, I was rather surprised. I reread it, and made sure that it was actually you, the Doctor and Rabbi whom I believed to be an intellectual, writing this piece. I couldn't believe my eyes. Is this the real summation of a person coming up with doubts? Is this in any way doing justice to that twenty-something asking this naive question on his journey of self-discovery? I was terribly disappointed to have to reread this and confirm that this is actually your article. Is it that you have only two options for the intellectual mind unfortunate enough to be born to Chareidi parents? Either his doubts are resolved by gedoilim [sages], or he should be trained by therapists to stop doubting? How can any secularly informed man not be aware of the eerie reminiscence this carries to the communist regimes of yore, labeling their dissenters mentally disturbed and sending them off to re-education camps? . . . Will we, the Marrano [i.e., double lifers] community, actually be subjected to an inquisition led by none other than our esteemed mental health community? Will our trust in Psychology be our very undoing?

I hope you can clarify this article for me in a way that will alleviate some of the pain wrought by it.

Sincerely,
Marrano Jew

Rabbi Tessler wrote back, and I summarize his response because I do not have his permission to quote directly from the letter. He told Shimon that having philosophical questions about *emuna* was actually quite healthy and normal. Someone with questions should then search for answers and if they were unable to find resolution, they should just live a religious life with doubts. However, a person with philosophical questions had to be distinguished from the one with repetitive thoughts, such as "there is no God," which led to depression and dysfunction. Rabbi Tessler defended his suggestion that a person who was suffering from *emuna* questions should check with a professional to see if the doubt was healthy or perhaps actually a symptom of OCD. Finally, he reminded Shimon that he was a psychiatrist first, so he would not argue with him about faith.

Shimon wrote back, attempting to get Dr. Tessler to acknowledge that religious doubt was more complex, emotionally and intellectually, than he was proposing:

> Thank you for giving of your precious time to respond; it means a lot for me and am deeply honored by it. I am reaching out to you, the special person who has the unique insight that can only be had when serving in the dual positions—Rabbi and Psychiatrist. This dual position lends you the distinctive ability to understand and empathize with people suffering within and from the religious sphere.
>
> I cannot fathom that you only see OCD as a resolution for the tormented doubter becoming depressed and dysfunctional. You allow for a resolution to his philosophical doubts only in the affirmative, while stating that "having philosophical questions about emunah is quite healthy."
>
> I would specifically take umbrage with your statement "people who have philosophical doubts can search. If they cannot resolve their doubts, they can live with them." You summarily dismiss the reality of life for people who identify themselves as Marranos with

all the difficulty of living in a belief system they did not choose nor they can make peace with. They cannot live with it for their unfortunate lot of having found the opposite side of the debate compelling, and they cannot live outside of it for various socioeconomic reasons. The emotional pressure this can bring on is perhaps vast and traumatic and I can see a number of psychological ailments coming his way, but how does this bring one to suspect OCD?

Your solution of them dealing with "it" in the traditional way with sifrei mussar [religious books] etc. is evidently not an option, and within the realm of possibilities that you describe, that leaves only the option of an OCD diagnosis. I will readily sympathize with your refusal to argue the validity of Emunah. However, if you accept the health of an individual reflecting critically on his Emunah, how dare you question his mental condition for coming to a different conclusion than what you consider the truth?

Rabbi Tessler wrote one final response (that Shimon showed me) before he ended their correspondence. Citing Solomon (Ecclesiastes 1:18), he noted, "As your intelligence increases, so does your suffering." He wrote to Shimon that his intelligence was not an ally in his struggle to make sense of a world that defies being understood. He concluded by wishing Shimon well and saying that if he knew how to resolve his dilemma, he would share it with him.

The Morality of Therapeutic Authority

Psychology was another lightning rod, like the internet, for ultra-Orthodox debates about life-changing doubt. Tanya Luhrmann describes the uneasy moral place of psychology in the United States in her ethnography *Of Two Minds*. Psychology, she writes, is located between medicine and religion, as it attends to the mind, between the body and the soul.[16] For some religious therapists, *kiruv* rabbis, and life coaches, the increasing professionalized attention to interiority helped explain how those exposed to "truth" since childhood might experience life-changing doubt. Rather than labeling them as unethical, these authorities showed that there were psychological reasons for doubt, not moral flaws of character. These practitioners held out hope that loved ones might be cured and returned to the fold. For them, the normative person was ultra-Orthodox, so doubt was blamed on biological illness in the mind and body, which blinded that person from accepting the truth. The ultra-Orthodox treatment of doubt innovatively transformed a non-Orthodox discursive tradition, psychology, while tacitly reproducing ultra-Orthodox moral authority.

For those living double lives, in contrast, therapy held out the promise of a nonjudgmental space where they could safely talk through the impossible position they found themselves in. Those with life-changing doubt, like Shimon, Dovid, Miriam, and Chavi, refused to be labeled as mentally ill or morally weak. In fact, Shimon made the claim, in the end of his letter to Dr. Tessler, that sacrificing his own happiness and beliefs for his family and children was the most moral, the most human choice of all:

> Indeed, if humanity is the measure, and selflessness the yardstick, the sacrifice we endure for the sake of our children, knowing full well that we will never be rewarded neither by God nor by man, shall surpass any mesiras nefesh [self-sacrifice] of the standard Chareidi [ultra-Orthodox Jew] living in our days.

Those living double lives used the therapist's office to stake their claims that they were still ethical Jews, perhaps more ethical than any ultra-Orthodox believer, precisely because they used their own judgment, their individual authority, to sacrifice for their families with no carrot or stick of divine or human reward.

Cultural and religious theories of interiority can be leveraged politically to challenge or uphold structures of authority. The history of psychology as a discipline itself hearkens back to struggles among Jews to exert authority over interiors, much as the Jewish Enlightenment did for two centuries before that. Freud's own secular Jewish identity, the notion that psychoanalysis was a "Jewish science" in the context of early twentieth-century Vienna, was part of a broader conversation over Jewish belonging and difference to the nation, one that continues to resonate with contemporary ultra-Orthodox therapists.[17]

Therapists may be authorized to diagnose mental health, but ethnography and history remind us that what constitutes mental health is also based on culturally normative ways of being and feeling. Some double lifers, like Shimon, equated their harmful experiences with religious therapy to the former Soviet Union, where mental institutions were used to lock away political dissidents. They felt their treatment had too often been simply a ruse to keep them quiet and religious. Psychology and medicine, as Foucault so famously argued, can be powerful forces to discipline those who do not conform.[18]

Similarly, my research with a few religious therapists brought me uncomfortably close to "Same Sex Attraction" or conversion therapy, which had striking parallels to Evangelical Christian conversion therapy. Both used spiritual explanations (*tayves*, spiritual weakness) for homosexuality in their efforts to support individuals' struggles with their own unacceptable desires. This was despite the fact that the American Psychological Association condemned conversion therapy as "pseudoscience" and in 2015, the Jewish organization for conversion therapy, JONAH (Jews Offering New Alternatives for Healing), was closed down by the state for promising something it could never deliver. Conversion therapy, so repugnant to me, reminds us of the limits of cultural relativism that anthropologists have struggled with.[19]

Despite this dark underbelly, religious therapy was also creating a new arena for exploring multiple forms of authority, which could be transformative for the individual and for ultra-Orthodoxy. With its very American value of individual personal transformation, religious therapy engaged with established ultra-Orthodox hierarchies of authority. The ultra-Orthodox individual did not really have the moral authority to choose exactly how to live. That's what tradition (*mesoyra*) and rabbis were for. The right to make individual ethical judgments, something claimed by double lifers and sometimes supported in their therapeutic treatments, could ultimately raise productive questions, questions that led to new ways of thinking about religious orthodoxy more generally.

Even as those living double lives sought help for themselves and their families, they continued to lead secret lives. Not only did they increasingly break commandments in private, away from the eyes of their families and neighbors, they simultaneously explored the city with others, a different public sphere where they knew they would not be discovered. Secretly, they tried on different ways of being, feeling, writing, and looking. These experiments drew on their ultra-Orthodox sensibilities and their imagining of secular Gentile life, which ended up changing both.

6

Double-Life Worlds

One day, Motti posted a "confession" on a WhatsApp group, a commentary on his double life:

> I will take this opportunity to make a confession. I live in two separate worlds. One life is in the real world and the other is in a virtual world. The virtual world is my community, extended family, workplace, etc. with whom I have little in common other than the bad fortune to have been at the same place in the same time. They are the people I associate with because I have to, not because I want to. It is a world based on power and fear.

> The real world is here. On social media, on WhatsApp, on forums and in bars. This is where I have the pleasure of living an honest and open life, surrounded with people who love me and respect me for who I am. The real world is what keeps me from going insane, given that I spend most of my time in a world which suffocates my true desires and beliefs. The real world is the place where I come when I'm completely fed up of living in a virtual and unauthentic world, to spend cherished minutes and hours with my dear, true friends.

Motti's public Hasidic life was a shadowy world of lies, fear, and imposed obligations that he had not chosen. The world he had made for himself on social media and at secret in-person gatherings was what mattered. For Motti, "real" life was not about a medium—writing on WhatsApp or hanging out in a bar. Rather it was about human relationships, rooted in honesty, shared morality, choice, and trust, wherever and whenever that happened.

Shared secrets rely on mutual trust, as anthropologists' work with all kinds of secret societies tell us.[1] The development of trust among those living double lives almost always happened first on the anonymity of social media, through carefully calibrated revelation of doubts, exchange of ideas, and referrals from trusted friends. Once trust was earned, many began to meet up in real life, where they sought out emotional connections and new experiences, "biting into forbidden fruit . . . to create an exciting life to fill the void of what feels so empty at home," as Nosson explained to me.

When invited, I followed as those living double lives explored new ways of being, thinking, writing, and feeling with like-minded friends. Many I met, especially men, felt that they had been cheated out of their childhoods, and they were determined to take back what they had missed.[2] This manifested in (a) rebellious, sexualized partying in the comfort of ultra-Orthodox settings and (b) sampling objects, tastes, writing, and experiences based on ultra-Orthodox imaginaries of the secular world, so distant, yet right around the corner.

Double lifers pursued, when they could, their newfound values of autonomy, self-expression, and personal fulfillment, yet their secret social worlds stayed close to the emotional attachments of ultra-Orthodox sensibilities. This is not surprising. Sociologist Pierre Bourdieu defined "habitus" as "the deeply engrained, lifelong habits, skills and dispositions" that shape who we are.[3] Ultra-Orthodox habitus, like any other, was hard to shake, but especially so since double lifers continued to live at least some of the time as they always had. Ultimately, secret double life worlds were mash-ups of the intimacy of ultra-Orthodoxy and ultra-Orthodox stereotypes of how the rest of New York lived. These mash-ups had different possibilities for double-life men and women, resulting in many women's exclusion from the heretical counterpublic, much as the Jblogs had done a decade before.

Those living double lives often socialized with those who had already left or were in the process of leaving, since these boundaries were rarely cut-and-dried.[4] Even though double lifers and OTDers had different stakes and often argued over who was more moral or honest or courageous, their social networks overlapped, so their socializing did too. My own presence online and in person was complicated. It was disturbingly easy to "lurk" on closed groups on social media, even though I had been invited to join. Unless I commented or "liked" posts, which I tried to do, my presence was invisible, an ethical dilemma specific to digital ethnography. In contrast, my physical presence at face-to-face gatherings was called out repeatedly, as people reminded others that I was there for research, speaking to the ongoing tension between not wanting to be "studied" and wanting to tell their stories.

Double-life experiments in recreation were mediated through the body, language, objects, and technology. Sociologist Lynn Davidman, writing about ultra-Orthodox Jews leaving their communities, notes that interior crises of faith were lived over time through changing bodies and sensibilities. It took time, for example, to get used to wearing jeans or eating *treyf* (nonkosher), like cheeseburgers, which often initially prompted disgust.[5] However, my time with double lifers revealed that that the body was not the only medium for changing one's habitus. There were diverse yet related networks of media through which double lifers experienced, created, and shared their secret lives. These media included language (written, spoken, and digital), such as Yiddish online poetry; material objects like bicycles or open-toed sandals; and digital technology, like Facebook.[6] Those living double lives engaged in these networks of media not to reject one habitus and try to inhabit another, but to live in two overlapping worlds at the same time.

Attending to relationships among diverse media moves the study of religion beyond the more obvious focus on sacred texts, rituals, and institutions. Bars, internet forums, and other explicitly nonreligious spaces were all important places where double lifers went to try out their ultra-Orthodox dreams of secular life, a different habitus, to be sure, but always refracted through ultra-Orthodox religiosity and its sensibilities. A question that only ethnography could answer was how those living double lives tried to secretly change while publicly staying just enough the same.

Building Trust on Social Media

Those living double lives almost always got to know each other anonymously first on social media before they would agree to meet in real life. Some, for example, joined the huge English-language Facebook closed group OTD (off the *derekh*, path) and interacted with a whole range of doubters from the closeted to those who had openly left, while others regularly posted on *Kave Shtibl*, the Yiddish-language forum, all without much risk of exposure. However, the more a person got to know others, the more danger there was of potential revelation. Many juggled different accounts and platforms (e.g., Reddit, WhatsApp, Instagram, Telegram, Snapchat) in their effort to keep their identities hidden.

Niks (nicknames) and profile pictures for Facebook and WhatsApp as material objects often revealed while they concealed, playing with insider knowledge of ultra-Orthodox Jewish life or the person themselves. [7] Just a sampling of Facebook niks included: historical civil rights figures (e.g.,

Harriet Tubman); generic names and places (Dave Brooklyn, Bob NY); talmudic or biblical names; linguistic puns playing with English, Yiddish, Hebrew, or combinations, for example, *baleboos* (male head of household) became Bill H. Boos.

Similarly, profile pictures could be obfuscating or meaningful for those in the know. Some used generic flowers or scenes from nature, and some used pictures of movie stars who had a passing or aspirational resemblance to the real person. Other images included the generic male silhouette Facebook generates; pictures of children; images that referenced a per-son's Yiddish name (Blimi, whose name means flower in Yiddish, used a picture of a daisy); nonconforming personality—a rainbow umbrella in a sea of black ones; or a pair of skis stuck in the snow, referencing the heretical experiments in bourgeois leisure activities that was part of many secret social lives. Some have begun to use bitmojis (cartoon avatars), which could change as the person did. For example, when Sheyndie changed her bitmoji profile picture on Facebook, taking off the hat from her wig, there were many comments asking about its meaning. Similarly, Yitsy's profile picture started out in 2013 with a bitmoji that lurked to one side of the frame, clearly sticking just his big toe in that world. In 2018 he updated his bitmoji to stand out front with a smartphone in his outstretched hand.

Danger of exposure always lurked from religious trolls, members of shadowy informal associations called *vaads* (committees), who stirred up trouble on comment threads and sometimes reported "invalid" pseudonyms to Facebook administrators, who could and did deactivate accounts. In some cases, like Yisroel's, a Facebook troll reported his activities to the *vaad*, who in turn reported them to rabbinic authorities, which created all kinds of real-life consequences for him, his family, and even extended family, since they told his parents, who flew in from Montreal to talk with him. Nevertheless, he soon opened up two new accounts with different pseudonyms.

Many told me that figuring out who people "really were" was a game that some played, with potentially frightening consequences. Sheyndie, for example, compared managing her secret identity to Cold War–era politics. She only divulged personal information to those who divulged as well: doubters' détente. Once Blimi had tried to find out who Sheyndie really was, and since then Sheyndie refused to have anything to do with her, even though Blimi had apologized, and they shared mutual friends.

Along with protecting one's real identity, there were also strategies even among friends or acquaintances for maintaining secrecy about where exactly one landed on the continuum of life-changing doubt. Digital media like smartphones could provide more opportunities for secrecy, while simultaneously leaving traces for discovery. For example, on Shabbes, when observant Jews do not use electricity, some turned off the feature on WhatsApp and Facebook that indicated if the recipient had read the message or not, so that no one would know they were breaking Shabbes by using their devices. Once, for example, I texted Sheyndie on a Shabbes on WhatsAppville Yinglish, and she didn't respond. I saw from the single checkmark that my message had been sent but not delivered or read. Knowing that she was regularly online on Shabbes and in a hurry for an answer, I switched to her private account. She immediately responded. When I asked, she told me that she wouldn't want everyone on our Whats-App group knowing she regularly broke the Sabbath despite being friends with most of them. Maintaining a double life meant careful calibration of who to trust with personal information and how much, including being careful to cover one's electronic and real-life tracks. Suri, for example, told me about meeting for a nonkosher dinner with a friend, who after ordering, turned to her suddenly anxious and asked her not to tell anyone she had ordered the rib eye. "I don't want everyone to know I eat nonkosher meat ok?"

Trust generated on social media created networks that spread transnationally across the ultra-Orthodox diaspora, while also bringing Hasidic, Yeshivish, Modern Orthodox, and even some Gentiles (often work colleagues) into regular written interaction. These interactions often included explanations of inside knowledge and translation of Yiddish posts for all who were not Hasidic. The diversity of Jewish and even some non-Jewish voices on social media all contributed to the formation of the heretical counterpublic. The ultra-Orthodox religious diaspora was sustained through kinship, marriage, and economic ties, but social media bound those living double lives and those who had gone OTD, which spilled over into face-to-face encounters to provide support. When, for example, a family tragedy occurred to a Facebook double-life friend in Israel, Shmuel raised money among all the "friends" and sent it to him. He was even going to organize a group to travel to Israel to visit the *shiva* (mourning ritual), but that ultimately proved too complicated for everyone, especially the mourning friend who would have to explain who these people from New York were.

Similarly, those with more experience living double lives helped ease some of the pain and fear for those newly doubting, by advising about divorce, custody battles, and therapy. For example, while I was interviewing Shimon, he received a call from a panicked married man in his twenties living upstate. His wife had just discovered he had stopped putting on tefillin, had had an affair, and had been hanging out with some prominent OTD people. She was threatening to divorce him and take custody of their five children. Shimon, in Yiddish, advised the man to immediately talk to a lawyer, not to sign or say anything to his wife or their families, and to find a secular therapist to go to with his wife.

On social media, in striking contrast to ultra-Orthodox social life, men and women interacted, exploring secular culture and politics, mocking the system together, much as they had on the comment sections of the Jblogs. Most mixed-gender postings were in Hasidic English or Yeshivish. Some women were not comfortable reading or writing in Hasidic men's Yiddish, and double-lifer men's English had generally improved from their widespread secular reading and digital writing. For example, on Facebook, Chavi posted a picture of eight books (literary and popular fiction) lined up and wrote, "Getting my yom tov [holiday] stash ready." Another responded, "I need something light for shul [synagogue], what would you recommend?" Many wrote reviews of television shows, movies, and plays they had seen and shared new finds in popular music, which often became the grounds for philosophical and political debates.[8] They also played with the boundaries between their shared knowledge of ultra-Orthodox life and their growing knowledge of popular American culture. For example, in reference to the challenges of some of the seemingly endless high holy days for a nonbeliever, one posted, "I survived #holidays5776!" (September 2015), combining then contemporary hashtag humor with the Jewish new year date (5776). Sympathetic comments followed.

Similarly, a posting forwarded to WhatsAppville Yinglish superimposed audio of Hebrew singing over a video clip of the Super Bowl trophy being carried to each member of the winning team (the Philadelphia Eagles that year), who kissed it as it passed. The Super Bowl ritual in fact bore an uncanny resemblance to the carrying of a Torah through a synagogue congregation, whose members also kiss it as it is carried around while singing. Superimposing religious ritual on a secular sports ritual mocked both while perhaps acknowledging the similarities of all rituals. This culturally relative insight was itself quite heretical.

There were frequent online postings of pictures of *pashkeviln* (posters hung on building walls and streetlights) with their various decrees about modesty or smartphones. By recirculating these posters, those online mocked rabbinic rulings and shared their outrage. Some even secretly video recorded events with their smartphones and shared them with heretical groups. For example, in 2017 someone posted a clip of a Yeshivish school where girls' hair was being measured with a ruler to ensure a modest length, with comments making fun of the absurdity of the extent of religious stringencies. The video went viral, eventually even getting picked up by the *Forward*, a secular Jewish newspaper.

Finally, there were smaller closed groups devoted to particular issues or interests. These were the most likely to either grow out of or lead to friendship circles in person. For example, one English- / Hasidic English–language private group, *Eyd* (witness), which had seventy-five members, was a site devoted to ethical debates and moral reasoning, and many of the people I got to know participated on it. The group's "about" page included an explanation of the group's purpose:

> The group attempts to function as a courtroom of ethics, where the members serve as advocates and arbitrators to discern right from wrong. This is a group to think, not groupthink [reference to Orwell's *1984*, which many read and found transformative]. We encourage independent thinking and welcome controversial and contrarian viewpoints. We encourage opinions based on empiricism and logic, and discourage opinion biased by agenda or based on allegiance to friends and society. We ask all members to respect the right of the individual to live according to his or her conscience.

This group was quite active for a while, but like many, it eventually died down, and people moved on to the next group and the next platform, part of the ephemerality of digital media.

English sites were open to men and women, but there were online spaces where women's lack of education in liturgical Hebrew and limited fluency in written men's Yiddish constrained their participation. Chavi, for example, who had been an excellent student in high school, told me about her frustration in joining a *khumesh* (Bible) WhatsApp group. Members of the group asked her why she was even interested since she "hadn't learned *khumesh*." That was extremely offensive," she told me, "I didn't learn it the way they learned it but I learned it my own way." The Bible group was conducted in *loshn koydesh*, and Chavi complained to the group, "Look, if it's in Hebrew I can't participate in it. Only if it's in English." While she never did join, she and another male member began having a private exchange about the Bible in English, which was itself something of a revelation.

Reclaiming Adolescence in the Intimacy of Ultra-Orthodoxy

A defining feature of ultra-Orthodox life and one often touted by its believers was the sociability, sense of belonging, and shared purpose structured by the rhythm of the Jewish calendar. However, for those living double lives, holidays instead often became pressure cookers, where they were stuck in synagogue, socializing with extended family, and having to keep up a front and perform what had become meaningless, boring rituals for days on end with no escape. Perhaps for this reason, double lifers often gathered on or around the Jewish holiday calendar to enjoy time with those who shared their heretical beliefs and values, creating different kinds of celebrations. For example, Zalman and a mix of OTD and double-life men got together regularly to learn Talmud, just as believers did. None of them were believers any longer, but this only enhanced their enjoyment of the texts because there was no need for reconciling truths. Studying Talmud became a way to participate in shared intellectual history in the comfort of what Zalman called the *haymishkayt*, the intimate familiarity of Hasidic male religious study.

Get togethers were regularly organized in between, before, or after family holiday celebrations. Parties, often hosted by someone OTD, offered private spaces to enjoy the familiar sensibilities of ultra-Orthodox food, singing, dancing, and schmoozing, combined with the experimental letting go of college-dorm or frat parties. The few all women's get-togethers were quite different (see below). Here are three ethnographic snapshots of different parties: Purim, Thursday nights (*leyl shishi*), and summers when wives and children were "in the country" (i.e., the Catskill Mountains). The get-togethers included men and women engaging in religiously forbidden activities (e.g., men and women dancing and singing together) in a comfortable ultra-Orthodox context. Party goers lived a rebellious adolescence they had never had, but with others who spoke their languages and enjoyed the same Jewish foods, music, and sensibilities.

A Purim Masquerade Ball

Purim is a holiday of inversion: a Jewish carnival that includes the reading of the scroll of Esther, a Jewish queen who saved her people from the archvillain, Haman, in ancient Shushan (Persia). It's common to dress up, and relatives exchange baskets of food and wine (*shalokh monos*), host festive meals, and donate money to charities. At our very first interview, Blimi asked me if I would be interested in going to a different kind of Purim celebration, with "people like her." Friends of friends of hers, a wealthy OTD couple, were hosting a masquerade ball, a perfect occasion for a wild dance party that would last until dawn. Guests were invited to wear masks, and I felt a certain protection from my own gold-feathered mask as I walked into the white-tented roof deck in Flatbush, warmed by space heaters and lit by tiki torches. Similar to the over-the-top luxury aesthetics of a Hasidic wedding, there was a full bar with ice sculptures, waitstaff handing out masks, a large dance floor with a blue strobe light, surrounded by white velvet couches, a DJ, and security with a guest list.

As I got used to the low lights and the throbbing music, I saw guests dressed up in Purim costumes—well, Halloween costumes used for Purim. There was a couple dressed as Disney's Beauty and the Beast, Bat Girl, a belly dancer, Freddy Krueger, and someone in a full gorilla suit and a long blond wig. Almost everyone who wasn't wearing a full mask wore a half mask, covering eyes and nose. In a dark corner, I saw a man dressed up in full Hasidic Purim *levush* (clothing), his holiday *shtraymel* tossed on the couch next to him. Was that a costume or his real clothes? Some women were wearing slinky, sexy dresses, and others had added modest leotard-like shirts (shells) underneath their gowns, along with wigs and masks. Many men wore black tie or suits. I finally spotted Blimi, drinking a cosmopolitan and dancing close with Moishy. Ultra-Orthodox men get drunk on Purim; it's a *mitsva,* actually. At this Purim party, it was both men and women who drank and danced with close friends, lovers, and perfect strangers.

Bodies touched all night—hugging and kissing hello, sitting on laps, dancing together, making out: men and women, women and women, men and men. There was a lot of drinking and drugs. I was introduced to a very young man, who kissed my hand, told me his name in English (Simon, not the Yiddish "Shimon") and asked me to slow dance. I did, awkwardly, since he looked to be about my own teenage son's age. I was grateful when the music changed to the K-Pop hit "Gangnam Style." Suddenly a group of men linked arms and began dancing round and round in a circle, just like at a Hasidic wedding. I found myself also holding hands and twirling in a circle with Simon, a woman in modest dress, wig, and mask, and the man in the gorilla suit and blond wig.

The party was a safe yet public space to do and be all that was forbidden, which ironically was in the very spirit of Purim. For the ultra-Orthodox, though, the transgressions and the inversions of Purim celebrations ultimately valorize the system. Ultra-Orthodox Purim revelers break rules in culturally sanctioned ways, and they return to "normal" the next day. The double-life/OTD Purim celebration fundamentally challenged the system by breaking even the rules for rule breaking, but doing so in a *haymish*, familiar kind of way. And the next day, the party goers returned to their (double) lives too.

A *Leyl Shishi* (Thursday) Party

Leyl shishi is the Thursday evening before Friday's Shabbes, a time when men traditionally studied all night in synagogue and have a taste of the Sabbath food to come the next night. Today it has become a night for going out, mainly for men, an ultra-Orthodox version of TGIF. The *leyl shishi* party at Mashy and Mendy's apartment had a Hasidic sensibility of a pre-Shabbes get-together juxtaposed again with a dorm party, with men and women drinking, singing, getting high, letting loose, and having deep philosophical conversations. In contrast to the Purim party, this was smaller and cozier, invoking the sense of hanging out before Shabbes. All kinds of people, however, were welcome as they were, no questions asked, and nothing required.

I had been visiting with Chaim one Thursday afternoon, and he called ahead to ask the hostess if I could join the party. The large apartment looked like many other Hasidic homes I had seen—a long dining room table, no rugs, a big leather couch, and the ubiquitous "breakfront," a cabinet with silver ritual objects and religious books. The meat and bean Shabbes stew, cholent, was simmering on the stove, and the long dining room table was spread with liver and farfel, kugel, mini-hot dogs on toothpicks, fruit, and some boxes of candy—all familiar smells and tastes of an Orthodox Jewish home. Some people there were openly OTD, and some were still in the closet. I sat next to a couple who looked Hasidic, but spoke very little, just looking around, taking everything in. "Sit closer to each other!" someone yelled at them. I heard a man ask a woman, "What's your story?" She said, "I don't want to talk about my story. It's too sad." So he told her his story about his divorce and the loss of custody of his one-year-old. Meanwhile, I talked to an OTD acquaintance about Chomsky and linguistics on the porch, where people were smoking and getting high.

Back inside Mendy soon took out a guitar, and everyone began singing *zemiros*, Jewish hymns in Hebrew, Aramaic, or Yiddish, traditionally sung by men around the Sabbath table. But in this party, when they knew the words or even if they didn't and just hummed, women joined in, something forbidden because men are not allowed to hear women sing. There was beautiful harmonizing as men and women lifted their arms into the air to beat time, a very emotional Hasidic gesture of transcendence. Mashy, the hostess, got up to make sure the curtains were drawn and the windows closed, so their nosy religious neighbors wouldn't hear or see them. The next day a guest posted on Facebook, "Thanks Mashy and Mendy, for hosting such a fun gathering of drunks and stoners. Hope we can do this again soon."

Ven de Vayb Iz in de Kontry (When the Wife Is in the Country) Party

I got a Facebook notification one summer day that I, along with fourteen others, was invited to party hosted by Blimi and Jakob Frank, a nik referring to the controversial eighteenth-century libertine who claimed to be a reincarnation of the seventeenth-century self-proclaimed Jewish messiah, Sabbatai Zvi:

> Since the brewing of the Borscht Belt, "die vieb iz in deh Kountry" [the wife is in the country, i.e., away in the Catskill bungalow colony for the summer] has been an

excuse to celebrate and to let loose. Since we are traditionalists, and Jakob's abode is free of kin and kinder [children], let's grab the opportunity to get together and have a fun time.

Using a "traditional" Jewish demarcation of time and Hasidic English, a mix of double-life and OTD friends were invited to a "wine-and-cheese" party. Jakob (who turned out to be Chaim) worked at a fancy kosher restaurant, and he had brought a selection of cheeses and spreads, an elite body of foodie knowledge, to try in the privacy and familiarity of a Hasidic and OTD gathering. Yitsy, who had only ever eaten cottage cheese and American cheese in his life, posted on Facebook the next day, "Thanks guys. It was amazing. And thanks to Chaim and Ayala, now I know the deal with cheese. Let's do it again soon."

There was the pleasure, along with perhaps a frisson of danger, in meeting someone in person after only interacting anonymously on social media. Benny, for example, posted on Facebook the next day, "It was great meeting some people and matching names to faces." Some remained anxious not to reveal their real names, fearful of possible repercussions, especially with OTD guests there, whom double lifers felt had less to lose. When I introduced one person to another using his real name, he quickly corrected me and said, "Use Jake instead." It was strange to see men and women shaking hands when they were introduced, since ultra-Orthodox men and women do not touch in public. In this safe space they could.

Because the party was in a Hasidic neighborhood, many came dressed as their religious selves, which was revealing of their family's religiosity in their public lives. For example, Mashy said to another woman, "Oh, I've only seen you with your own hair [when they were hanging out, and she had taken off her wig]. I didn't know your wig was so long." A long wig is generally less religiously stringent than a shorter one.

My ambiguous position as anthropologist and friend/guest was good-naturedly pointed out by Joe, a well-known OTD figure, who repeatedly reminded everyone that I was doing research. "Are we mice?" Bentsy asked me, "Are you observing us?" "I see your racket," joked Miriam, "You use your job to come to fun parties."

The party was predominantly an intimate male space. Women double lifers often had young children and were unable to come out on a Thursday night. As the guests relaxed, the men began to speak more and more Hasidic Yiddish, especially outside on the driveway, where they were standing around getting high. Miriam had told me at a different party that she felt left out when men all reverted to Yiddish in these situations. At this party, too, there was singing, with men belting out *khazunes* (cantorial music), and women joining in—at least, when they could.

Almost all the guests were Hasidic, but from different groups. This provided an opportunity to tease each other about Hasidic loyalties, which seemed hard to ever completely let go of. For example, in the middle of taking a puff from a joint, Mashy pointed to a picture of Chaim's rebbe on the wall, laughingly telling him to take it down. "He's staring at us," she said. "We don't put the rebbe's picture up," another said, "because it's not really ok to have an image." Another made fun of a different rebbe who was known not to be very intellectual. "What would you be if you could choose?" asked Avrum. Yitsy said he would be Satmar and Blimi agreed, saying, "They really know how to live, how to enjoy themselves." Mashy told a story about how special her *rebbetsin* (wife of the rebbe) was to hoots of mocking laughter from the table. The next day Mashy posted to the group: "Last night was entertaining and *geshmak* [delicious]. I hope I converted some of you to my *hasidus* [Hasidic group]. If not, there's always next time."

Gentile Leisure Worlds

Life-changing doubt and its alternative morality included desires to explore activities, objects, and expressive forms that had previously been forbidden, what they imagined was *goyish* (Gentile) or secular recreation. There were plenty of activities and places in New York that ultra-Orthodox Jews did partake in as families, such as trips to Prospect and Central Parks, complete with row boating and biking. Many visited the botanical gardens and the zoos, water taxis, and the Museum of Natural History (with the exception of the dinosaurs on the fourth floor—problematic evidence of the theory of evolution, which the ultra-Orthodox do not believe in). These kosher excursions were often taken during Jewish half holidays when families were all together.

Those living double lives, in contrast, explored the city by themselves or together, to try on new ideas, to feel different things in their bodies, to try different tastes. They created get-togethers with distinctive ideas of sexuality, friendship, and kinship; and they used languages to express their changing sense of who they were or might become. They chose some experiences to make up for what they had missed out on in childhood, much like drinking or getting high at Jewish parties did. Other activities, places, or objects provided a sense of excitement, newness, and perhaps the thrill of deviance.

Bodies, Language, and Material Culture

Bodies, clothing, language, and food mediated—made visible, social, public—changing senses of the self. Men and women living double lives, for example, told me similar stories of changing relationships to their own bodies as they tried out new sports or recreational activities. Learning to ride a bicycle almost became a rite of passage for many living double lives. Though some ultra-Orthodox adults, especially women, worked out or "walked the [Williamsburg] bridge," bikes and other recreational sports were generally frowned on in Hasidic communities, especially for boys after bar mitzvah age (thirteen) when they could be studying the Torah. Those living double lives, in contrast, often posted pictures of themselves on social media or told each other about learning to ride on the rental Citi bikes, available in neighborhoods beyond their own. Toby, for example, had gone to Staten Island to practice. Some even proudly displayed scraped-up knees on Facebook. An intimacy with one's body, a feeling of strength rather than shame, was something that many wanted to establish.

Similarly, others learned to ski, perhaps because skiing involved leaving one's community, away from judging eyes, and was so evocative of Gentile upper-middle-class leisure, at least for the ultra-Orthodox. This sport was often documented on Facebook, too. Esty, for example, posted two pictures of herself in full ski regalia (pants!). One friend posted: "Respect. Just for taking the challenge." She responded: "I skied, I fell down, I got up, I fell down and got up most of the time!" Some couples spent weekends away. Experimenting with leisure activities that most ultra-Orthodox Jews did not participate in allowed those living double lives to dip their toes into their imaginings of bourgeois Gentile leisure in the safe company of others like themselves.

Changes to hair, head-covering, beards, or clothing were often shared and celebrated as staking autonomous claims, asserting individual authority over one's body. In part this was because the embodied demands of ultra-Orthodoxy came to feel restrictive, uncomfortable, and boring, as did some religious rituals, which had ceased to be meaningful. When double-life women got together themselves, for example, talk often turned to these changes. At a play that Esty, Blimi, Toby, and I all went to, Blimi complimented Esty, who no longer wore a hat on her wig, telling her, "You look so good." Esty told us that she had not only taken off her hat and replaced it with a headband, but she had stopped shaving under her wig, too. "You'll see," said Blimi, "soon your band will get skinnier and skinnier until no one even notices it's gone!" Blimi told us she never would have "dared" wear sandals (red with open toe and back) before, but these days she did.

Later, Esty suggested to me privately that maybe Blimi got away with so much because she came from a "good" family with money and rabbis on all sides. Esty thought Blimi's extended family provided her with more leeway. "With my family," said Esty, "I wouldn't be able to get away with what she does." Actually, I had been unable to figure out exactly how ultra-Orthodox social class, with its mix of genealogy, wealth, male scholarship, female beauty, and levels of piety, affected living a double life. As I noted in chapter 4, some prestigious families did seem to have more flexibility in terms of conforming to communal standards and norms. Perhaps this was like the wealthy donors to anti-internet campaigns I heard about on Facebook, whose own unfiltered smartphones were never a topic of conversation. On the other hand, a number of people also told me that prestigious families actually were more in the public eye, as role models for others. In those cases, there might be less tolerance for anyone pushing the boundaries of acceptable behavior.

Bodies were not the only medium for boundary pushing. Some changed their English lexicon (vocabulary) to include both more profanity and sophisticated, more literary English words, probably a result of their secular movie watching, voracious reading, and digital writing. Cursing, *nivul peh* (profanity), in any language, was considered by the ultra-Orthodox, if not exactly sinful, not fitting for a refined (*aydel*), morally pure Jewish person. Refinement was less about social class and more about the innate differences between Jews and Gentiles, manifested in their language. Gavriel told me, for example, that the first time he heard a Hasidic person say "fuck" he was twenty-five and was deeply shocked. In contrast, those living double lives, both men and women, used common English profanity in speaking and writing online, making them sound, to me at least, more like everyone else in New York. At the same time, many also used English vocabulary gleaned from reading. Sometimes they mispronounced words or asked me about pronunciation during interviews, a legacy of being autodidacts, part of a secret intellectual life. Shmuel also told me that among themselves some would discuss pronunciation of words they had only read or resort to digital aids, such as Google's text-to-speech app.

Fluency in Standard English did not necessarily correlate to other semiotic signs of social class in wider New York. Ultra-Orthodox food, for example, was something double lifers were proud of. Indeed, several people told me there was less interest in experimenting with nonkosher food because "kosher food is delicious." The kosher food that most Hasidim ate was typical heavy eastern European cuisine. When they did try out non-kosher food, they often defaulted to the stereotypical and (IMHO) unexciting, such as bacon cheeseburgers at McDonald's, rather than explore international cuisines or what are considered elite foods in secular circles (e.g., locally sourced foods, craft beers, artisan breads). Boruch told me the first time the RM group met up, they went to an Olive Garden outside of the city, a recognizable Gentile chain that was cheap, accessible, and of course not kosher. When I ate at an Indian restaurant with two OTD guys, they remarked on the spiciness of the food and seemed unfamiliar with a cuisine that many New Yorkers take for granted. Similarly, when I invited double lifers to lunch for interviews, I sometimes had to help make sense of the menu; a number of men asked me what mesclun was, for example. There were, of course, exceptions, such as the recent Facebook request for suggestions about exploring new foods or the double lifer who explored all kinds of New York restaurants. Perhaps, though, the real experience that many of those living double lives sought was experimenting with ultra-Orthodox imaginaries of nonkosher food.

Hanging Out in Bars

A key part of many double-life secret worlds was experimenting with sexuality, especially for those with unhappy marriages. I heard about casual hookups and long-term love affairs. Some women recounted angrily how often Hasidic guys harassed them on Facebook. They complained that Hasidic men online assumed that any woman on social media was open to casual sex, reaffirming the double standard for doubting men and women.

Mixed-gender get-togethers in secular spaces, like bars, were important opportunities for double lifers to explore sexuality and friendship among themselves and casual interactions with Gentiles and secular Jews. One evening, for example, the RM group told me I could join them (just that once) for their weekly get-together at a bar in Park Slope, a gentrified neighborhood adjacent to, but worlds away from their ultra-Orthodox neighborhoods. When I arrived first, at 11:00 p.m., I asked the tattooed bartender if she had noticed a group of Hasidic Jews who hung out weekly. "Oh yes," she said, "They'll be here soon. They're all in their garb. They're very sweet. They don't know much about bar culture, and they'll come ask me about drinks. Sex on the beach. They're cute."

Soon enough, Gavriel, Miriam, Shimon, Chaim, and some others I didn't know in ultra-Orthodox dress walked in, ordered beer, and went to sit down. The whole group knew who I was and began asking me about my research. It felt like an interview. A married Hasidic man and his long-time blond non-Jewish girlfriend, Megan, joined the table. Gavriel asked her to teach them some songs, "secular" songs, but instead, she began to make out with her boyfriend, which no one commented on.

A few more women arrived, dressed in tight jeans and blouses, no wigs, and high heels. They were there with their husbands who had slightly trimmed beards and were in jeans too. Everyone introduced themselves to me using their Facebook pseudonyms, not their real names. As the women sat down, they noted how awkward it still was for them to sit in jeans, which often slipped down (low-rise jeans were a thing then). One of the women described how "sexy" she felt the first time she wore jeans, a tank top, and "her own hair." Another opened her bag and showed me where she had stowed her wig and stockings, which she had taken off on the subway and would need to put back on before she went home. Yet another described the revelation of feeling the wind blow through her own hair as she walked down the street.

The conversation that night ranged from the way their own noncon-forming behavior affected their children's summer camp admissions to wondering about the effect of the internet on religious doubt. Many asked me upon introduction if I was Jewish and if I believed in God, perhaps checking to see how openly they could talk. The bar was a place where they could hang out together, drink, and be like everyone else. Except they still looked and sounded distinctive from all the other Brooklynites there, and they sat by themselves, often talking in Yiddish and English about topics only relevant to themselves.

Later, Sheyndie would tell me that, "Hasidic [double-life] guys don't know how to behave," something some other double-life women had mentioned. She described being at a party where a guy asked her if she would sit on his lap. When she refused, he actually asked her husband if she could. She asked me, "Is it my *frum* upbringing or are these guys really inappropriate? Are they being weird?" "Maybe they just don't know how to be with women," she said. One man still living a double life after a decade reflected uncomfortably back to when he was still "green," and was, he felt, verbally inappropriate with women doubters he met. He had since apologized to some of them, blaming the "warping" of his sexuality on his ultra-Orthodox upbringing until he finally realized "what was normal and what wasn't." Eventually, negative encounters that were discussed on one of the closed double-life Facebook groups led a man, accused by a woman of sexual misconduct, to be expelled from the group. Since then, some had decided to either meet in smaller mixed groups or in same-sex groups.

Intellectual New York

Since the morality of a double life was legitimated, in part, by intellectual explanations for doubt, those living double lives often sought out spaces where they could be exposed to new ideas and bodies of knowledge, such as classrooms, performances, concerts, and lectures. At the same time, however, they often veered toward Jewish events. Enrolling in a local community college, like Touro College, for example, was often a stage in life-changing doubt. With separate courses for men and women, students could remain in a relatively kosher environment, while reading and discussing forbidden texts like Freud. Many of the teachers were themselves ultra-Orthodox, and the students, at least from the sociology class I visited, included Modern Orthodox and Hasidic, so that there were a range of Jewish Orthodox voices.

Others were intrigued with how ultra-Orthodox Jews were represented in academic and cultural events. Some came together, for example, to my talks about them at New York University or the CUNY Graduate Center. One of my colleagues asked me wryly if I always brought so many "rabbis" with me. Those who attended often gave me detailed feedback afterwards, speaking to the particular political investments of fieldwork at home with those who are so engaged in their own representation.

On social media I saw that many went to secular Yiddish plays, like the revival of Sholem Asch's *God of Vengeance*, fascinated to see as one woman posted, "The holy language of Yiddish" used by boys and girls to talk about "lust and *libe* [love]."[9] Many went to see *Fiddler on the Roof*, seeking to experience a Broadway show that felt *haymish* (ultra-Orthodox). Similarly, as I noted, Blimi, Esty, Toby, and I went to a play together, using me as their cover ("I'm meeting that professor again"), and making sure to pay in cash when we went out for nonkosher sushi after the play, so their husbands wouldn't know. Many of those living double lives ventured out into New York City, but not too far, usually not exploring places or things that were completely alien.

Double-Life Women's Sociality

Double-life women I knew rarely seemed to get together themselves to hang out as so many of the double-life men did. It was only as recently as 2016, in fact, that an all-women OTD closed group formed on Facebook. There were structural reasons, as I noted, including that it was very complicated to plan social events out alone, since they already had extensive family obligations at home and at weddings, bar mitzvahs, etc. There were times, though, when they managed. I heard of double-life women getting coffee together, meeting for a birthday celebration with others in restaurants, going to plays together (see above), and going to each other's family celebrations. Indeed, I went to Toby's son's bar mitzvah and another son's wedding, where I sat with the same group of women who were questioners and nonconformists both times. Below are two all-women occasions where the intimacy of women sharing a meal, so common in ultra-Orthodox life, was extended to those who doubted or had left. In these gatherings, in contrast to men's and mixed-gender get-togethers, there was little drinking and no smoking or drugs. These occasions were about spending time together with friends, without any judgment, rather than recouping teenage rebellions they had never had.

Memorial Ladies' Night Out

A group of OTD and double-life women friends—among them Blimi, Chavi, Esty, Toby—decided to have an evening out, and fortunately invited me along. The evening was notable for its sensitivity to and tolerance for those at very different points along the continuum of religious doubt. It began with a closed Facebook page Esty set up to organize the party called "Memorial Ladies' Day/Night Out." It took two months of Doodle polls, way past Memorial Day actually, to figure out a date given family obligations (weddings, bar mitzvahs) and the Jewish calendar (the holiday of Shavuos fell on Memorial Day that year). An OTD woman, Chaya Suri, offered her back deck for a barbecue, and as the group signed up for food to bring, Yidis raised the delicate question about kosher food and a kosher kitchen:

> Yidis: It sounds like we could still use some fruit and chips or something. Any takers? I'm sure the last thing this event needs is a rebbetzin [a rabbi's wife], but I can't let the slot go unfilled 😊 Observance in this group varies, but please let's try to keep a standard of kashrus [kosher food] everyone can be comfortable with. Thanks, and here's the mic back to you, food guys (🍴).

> Chaya Suri: :clears throat: in case anyone is too diplomatic to ask. My kitchen and grill are 100% kosher (🍴).

The *rebbetsin* reference was a play on the moral authority of a rabbi's wife to maintain a certain level of religious practice, usually a form of gatekeeping. Yidis and Chaya Suri's exchange was pitched toward inclusivity rather than exclusivity, but Yidis's comment reminded the guests that religious observance varied in the group.

As we traveled to Chaya Suri's house, I noticed how assertive these women were in ultra-Orthodox male-dominated public space. A few of us took a private ultra-Orthodox bus from midtown Manhattan, which had a curtain that divided the men's and women's sections. On the way, Blimi and I talked loudly, and men kept looking over at us. When the woman in front of us turned around and shushed us, I sank into my seat, but Blimi seemed unfazed. Yidis, who picked us up in her car, laughed at the story and told us she had no problem talking back to men on that bus. When there weren't enough seats on the ladies' side, she simply pushed aside the curtain and sat in the men's section, though men scolded her, saying in Yiddish, "It's not nice." Since these two in particular no longer believed in men's moral authority, perhaps they no longer felt constrained to behave in a modest, self-effacing way in the male public sphere.

As the other women arrived to sit on the back deck in the perfumed June evening, I realized I needn't have worried that I had come as myself in a sleeveless sundress. Some were in full Hasidic dress and others were wearing leggings, short sleeves, and uncovered hair. The conversation that evening included kids, families and schools, childhood memories and current events, as well as Hasidic politics, especially the corruption of leadership. When Chavi passed me a DVD she had saved for me of an anti-internet rally from her son's yeshiva, the women laughed and made fun of the anti-internet movement, calling it *pekh in shvebl* (fire and brimstone). Everyone there that evening was questioning something, despite the diversity of where they landed on the continuum of life-changing doubt.

My own status was questioned as well. I had explained who I was on the Facebook invitation since I had not met all the guests. When a latecomer arrived, she asked me about my work, saying she felt uncomfortable. Feeling guilty, I passed out the verbal assent forms I had meant to give out to everyone earlier, but which had felt too awkward. As the deck fell silent, Toby turned to me and said, "Wait, so this is research too? Is there ever a time we just hang out as friends?" After a beat, she laughed and said she was just teasing. But in fact, Toby had hit on an uncomfortable moral tension inherent to the very nature of anthropology, one that I often struggle with myself.

We had to hurry to catch the last *khasena* (wedding) bus at 12:00 a.m., which ferried women and men back to Brooklyn from weddings. We stepped onto that bus like Jewish Cinderellas, searching for seats among the ultra-Orthodox wedding goers in all their finery. Except Cinderella is a *goyishe mayse* (Gentile story) that Jewish daughters of *Hashem* (God) don't read.

Queer Family Parties

Another all-women group I got to know was a loose network of mostly queer OTD and double-life women whose get-togethers redefined the very nature of Jewish family and kinship. These women regularly met and brought their children to picnics in Prospect Park or parties at Tsippy's house right in the heart of Williamsburg. Many gay ultra-Orthodox men and women, especially those who came out before marriage, left their communities altogether, going OTD. Tsippy told me, "It's very, very rare for someone to remain *frum* and be queer. . . . [It's] too difficult to balance the contradictions. . . . it's too tough to find love and happiness when trapped in a community whose largest focus is on family and marriage."

The first of several parties I went to was a birthday party for Tsippy's oldest daughter, fourteen-year-old Matty, who had chosen to have a Harry Potter–themed celebration, already a rather controversial choice, since American birthdays, wizards, and magic were not exactly the stuff of ultra-Orthodox childhood. I was invited because my own daughter, Talia, was the same age. The girls had met once before in a Brooklyn pizza shop and had become friendly, a reminder of how blurry the line between fieldwork and friendship always is. Other guests at the party included women in hat-covered wigs, modest skirts, and seamed beige stockings; a woman wearing overall shorts, Doc Martens, a crew cut, and a nose ring; and an OTD transgender man. They all knew each other from Hasidic schools or camps and now knew each other's children too. One woman's child had recently decided to use the male pronoun "he" instead of "she." No one batted an eye.

Some months later I went to another party at Tsippy's, for adults this time, on the second night of Rosh Hashanah, the Jewish new year. There, I spoke with Miri, an outgoing OTD woman, who told me that she had lived a double life as both a lesbian and someone who had chafed at the system for a long, long time. Miri had had her first romantic experience with a woman as a teen in a bungalow colony. She had been sent soon after to consult a rabbi for both her sexuality and religious doubts. However, she wanted to have children, and she did not want to leave her community, where she was a respected teacher. She was also a "believer," she told me, and a "proud Jew." So when a matchmaker proposed a groom who, Miri said, everyone knew had a long-term boyfriend, they all decided it was a good match, speaking to the flexibility of religious authority as long as the business of reproduction and religious continuity are taken care of, and any deviation from normative behavior remains private.

About a year ago, however, Miri's ten-year-old daughter made a case for abandoning what had become their shared double life. Miri described how one Shabbes, as she was secretly texting in the bathroom, her daughter yelled through the door, "Are you texting? Why do you have to lie?" When Miri came out of the bathroom, her daughter told her that she didn't want to hide anymore, referring to not telling her friends or family that she watched television or that Shabbes ended "early" in their house or that her mother was gay. Miri was unsure, but then, after an argument with an OTD friend, she was outed (in both religious and sexual senses of the term) on Facebook. Miri was forced to come out soon after, which led to rejection by her family. Listening to Miri tell her story to me, others chimed in with their own stories about parents who could not deal with their "lifestyle" as lesbians, with one woman remembering how her own mother called her a "whore." Some parents had even tried to take their daughters' children away from them, testifying against them in civil family court in order to "save" the children from any secular influence.[10] As the women talked, it seemed to me that by coming together to celebrate a Jewish holiday or a birthday, that they were creating new definitions for what constituted Jewish families, since so many of them had been rejected by their own.

Enlightened Hasidic Yiddish Online and Beyond

In contrast to double-life women, men got together all the time, given their mobility and independence. I hung out with a few double-life men in a small group, but when I tried inviting myself to some of the larger all-male gatherings on Friday nights after the Shabbes meal, I was told I wouldn't feel comfortable. And maybe I wouldn't have. Or maybe they wouldn't have.

One place I could go, though, was men's online Yiddish sites, where *ofgeklerte* Hasidic men were reimagining how and what their Yiddish could express. In contrast to the Jblogosphere, where the majority of posters were Yeshivish and wrote in varieties of English, by the first decade of the twenty-first century more Yiddish-speaking Hasidic men used smartphones, which made writing Yiddish in the Hebrew alphabet more accessible. This led to the emergence of Enlightened Hasidic Yiddish, a variety of Yiddish for and by open-minded Hasidic men with its own emerging standards, aesthetics, and language ideologies, that is, cultural ideas about language (see chapter 2). Enlightened Hasidic Yiddish had a familiar form—but it was used to express new ideas, explore secular knowledge, and engage in open-minded debates. In fact, Enlightened Hasidic Yiddish lived a kind of linguistic double life, much like the Yiddish of Jblogger Katle Kanye a decade earlier: it looked Hasidic on the outside, but its intent and content was often subversive and sometimes heretical. Rooted in the casual vernacular of online Yiddish forums, WhatsApp groups, and other social media, we might think of Enlightened Hasidic Yiddish as a "medialect," a distinctive form of a language spread by media, as anthropologist Janet McIntosh has described for texting in Giriama and English among youth in Kenya.[11] Enlightened Hasidic Yiddish was by and for men who were open-minded or more, making it a medialect for participants in the heretical counterpublic. And while Enlightened Hasidic Yiddish began online, of late it has expanded beyond screens to print Yiddish publications. The very fact that Hasidic Yiddish was being put in the service of men's leisure reading and exploration rather than their religious study could be its own kind of heresy too; it was a form of *bitl toyre*—a waste of time for men who were morally obligated to study Torah in order to eventually hasten the messiah.

The existence of Hasidic Yiddish forums where writers were known to be enlightened contrasted with other kosher Yiddish forums such as *iVelt* (*yiddishe velt*, Jewish world), which were mouthpieces for rabbinic authority and heavily censored by the adminstrators. On sites like *iVelt* Hasidic Yiddish was never allowed to be a medium for open-minded ideas, let alone heresy. Zalman explained to me on WhatsAppville Yinglish, "[Ultra-Orthodoxy] is supposed to be a culture of purity, and therefore Yiddish is a language that doesn't express heresy ... heimishe [ultra-Orthodox] Yiddish isn't a medium that is supposed to house heresy."

However, in 2012, frustrated that any criticism of rabbinic leadership or the system was routinely censored on *iVelt*, a group of Hasidic men founded *Kave Shtibl* (KS) (coffee room, the break room in a yeshiva or synagogue): an alternative, borderline kosher forum explicitly committed to open-minded debate, including social criticism, secular literature, science, art, politics, and poetry.

The homepage shows two figures sitting at a table drinking coffee, with the Yiddish caption, "kave shtibl, a ruig vinkl tse shmuesn un farbrengn" (*kave shtibl*, a peaceful corner to chat and enjoy). Through online reading and writing on KS, Hasidic language ideologies about Yiddish began to

change, as did some aspects of Yiddish writing.[12] Anyone could sign up for KS, but they had to have a male username and icon, and most everyone wrote in Yiddish. When a woman I knew wrote in English with a feminine pseudonym, an active member wrote to her and suggested she use a male username and write in Yiddish, so everyone would understand her. Though the administrators of KS drew the line at outright heresy, they took a few hours to delete such posts, eventually putting up in its stead, "This post was removed due to heresy." In short, KS was known to be an unusually tolerant site where diverse ideas, bodies of knowledge, and individual sensibilities could all be expressed in Enlightened Hasidic Yiddish. In fact, a number of kosher filters now routinely block KS.

Kave Shtibl users spanned linguistic competencies and religiosities, though most were at least interested in open-minded debate. One writer described the most active posters as, "The old guard [referring to the Jblogs] . . . and *maskilic* giants." There were some who just read others' posts because they themselves had trouble writing in Yiddish, a legacy of their yeshiva schooling. Aron, for example, told me that he often enjoyed reading the posts, but never posted anything. He explained, "For me to put together my thoughts on paper is very hard. You never had to articulate your thoughts [in school]. You never had to think even." Another explained that unless you had gone to *kollel* where you might take notes in Yiddish on the Hebrew texts, there was no reason to ever write in Hasidic Yiddish.[13]

KS discussion threads (*eshkol*s) encouraged open-minded content in the kosher, *haymish* medium of Hasidic men's Yiddish. For example, there were reactions to secular films, art, music, and literature that only enlightened men would expose themselves to. There were insider political debates about the ultra-Orthodox "system," for example, discussions over ultra-Orthodox racism, limited secular education for boys, or what one poster claimed were unreasonably stringent *takunos* (proclamations by rabbis) about girls' modest clothing.[14] There was even a closed section on

KS for married men called "In the Bedroom," with frank talk about sex education, something unheard of in Hasidic circles.

Some posters on KS subtly undermined the ultra-Orthodox semiotic ideology (cultural beliefs about signs) that if a medium looked or sounded ultra-Orthodox, one could assume it contained pious Jewish intention and content. For example, KS writers played with a common American Hasidic strategy of transliterating or translating English phrases into Yiddish (i.e., making them Jewish), but not in order to make English kosher; rather they used English in Yiddish for the purpose of sharing their growing fluency in secular American culture, while also poking fun at ultra-Orthodoxy. For example, one poster translated Taylor Swift's song, "Shake It Off" into Yiddish (*ikh shokl es avek*), but wittily replaced the word "date" with *b'shou*, the short visit between a young man and woman that is part of Hasidic matchmaking.[15] Perhaps this substitution, along with the Yiddish translation, made Taylor Swift's song speak to ultra-Orthodox experiences, a kind of conversation with secular American culture, where a *b'shou* was not all that different from a date.

Others used Yiddish transliterations of English idioms to fill in what they perceived to be expressive gaps in Hasidic Yiddish as a language. For example, posters used "ey kat above de rest" (a cut above the rest, עי קאט עבאוו די רעסט) or phrases like "who keyrs?" (who cares, האו קעירס).[16] An administrator explained to me that these English transliterations filled gaps in Yiddish to indicate certain emotions, especially once men became more fluent in English. This was a new kind of language purism that some of the Jbloggers, like Shtreiml and Hasidic Rebel, had articulated too. Shtreimel had suggested back in 2008 that while Yiddish was "juicy" and good for use in "curses, idioms, colloquialisms," it lacked "words, definitions, synonyms." In 2014, a frequent poster, Efraim, told me that writing "who cares" in the Hebrew alphabet of Yiddish expressed "a half-serious, half-sarcastic, informal effect" that the Yiddish language just did not have. Of course, the Yiddish language does have a full range of expressivity, especially that of pre-Holocaust eastern European Jews. What Efraim and Shtreimel's explanations of Yiddish's deficiencies really speak to is a growing dissatisfaction with the English component of contemporary American Hasidic Yiddish. Those writing in English or Enlightened Hasidic Yiddish seemed to be suggesting that their Yiddish should not have to rely on English or even *loshn koydesh* to express the diversity of human emotion and intellect.

Writing and reading in Enlightened Hasidic Yiddish led to a heightened awareness of language itself, evidenced in metapragmatic posts or talk about talk. For example, some on KS criticized grammatical and spelling errors in vernacular written Hasidic Yiddish, defined as it is by its lack of concern with standardization. One person posted a picture of a letter their children's Hasidic school sent home to parents reminding them that their children should only speak in Yiddish. The poster pointed out twenty-three spelling and grammatical errors in Yiddish on the very first page.

As some KS writers were increasingly writing and reading English, Yiddish, and Hebrew literatures, their own writing practices began to merit discussion. There were explicit conversations about how English words should be incorporated into written Yiddish. For everyday speakers of Hasidic Yiddish this was rarely a topic of concern. For example, a poster on KS introduced the topic of "the creation of new Yiddish words" (*dos fabritsirin naye yiddishe verter*). Take the word "elaborate." He wondered in his post if the Yiddish should be *elaborirn* (adding the Yiddish suffix to an English verb stem) or simply the English verb transliterated into Yiddish orthography. The writer prescriptively posted his conclusion that English words should not be incorporated into Yiddish grammatical structure. Instead, English words should simply be transliterated into the Hebrew alphabet to visibly maintain their English language origin, as "their grandfathers had done." (Translation from Yiddish, Rose Waldman. Italics added for clarification. The entire post was in the Hebrew alphabet.):

> (a) person wrote *terminen un konditsyes* [instead of transliterating "terms and conditions"]. Oh, come on. Well, okay, *terminen* has become a Yiddish word by now. But *konditsyes*? I mean, what kind of new plague is this? Either write it in English [i.e., code-switch] or write the way our grandfathers did [English words transliterated into the Hebrew alphabet]: *terminen un konditions* [טערמינען און קאנדישאנס].[17]

These kinds of posts suggest a growing interest among the enlightened in standardizing how Hasidic Yiddish incorporated English, making it a language that needed shared conventions and patrols along its linguistic borders, like any other national language. Perhaps these are the linguistic seeds that will lead to the flowering of Enlightened Hasidic Yiddish across media.

Writers on KS also began to experiment with Enlightened Hasidic Yiddish as a medium for individualized artistic expression. This was an innovation from existing ultra-Orthodox expressive Yiddish culture, like Hasidic music, poetry, or art that aimed to inspire, morally uplift, or educate other Jews in a religious idiom. Menashe told me once, for example, that while arguing with his father about his desire to visit an art museum, his father said, "We [Jews] are supposedly above art. We have the *toyre* [Torah], and it is better than art. We don't need art the way nonspiritual people do." Art, he meant, was a poor man's substitute for the emotional, spiritual life of Jewish Orthodoxy, which did not need any additional human-made beauty to be moved.

An argument over a poetry contest held on KS, inspired by a rival poetry contest on *iVelt,* revealed how some were trying to transform Hasidic Yiddish into a medium for individualized aesthetic expression. Since the postwar period, Hasidic newspapers and magazines have published Yiddish and *loshn koydesh* poetry in the United States. The *iVelt* poetry contest used shared religious metaphors and textual references to inspire pious feelings in readers, which some of the KS writers "poked fun at."[18] The KS poems did not differ greatly in form from those on iVelt: they too were either in a *loshn koydesh* or a formal register of Yiddish without any English code-switching. Like those on *iVelt,* KS poems almost all rhymed, and writers similarly drew on shared religious metaphors and imagery. However, the content and intent of the poetry on KS was subtly different than *iVelt's,* tending to be about individual emotions, for example, romantic love, beauty in the natural world for its own sake, or even disappointment in God.[19]

In a small Yiddish-world moment, the KS poetry contest was reviewed by Yiddish writer/poet Shalom Bernstein for the secular Yiddishist paper, *Der Forverts.*[20] Bernstein described the KS poetry as honest, sincere, and emotional; however, he complained about the uninspired rhyming form of the poetry, which he said was "filled with platitudes." Mischievously, he then reposted that article on KS, where in fact he regularly posted his own (nonrhyming) modernist Yiddish poetry. The way that some responded to him hints at an emerging Enlightened Hasidic Yiddish reading public. This is a public with its own masculine sensibility and aesthetics, rooted in shared religious texts, but which uses Jewish languages for the purpose of individual expression. One frequent writer, "Gefilte," posted on KS (Yiddish translation, Rose Waldman):

> My response, Shalom, is that the [KS] poetry campaign caters to Chassidishe [Hasidic] Jews, according to Chassidishe Jews' flavor in poetry, and according to how they're used to reading poetry from Dunash, Baruch Chazak, Chassam Sofer [all important religious authors], introductions to seforim [religious texts] . . . and so on. When you put up your poems in the Shtiebel [KS] every so often, no one knows what the heck they're saying. Classical poets can't critique rap from Harlem. Both are artful. Each in its own way.[21]

Gefilte made a case for tolerance and pluralism regarding aesthetic values. Their Yiddish poetry, he argued, drew on religious Jewish texts, since that was the literature and languages that Hasidic men had been steeped in.

However, they used ultra-Orthodox language for different, enlightened purposes. There were, Gefilte implied, many ways to produce art, each with its own standard, its own history, and its own value. In fact, this was a radical idea, especially for ultra-Orthodox Jews reared on what many described as "black-and-white" notions of truth.

Significantly, in 2016, some of the KS writers began a printed Yiddish magazine aimed at Hasidic men, *Der Veker* [The Awoken], a name taken from an earlier twentieth-century Jewish Enlightenment printed publication. Striving to entertain or inform its readers rather than morally uplift or instruct, one of the *Veker*'s founders and editors explained its innovation in a WhatsApp text to me (ironically echoing Bernstein's critique):

> The standard Hasidic literature, the magazines and newspapers, they're all written in a formal style, basically there is very little expression, lots and lots of clichés, also very little personal, people don't share vulnerabilities. *Der Veker* embraces every style, whatever goes anywhere can go in the *Veker* as long as it's not *kefira* [heresy] or *nivel peh* [profanity]. So whatever people can share about their life, they can say anything, say new ideas and the way they write, it doesn't have to be formal.

Der Veker editors were committed to professionalism, itself something of an innovation for Hasidic Yiddish publishing. They copyedited for spelling, some grammar,[22] and rejected code-switching into English when there was a clear Yiddish equivalent. An Enlightened Yiddish magazine for men's leisure reading (when they could be studying Torah) by default could set a dangerous precedent. That's why if you wanted to buy this magazine, you had to order it online from Amazon, which then delivered it to your house in a brown paper cover. Note that deliveries from Amazon to Hasidic doorsteps had become commonplace by this point. There were other similar Yiddish publications, including a straightforward Yiddish news magazine, *Moment,* and a new Yiddish book analyzing and critiquing Hasidic boys' education by none other than blogger Katle Kanye (see chapter 2). These Hasidic writers are creating a vibrant Enlightened Hasidic Yiddish (online and in print) with new spaces to read and write, expanding the heretical counterpublic for open-minded Hasidic men. In fact, an Amazon review of Katle Kanye's new book claimed, "A must read for every Chasidic guy." Another Hasidic "guy" explained:

> When I grew up, I mean, before the internet, there wasn't anywhere to write. Even if a Hasid wanted to write in Yiddish, he had no place to write. You understand? Nowhere. Now you can write online or

WhatsApp. People want to write, so automatically Yiddish becomes a language. The language is reborn, in a certain sense.[23]

I would add that the language is perhaps "reborn," but it is exclusively so for men who are fluent in writing and reading Hasidic Yiddish.

Secret Social Worlds and Change

There were some whose secret lives accentuated the moral compromises they made and the price they paid for them. For example, when I was quoted by a journalist saying that those living double lives still felt an attachment to ultra-Orthodoxy as a lifestyle, Benzion posted a long text on WhatsAppville Yiddish voicing his complete disagreement with my assessment:

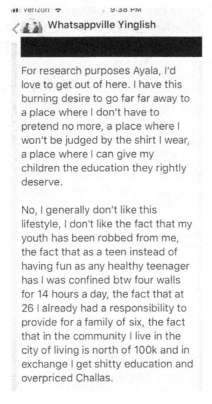

He concluded, "Of course, I'd rather not lose my friends and family, but that has nothing to do with the lifestyle. The only thing keeping me here is that I can't stomach all the pain my leaving will cause my wife and my family and ultimately my kids. Shoin [That's it], research."

Despite or perhaps because of their frustration, double lifers created ways to socialize together in face-to-face and digital spaces, to try out different ways of being. This recreational life happened through experiments on bodies, with languages, objects, and technology. Once those living double lives built trust, they created get-togethers in places that felt familiar and comfortable, an emotional repertoire of ultra-Orthodox objects, sounds, tastes. In these safe spaces, they tried secular foods, drugs, music, and sex, though not without consequences, especially for women. They also ventured out into New York City, exploring the leisure activities and spaces that other New Yorkers did, but that ultra-Orthodox Jews specifically did not. Their secret worlds stretched their bodies and their minds or maybe just numbed their pain.

There were a few lucky ones who were able to negotiate a double life that felt like the best of both worlds, something many still-religious people accused them of wanting. For example, Moishy, in contrast to Benzion's message above, posted on Facebook:

> What many of us don't realize is, that though the majority of the things we do are religiously motivated, they have, inadvertently, also become part of our culture. While the Friday night Shabbos meal has religious meaning to it, it has become a meaningful way for us to connect and spend time with our families as well. . . . The food, the music, all of it, they may seem just like tasty Hungarian [Hasidic] dishes and outdated melodies, but they are more than that: they are part of who we are, part of our fabric. So why strip all that and risk leaving yourself and potentially your kids scarred?

Moishy was right in a way. For those living double lives, ultra-Orthodox habitus, lived through music, food, language, ritual, etc., was part of who they were and sustained their emotional connections with their families and their histories. Even for those like Benzion, who desperately wanted to leave, his double life and those of others were inextricable from that ultra-Orthodox habitus. At the same time, double-life ultra-Orthodox habitus changed in private as well as some very public ways because of secret forays with others into new realms. Double lifers lived those changes at home, not only with their spouses, but performed them with and for their children, too, consciously and unconsciously. This meant that many double lifers found themselves in the morally ambiguous position of trying to sub-rosa undermine the very worlds they were helping their children reproduce.

7

Family Secrets

One day Toby posted the following exchange she had had with her then fourteen-year-old daughter, Leyeh, on Facebook:

> Leyeh: Mami, I'm a very spiritual person, and you are not.
> Toby: What do you mean?
> Leyeh: Don't play stupid, Ma, you know you don't have strong belief. And because I am just like you, I am so worried that when I will be older I won't be a spiritual person either :(

Toby wondered how to respond to Leyeh's worries about her spirituality, since it was Toby's own double life that had created them. What were the ethics of keeping secrets from one's own children? Of trying to model other ways of being, while children continued to live ultra-Orthodox lives? What were the implications for children and teens, sensitive as so many were to what was not said? How did one parent's life-changing doubt, even kept secret, instigate changes for the rest of the family, while things looked more-or-less the same from the outside?

When I asked men and women living double lives what they hoped for their children, they consistently told me that they wanted their children to have a choice in how they lived their lives, something they felt they had never had. Ending up ultra-Orthodox or secular was less relevant than the opportunity for their children to choose their own paths. This involved teaching their children that living as ultra-Orthodox Jews was not the only way to be moral Jews, that questioning was healthy, and that they should pursue their own happiness, wherever that took them. Double lifer Boruch told me, for example, "My job is to make them comfortable that they're allowed to question, and it's normal to question, and it's normal for people to have different opinions about everything. Most important to be tolerant of somebody who has a different opinion." Blimi used the language of happiness and self-fulfillment to describe her dreams for her children. She told me that she wanted her kids to be "the best they can be" no matter whether they stayed Hasidic or left, and she hoped that they had happy, loving marriages, and if they didn't, she hoped they "cheated." Double-life parents told me they wanted their children to have choices they had not had as children, just like so many other parents do all over the world.

Double lifers' commitment to their children's right to make their own choices was not neutral or history-free.[1] Choice was part of the double-life moral system, one which, in direct contrast to ultra-Orthodoxy, aligned with contemporary American liberal values about the individual. In double lifers' moral framework, individuals used their autonomy to make ethical choices in the context of their secretly shared liberal values of pluralism, tolerance, and striving for personal fulfillment. This was a very different model from what they had grown up with or what their own children were learning to participate in. Part of the Ultra-Orthodox alternative modernity I have described also engaged many of the same categories of the self as American liberalism. However, the ultra-Orthodox faithful came to very different conclusions. This was especially evident in the ultra-Orthodox rejection of those same values of pluralism, tolerance, and personal fulfillment for their own sake. For example, in ultra-Orthodoxy, individuals have moral autonomy, but the process of growing up included learning to use that autonomy to submit to hierarchies of religious authority. This was what defined mature Jews, who understood their responsibilities to the Jewish people and God, not to mention their own families and friends. In the Hasidic homes and schools I spent time in, Gentiles were often portrayed to children as selfish and immature because they simply did what they felt like, prioritizing themselves above others. Freedom, or individuality, in that schema, was actually a negative value, because it spoke to the unwillingness or inability to discipline the self for the greater good. In contrast to those living double lives, the ultra-Orthodox faithful borrowed the familiar North American language of happiness and fulfillment in order to distinguish themselves from the world around them: children and teens learned that their increasing ability to "fit in," to discipline themselves, and do what was expected would actually lead to true happiness and fulfillment, in this life and the next. These were concepts that Gentiles could never understand or live out.[2]

By embracing certain liberal values, however, those living double lives were in an ethically tenuous position. They were socializing their children to reproduce the very system that they felt was morally wrong, while subtly encouraging them to become critical thinkers, to develop tolerance for difference, and to fulfill their own individual dreams that might conflict with communal expectations. By secretly introducing a different structure of authority into the intimacy of the home, double-life parents tried to quietly encourage values antithetical to ultra-Orthodoxy without going too far out of the lines, lest they draw the unwanted attention of school, rabbinic authorities, and extended family.[3] This led to competing moralities at play in most double lifers' everyday homes. The fear that there was a growing population of those living double lives also led to a mounting concern among the ultra-Orthodox about the moral confusion that might result from "mixed marriages" between a religious and nonreligious spouse. The moral inconsistency of being exposed to parents with different beliefs was thought to put children "at risk" for life-changing doubt.

The contemporary anthropological study of morality and ethics has tended to focus on the individual cultivation of virtue, as I noted in chapter 4.[4] Within this approach, fewer have focused on morality and ethics in the context of families, especially in childrearing, with its gendered dynamics. This is especially the case in ethnographies of religious orthodoxies. Perhaps this is because children trouble the imagined individuals of moral philosophers: rational adults who make considered ethical judgments for some good, or as anthropologist Cheryl Mattingly describes it more accurately, among conflicting "best goods."[5] However, it is precisely the diversity of individuals with different forms of agency that make families such rich and complicated sites for the study of morality and ethics. Family dynamics, especially across generations, often include negotiations between competing moralities with their attendant gendered sentiments. Families are also junctures, where different relationships of obligation and scale meet, from the institutional to the individual, the public to the private. Anthropologist Merav Shohet's work, for example, on a Vietnamese woman's search for romantic love or a mother's grief at her son's death from AIDS, were narrative accountings that exposed inevitable discrepancies between official state ideologies and personal experiences.[6] Family dynamics, as anthropologist Veena Das shows us in her analysis of a forbidden love match between a Hindu young man and a Muslim young woman, have political implications way beyond the family, speaking to the formation of broader political categories of belonging and difference.[7] Double-life stories about childrearing practices and their children's experiences having a double-life parent, highlight the poignant, ethical dilemmas of trying to instigate change while staying within the system.

Double-Life Parenting: Moral Changes According to Age and Gender

Double-life parenting was shaped by gender and age. Very young children would rarely notice how often their father put on tefillin or question why their mother let them watch Barney on the iPad. However, once children entered gender-segregated schools (around three years old), there was consistent continuity across home and school, by design. At that point, children often began to notice discrepancies in that continuity, which could require them to be complicit in the secrets of their double-life parent to everyone's moral discomfort.

Further, as children matured, mothers were increasingly in charge of their daughters' upbringing and fathers in charge of their sons'. Toby, for example, told me that she had been able to have such an active double life because she only had one daughter, Leyeh. The rest of her children were boys, who were off in yeshiva from early in the morning until late every evening, giving her freedom and privacy to do as she pleased. At the same time, for double-life parents with the same gender children, there was the possibility of sharing secrets, since as children grew their lives were increasingly structured by gender. The intimacy of revelation, though, was a double-edged sword when pious teens felt betrayed or called out the hypocrisy of a double-life parent.

Double-life mothers and fathers encouraged their children to make choices and think critically based on their own gendered positions of authority within the family. Chavi, for example, used everyday interactions around domesticity as opportunities to encourage tolerance for Jews and for Gentiles. She told me that she corrected her children when they told her that the *goyte* (Gentile cleaning lady) had arrived, a very common expression among Hasidic children and parents. She told them that it wasn't "nice" to call someone a "Goy." Instead, they should learn her name. She said, "I try always to say all human beings have the capacity to be good, just because you're different doesn't mean you're not good. You know, you can have a Jewish person who does really bad things and you could have a non-Jewish person who does really good things." Chavi told me her eight-year-old son who was in school had the "hardest" time with that message, since his teacher told him many stories about how "the Goy is so bad." When he would repeat what his teacher said that day to his mother, he would qualify his use of the term "Goy" as "I'm just saying what my rebbe told me. I know you don't like this story."

Chavi also used her own changing standards of modesty and feelings about her body to encourage tolerance for Jewish difference, though she did so less openly than tolerance for non-Jews. She had recently begun wearing pajama pants to bed, something her younger children did not question. Her son, however, asked her point-blank why she was wearing pants, something Hasidic women never do. She told him they were actually more modest for bed since they "didn't roll up," which he grudgingly accepted. Her goal, she told me, was to accustom her children to seeing her in pants, and perhaps accustom them to think more flexibly about what constituted modesty, not to question modesty itself. Soon she began wearing leggings under her skirts in cold weather and when she got home, would take off her skirt and hang out in leggings. By then, however, her son had an explanation for her pants, and when he came home from school and saw her in leggings, he merely said, "Oh, you're in pajamas already?" I was struck that he was so clearly anxiously keeping an eye on her and her clothing to begin with, not something that many eight-year-old boys would. Clearly Hasidic boys are different.

More upsetting for him was when Chavi stopped shaving her hair, and, if her husband wasn't home, left it uncovered after a shower to dry. Her preschool-age daughters were curious and asked to touch her hair, but they did not seem troubled. When her older son saw her, though, he recoiled, saying, "Oh, you're not dressed yet. I'll come back when you're dressed." She was, of course, fully dressed. Chavi told me she asked him why he found her hair so "jarring" and he said (in Yiddish), "A mother, who is supposed to protect me, who loves me, looks almost like a person who is scary [i.e., a non-Jew]." Note he still avoided the use of the word "Goy," since he knew Chavi didn't approve. She told me, "That he didn't feel safe with me, that bothered me, so I got into it with him, telling him I'm always going to be his mother and that no matter what, I'll always love him."

Not shaving her hair and experimenting with "pants" were all part of Chavi's changing attitudes to modesty and her own body, which she continued to share with her children. When, for example, Chavi's three-year-old daughter ran out of the bath and danced around the living room naked, her oldest son yelled in disgust, "She's a *khazer* [pig, implying a pervert]! She's a *khazer*!" Chavi told me she immediately tried to teach him the difference between "privacy and shame." In fact, other women who had curvy bodies had told me about their own senses of shame, also using the image of that most unkosher of animals, the pig. Sheyndie told me her mother had made her and her sisters wear a girdle once they hit puberty, so they would not look like such *khazers*. Chavi was encouraged that her young daughters so far seemed to be unembarrassed about their bodies even at ages three and four, unlike other girls she knew, who were already aware of and worried about covering their knees and arms to be modest.

Nosson and his wife, living a double life together and each pursuing a career in social services, were similarly concerned with offering a more tolerant, matter-of-fact education about the body for their four young children. They had already introduced the concept of reproduction and had books at home on the way the body worked. This was rarely discussed at all in ultra-Orthodox homes. Nosson told me that his professional training shaped how he and his wife had decided to rear their children.

Men living double lives, in contrast to women's domesticity and modesty, were able to use their positions as the leaders of spirituality (*rukhnius*) and ritual in their homes to challenge the very basis for certain beliefs, often using that very dangerous register, *leytsones*, mockery, to drive home their point. Leyzer, for example, told me a story that his close friend, Naftuli, had told him. Every year around Rosh Hashanah, the Jewish new year, Naftuli's children would come home from school having learned that pomegranates graced the holiday table because each fruit had 613 seeds, the exact same number as the Jewish commandments. Leyzer remembered (my translations):

> Every kid comes home with a paper at the *seuda* [the celebratory meal] and . . . Naftuli tells his little kids . . . every single time, how about we open up and we start counting? Every time his wife storms away. But he still does it because it bothers him so much. He told me it bothered him when he was still extremely *frum*. You take bullshit and you make it like this is the real deal. . . . His kids all start laughing . . . it becomes a joke in his house. His wife doesn't like it.

As the leader in his family, Naftuli was able to challenge what his children were learning in school with a fact-finding, hands-on experiment based on his own religious authority. He had even found an online article that he had shared with his children that showed the incredibly varied numbers of seeds in pomegranates. Naftuli juxtaposed this article, his children's own experiences, and what they had learned in school, which he showed to be false. He offended his wife, but his children just laughed, apparently used to their father's questioning the authority of their teachers, and by default, the whole system. They knew, though, even the little ones, not to talk about their father's pomegranate challenge in school, which would have gotten everyone in trouble.

Similarly, Boruch's gradual move to atheism shaped his own choices as the family leader in ritual. He told me, for example, that when the family lit candles to commemorate the anniversary of a death (*yortsayt*), the responsibility fell to him to choose to a religious text to share. He explained,

> So I would always struggle which story to pick because if the story has any spirituality in it, or any superstition, I can't relate, I can't tell the story. So I would always look for a story that just says nice things about the person, like he was so nice because this and this, these nice things. So that's the message I try to convey.

Boruch's changes were subtle in that he still chose standard religious texts, and he still led the family ritual. However, by exclusively presenting texts with moral, more humanistic messages, he effectively made his case to his family that one could be a good person without, as he said, "spirituality or any superstition." In fact, Shmuel told me that since men were often called upon at family gatherings to provide a short inspired discourse on the Torah portion of the week, some double-life friends shared and discussed which interpretations and passages might be less offensive to their changing sensibilities or have the possibility of offering a more humanistic interpretation.

Leyzer, Boruch, and Naftuli's still-religious wives, though, were all put in an ethical bind by their double-life husbands, in some sense similar to that of Shoshana, the still-religious spouse in chapter 4, who had to make kiddush for her family when her husband became an atheist. Because of women's more limited fluency in religious texts and their subordinate positions to their husbands as faithful wives, they were effectively silenced from contradicting their husbands' efforts to undermine religious authority or take on that religious authority themselves. Naftuli's wife, for example, stormed off when he annually posed his pomegranate-seed challenge, angry but unable or unwilling to confront her husband in front of the children.

Boruch told me sadly that his wife sometimes tried to be more of a religious leader at home, but she just did not have the knowledge to do so, a legacy of gendered education. For example, he told me that he never verbally marked the importance of certain special days of Jewish holidays to his children, a practice the man of the household usually did:

> So I wouldn't say, "Today's a big day." I never say it. Even on Rosh Hashanah and Yom Kippur I wouldn't say it. So *zos khaneka*, the last day of Hanukkah, while I was *tsinding* [lighting] the candles, she says, "Kids, today is *zos khaneka*, it's a big day." And I felt so bad for her because she doesn't know what to say anything beyond those words. And she was hoping I would take over from there. But I didn't.

At the same time that still-religious wives were disappointed or silenced, they were hearing from other male authorities—a father, a rabbi, a brother-in-law, a therapist—that they should, in fact, be trying to do it all: keep peace in the marriage by capitulating to their husband's religious changes, uphold the level of religiosity to the best of their ability in the home to protect the children, and wait patiently for their husband's eventual return to *emuna*. Still-religious wives were, in essence, given an impossible set of tasks to protect their own homes with no regard for their own religiosity.

Both fathers and mothers living double lives valued fluency in English, the language and culture of American childhood and popular culture, especially for boys. Still-religious spouses often shared this goal since boys' limited English and math skills have become a real concern among many. However, encouraging boys' English proficiency, through leisure reading, often on an iPad, a phone, or in the library, was subversive, since it took time away from Torah study. English literacy also prepared boys to participate in the wider world if they chose as they grew up. Indeed, a number of Hasidic men living double lives I had met felt their own shaky English was one reason that they were trapped and had stayed; they wanted their sons to have more options than they had had.

Women living double lives, much more fluent in English than men, agreed. Many bought English books, exposed their sons to English-language children's television programming, and used time together, for example, setting the Shabbes lunch table, to introduce new English words. Blimi offered her sons a monetary incentive for learning new English words—a dollar a word. Suri did what, she told me, many Hasidic parents did. She had her son's English assessed by outside literacy professionals in his yeshiva. Since he was below grade level, he qualified for free tutoring, which was basically a way to get the school to provide free English instruction after school.

The Intimacy and Complicity of
Shared Family Secrets

Learning to Keep Secrets from School

Double-life parents generally tried to keep their own breaking of *mitsves* hidden from their children as much as possible. Leyzer told me that he sometimes adjusted the air conditioner on Shabbes, but he never let his children see him do it. Others took their phones into the bathroom on Shabbes or closed their bedroom doors and texted under the covers. One man living a double life described on Facebook how he would move his tefillin bag around the dining room table every day, so it would look like he had gone to pray. When I asked Boruch how much his children knew about his religious practice or lack thereof, he said, "They know I'm open-minded. But I don't want them to know the extent. It's going to cause too much conflict for them."

As children grew older, what they were learning at home from their double-life parent, or observing as children do, clashed with what they were learning in school, especially in the usage of digital technology. Children and teens had to keep their parent's secrets from their teachers or even from a still-religious parent, both in order to protect a double-life parent and/or to continue to use the technology. In their efforts to introduce tolerance or critical thinking, double-life parents might expose children to technologies that their schools expressly prohibited. For example, most of the Hasidic schools for boys and girls did not allow internet at home. However, in his effort to teach his teenage daughter to think critically, Yonah helped her write an essay on the differences between science and pseudoscience, and "secretly" taught her to use Wikipedia, without his wife knowing. His goal was "to tell her [his daughter] that everything that someone says is science, another person is going to call pseudoscience. I want to teach her to form her own opinions." However, his daughter innocently told her class during the presentation of her essay (all in Yiddish) that she had gotten her information from Wikipedia. Yonah told me that the next day he got a call from the principal, who told him that there had to have been a "mistake." Their school was not one where students could see anything on the internet, she elaborated. Yonah's daughter soon found out that her principal had called and was "devastated that she got him in trouble." She asked him, "Why didn't you tell me not to say anything?" Yonah told her that he would never let her do something she was not allowed to, though technically he had. He explained to her that her school had a problem with the internet not because of Wikipedia, but because of other things on there. He remembered he said, "As a big girl you have to use your judgment about what to talk about and what not to talk about. You will never hear me tell you 'don't say anything' unless I'm buying your mother a gift."

Yonah told me that from his perspective, anything he introduced his daughter to was fine, and she could tell whomever she wanted. He said, "I didn't want to make secrets." But Yonah ended up giving his daughter a mixed message. While he denied any wrongdoing by himself or her, Yonah also told his daughter that she needed to use her own ethical agency, her judgment, about what she chose to reveal and to whom. Was the real point that the school's rule was to protect her from something much worse than Wikipedia, which legitimated their using it and thus breaking the rule and perhaps lying about it? Or was the real takeaway that she, as a "big girl," was able to make a moral determination all on her own, something that for the ultra-Orthodox really was an unacceptable form of individual authority, a slippery slope that could certainly lead a girl off the *derekh* (path)?

Other parents living double lives similarly struggled with moral ambiguities, secrecy, and lying about the use of technology. None wanted to tell their children to lie about what they did at home with them, but double lifers found themselves having to say point-blank: if you want to continue, for example, to use the iPad or watch television on the computer, you have to know who you can tell and who you can't. This was often framed as a mature "smartness" about figuring out what was appropriate in a range of ultra-Orthodox contexts, which could give a child a sense that morality, and even truth, might be relative—again, a potentially dangerous threat to the authority of ultra-Orthodoxy. Chavi told me, for example, that when she let her school-age kids use the iPad, she gave them this mixed message about truth and lies:

> I'm not looking to confuse them, but I do want to open their minds, so I did explain to them look, the school does not always allow this. Ok, I happen to have the iPad because I need it for work. . . . and I hate telling you to keep secrets, but just be smart, that's all. You don't have to keep a secret, but if you don't keep it a secret we're going to just have to stop watching it. Not like, don't tell anyone about it.

New media, like cell phones, iPads, or the internet do not themselves necessarily traffic in secrecy or challenges to authority. What they can do, though, is create new avenues for how knowledge travels, who gets access to it, and how that knowledge might be concealed. For example, anthropologist Julie Archimbault's research in Mozambique describes the text messages on cell phones that young women used to arrange illicit trysts with men, where money and goods were exchanged for sexual favors. Whole families benefitted from these arrangements, but since girls' parents never saw the texts they were able to publicly avoid the "unpleasant secret," which put food on the family table.[8] For double lifers and their children, access to digital technology was a shared pleasure, but one that required that all be complicit in the fact that their watching or game playing or listening actually was against school policy and hence, communal rules. By allowing children to participate in forbidden media, double-life parents were asserting their own authority to make decisions that might differ from school, which was directly linked to rabbinic authorities. Their choice to do so revealed a chink in what had been designed to be a united front of parental, school, and religious authority.

Shared Gendered Secrets at Home

Secrets were sometimes kept along gender lines at home. Take the unusual case of Avi. He had one son and four daughters, and he had an agreement with his still-religious wife: he would be in charge of his son, and she in charge of their daughters. One night, over dinner, Zalman and Tsippy told me about the "secret" that Avi and his son had together. From the time he was nine, Avi had chosen to include his son in his double life, who, according to them "didn't have a problem with it." He had come completely clean to his son, who still continued to go to yeshiva. However, every Friday night and on Jewish holidays he and his son drove away to spend the weekend elsewhere. His wife and his daughters were all still religious. Zalman and Tsippy were unsure about the ethics of this. They were, as they told me, "struggling with it, debating if it was healthy or not." On weekends, Avi had a tutor come and teach his son about American popular culture and English. They did martial arts together and visited other double-life friends. The one thing they never did was go to synagogue. Avi was in touch with a therapist, someone who knew the community but was not Jewish himself, who helped guide him in this unusual parenting. What are the ethics of including one of your children, but not others, in your double life? Avi's son not only had to keep his father's secret from school, but he also had to keep his own secrets from his mother and sisters. The distance that Hugh Gusterson describes for secrets kept in families (see chapter 4), include children whose lives are changed in all kinds of ways as they are obligated to keep secrets of many kinds.

In some cases, a child, influenced by his double-life parent, might come to have his own doubts in ultra-Orthodoxy. In that case, parent and child quietly and less explicitly than Avi shared a secret from the rest of the family without actually physically separating themselves. Leyzer's son, for example, had decided for himself early on that, as Leyzer said, "What *rabbonim* [rabbis] say is just nonsensical." In a variety of ways, Leyzer's son let his father know that he was allied with him. Once, Leyzer remembered, his son brought home a note from school letting parents know that any food students brought in had to have a particular rabbinic stamp of approval (*hekhsher*). The class had learned that eating any food with a different kosher stamp would clog up or pollute their minds (*farshtupn de kop*) and make learning difficult. Leyzer proudly told me that his son had said to him, "I don't understand. So this *hekhsher*, it's obviously kosher for someone else, but not for us. How does the food know not to clog up someone else's head?" His son asked the question in a way that Leyzer felt required no answer; he was merely pointing out the silliness of the system and expressing his alliance with his father.

Sometimes a double-life father, like Chaim, gained the allegiance of some of his children, who then kept his (open) secrets, along with their own, from their still-religious mother or other, younger siblings. Two of Chaim's ten children, his oldest son and daughter, had both started questioning, which actually led to rabbinic pressure on his wife to divorce him after many years. Chaim told me he had caught each of his children texting on Shabbes, something he did too but never in front of them. His eldest son soon quit yeshiva when he turned seventeen and secretly got a job for the summer. He begged Chaim not to tell his mother, and he didn't. Soon after, Chaim's sixteen-year-old daughter began to experiment with boys. She asked her father to keep a pair of jeans in his car for her, which he did next to his own secret pair. She even told him when she had her first kiss, something neither he nor she could ever tell his wife. When his daughter wanted to see a pet dog (something an ultra-Orthodox religious family would never have), he arranged for her to go visit an OTD friend who had one. She even took the bus on Shabbes there while he "covered for her." What kind of ethical choices did Chaim and his teens make, constrained by the structure of their lives, which included secrets kept from a still-religious mother, which eventually led to divorce?

Double-life women and their older daughters were similarly often allied, though this could backfire. Toby, for example, often confided in her daughter, Leyeh, walking a fine line between protecting Leyeh, while simultaneously pushing her to question authority. Leyeh, an intense teen, often confronted Toby with difficult existential questions about faith and truth. Toby told me that after one interaction, she finally conceded that she didn't know what she believed about divine revelation. She remembered telling Leyeh, "Nobody knows, and whoever tells you they know, they're lying. They haven't been there. Whoever tells you they know for sure, they're lying." This was a very different message not only from Leyeh's school, but from her own father and siblings.

Others living double lives, like Sheyndie and her husband, decided not to share their double life with their daughters, at least explicitly. She told me, "We've talked about it, and it's too big a burden for them to keep." However, by the time her eldest daughter was in high school, Sheyndie thought she had figured them out and was probably living a double life herself. Her youngest daughter, though, was a "real *rebbetsin* [a rabbi's wife]," earnestly religious. She watches us, Sheyndie said, laughing a little. She tells my daughter and me to pull down our skirts.

As Sheyndie and her husband got more involved in a small double-life group and grew bolder, they eventually spent part of Passover break away with an OTD family. On that vacation, the youngest daughter realized that the other family was not fully observant. She pulled her mother aside and anxiously asked her, "You would never answer a phone on Shabbes, right? Or do those things?" Sheyndie told me she had reassured her daughter because it was clear that she "needed her to." As she said, "Sometimes lying is the right thing to do."

The intimacy of a mother-daughter or father-son relationship could be comforting to double-life parents, who felt guilty, though they were trying to do the right thing. However, sometimes parental relationships with children across gender lines caused anxiety. For example, Blimi told me that she was "pretty sure" that once her daughters found out everything about her, "They wouldn't blame me. They will understand." Blimi wasn't so sure though about her sons, whom she described as "really *frum*." They might judge her harshly if they knew who and what she really was. She said:

> See, the things that do bother me—the only things—sometimes I think to myself, oh my God, if they would know what I do . . . that my kids would judge me and hate me. That's the piece that I really . . . more than anything else. It sometimes hits me.

Nosson, the social worker, who had, in his own words, "heretical ideas," worried about the effects of keeping secrets in a family, from a professional and personal standpoint. He told me about a daring question he had asked one day at a lecture between a *kiruv* rabbi who worked with at-risk teens and a religious therapist, about secrets in families. During the Q & A session, audience members could write anonymous questions, which were read out loud. Nosson wrote, "Should a *frum* person tell his children that he doesn't believe in God?" He was terrified, he said, but he needed to ask not only for his practice, but also for his own family. Additionally, he told me, he had a "secret agenda." He wanted other professionals and rabbis to know that "this is a real thing."

The therapist responded first, with a joke, "Ok, I see it's time to go," indicating the question was a tough one. Then, more seriously, he answered that if a parent was struggling with issues that did not directly affect their children, there was no reason to share that struggle. A four-year-old, he said, does not need to know that you are doubting God. When a parent's struggle with doubt did affect the child later on, then it would be important to be able to discuss that in an age-appropriate way. The *kiruv* rabbi, in contrast, completely avoided the question, remembered Nosson, and recycled an old chestnut, that disbelief in God was a symptom of depression, and once treatment was given for the depression faith would return.

Double-life parents, within gendered spheres of authority, made their own ethical decisions about raising their children, rather than relying on rabbis, schools, or even a still-religious spouse. Moral ambiguity, the reliance on their own authority and their peers', were all in opposition to the moral certainty that ultra-Orthodoxy claimed. Double-life parents were also in the particularly poignant position of wanting to share their new, changing ideas with their children and provide them with chances they never had, and yet doing so could be their own, and their children's, very undoing, As Moishy said, when I asked him if he thought of leaving, "I might have, but I look at my kids, and I know the stigmas that they're going to face. And I just can't do it." Their only recourse was half-truths and secrets, as they slowly and gradually tried to expose their children to different experiences and ideas. Perhaps it would be a slow, quiet revolution or maybe it would merely be one idiosyncratic parent who had little effect at all. Only time will tell.

Teens of Double Lifers Talk Back

There were all kinds of reactions and outcomes—even within families—when teenagers figured out that one of their parents or even both were leading double lives. Some teens grew more fervently *frum* and others went off the *derekh* or led their own double lives until they could leave. Religious adults in their lives—a parent, a teacher, a relative—could make a big difference, keeping them in the fold. Some, especially boys for whom success in yeshiva could be socially rewarding, decided to continue to fulfill communal expectations regardless of their own belief and despite a double-life parent who did not. Benzion, for example, told me that when his eldest son turned eleven, his wife had begged him to start taking him to the men's *mikva* (ritual bath), as he would be expected to go regularly after his bar mitzvah. Benzion had refused because he found the *mikva* "disgusting and meaningless." Soon enough, with no discussion, his son simply began going to the *mikva* by himself at a little synagogue near their house. Benzion understood the situation this way:

> So I think he made the distinction. He's one thing, his father is something else, and it doesn't make a difference. For now, he's going to live the yeshiva *bokher* [boy] life, and he has a very good *kop* [head], so he is the top of his class, so it's part of the package. You can't be a very good *bokher* in your class when you don't do the other things. So he has to [i.e., go to *mikva*]. He does the whole program, why not?

Some children, then, stayed *frum* with little angst, comfortable enough with themselves and their double-life parent to tolerate the moral ambiguity. Sometimes humor helped a teen tell a double-life parent he was on to him and did not approve. One of Chaim's children was a "very *frum*" sixteen-year-old boy, not like the two eldest who seemed to be going OTD. Chaim told me that his son regularly teased him, saying, "Tatty, you're a complete *shaygets* [Gentile or a Jew who looks like a Gentile]." However, this teasing was, according to Chaim, done in a "totally loving way." Teens like these seemed to accept that their parents struggled with their own *emuna*, while they continued to live their own lives as "good" boys and girls. That is, their parent's moral struggle did not challenge their own *emuna*, though it might impact them when it came time for arranged marriages.

Identifying with the still-religious spouse, especially if the same gender, could provide an alternative moral model for a teen. Leyeh, a young woman who was herself deeply conflicted about her mother's double life (Toby), told me that one of her older brothers, Laiby, was able to separate himself from his mother in a loving way; this allowed him to retain his "black-and-white" morality, considered positive among ultra-Orthodox Jews. Leyeh told me the following story to explain what she meant. One day, she found some ice cream in their freezer, which had an Orthodox

Union (OU) *hekhsher*. This was not a *hekhsher* her family accepted, and ordinarily she would never eat OU. But there it was, looking delicious, right in her own home. She was about to scoop herself a bowl when her seventeen-year-old brother, Laiby, came into the kitchen, saw her and told her to put it back. Leyeh was annoyed, saying, "Excuse me! Mommy brought it home." He explained, "Mommy has her temptations, and she has to deal with them on her own. But we're Tatty's [Daddy's] children, and we have to go according to Tatty."

Laiby reframed his mother's transgressions as "temptations," that is, interior provocation from her inclination for evil. He was able to understand his mother's refusal to participate in the system not as heresy or intellectual doubt, but as an individual moral weakness, something that was her own particular burden to struggle with, not his. This was a similar interpretation to that of some of the life coaches or activists, who believed that religious doubt always had an underlying mental health explanation. It was also similar to some of the rabbis who suggested that social media awakened one's evil inclination or was even actually the evil inclination itself. These interpretations of life-changing doubt assumed that ultra-Orthodox life was morally normative and effectively neutralized any intellectual or emotional challenges to the system as simply a sign of individual spiritual weakness.

Not all teens were so confident in who they were, though. Some, especially girls who identified closely with their mothers, were troubled and confused by what they heard and saw at home, especially when it directly contradicted what they were learning from other adult women they admired in school. In some cases, a teen might fear that her own mother was a bad influence on her and lead her astray or hurt her chances for a good marriage. One teen, Faigy, whose parents were divorced and whose mother led a semisecret OTD life, told her, "Mommy I know you're going to tell me things that are not good for me to hear. Please don't tell me." Faigy never refused to spend her custody time at her mother's house, but she was fearful enough to remind her mother that she had to be protected from inappropriate things her mother might say when she came over.

One day while we were having lunch, Toby, who was ordinarily quite private, surprised me by offering to introduce me to her daughter, Leyeh. Toby's life was stable. She had a job that she liked and a relaxed husband who did not mind her independence. Maybe she wanted to know what Leyeh knew about her and how she felt. I don't know, but I jumped at the chance. As I would learn, Leyeh agreed to talk with me because she had her own agenda. She wanted people living double lives to know how "unfair" and "wrong" it was to confuse their own children with their "hypocrisy."

I met Leyeh for our first interview in a park on a summer day. She was sixteen then, dressed very modestly, with a dusting of freckles across her nose. I had told her simply that I was doing research on the internet and faith because I was not sure exactly how much she knew about her mother's double life. Leyeh described her own transformation from someone who "didn't want to be religious" to the stringently religious young woman I met that day, a change that began in her junior year of high school at a school with all kinds of Orthodox girls.

When she was younger, Leyeh told me, she knew her mother "wasn't your typical *hasidishe* [Hasidic] lady." That didn't bother her, though, since she herself "didn't really believe in *hashem* [God]." She had been exposed to forbidden media from a young age, often with her mother, watching movies, listening to Taylor Swift on YouTube, or passing around pictures of Justin Bieber with some bummy school friends. At that point, like so many teenagers, she was determined not to live like her mother, like a "hypocrite," imagining that she would not be religious at all when she grew up.

As she started high school, though, she began to change, influenced by her teachers and especially her school principal, all of whom she admired greatly. Her mother's hypocrisy, in contrast, began to bother her more and more, and she worried about its effect on her own *emuna*. Why, for example, should she have been exposed to so many movies for adults on an iPad, snuggled against her mother at night in bed? Why was she able to read any of the inappropriate English books lying around the house, like *Fifty Shades of Grey*? (Actually, her mother was upset that she had read that without her permission. She felt it was inappropriate.) Why did her mother go out at night with friends? Leyeh began to question and challenge her brothers and her father. "How could you be such a coward," she yelled at her father, "Why do you let her go off at night?"

Over the course of high school, Leyeh became increasingly observant. She traded in her smartphone for a kosher flip phone and stopped watching movies. Instead of college, something Toby had hoped for, even expected, Leyeh began planning to go to a teachers' seminary upon graduation. She prayed every day, hoping to be a role model, something she felt her mother was not. Her skirts got longer, her blouses were all buttoned up, and she stopped wearing long earrings. She began reading inspirational books on faith. One summer at the girls' sleep-away camp she went to every year, Leyeh met a new *rukhnius* (spirituality) counselor, Mrs.

Gold, who would become a mentor to her. Eventually Leyeh confided in her about her mother's double life.

As Leyeh began to tell me about Mrs. Gold, she got upset. Her voice broke, and she asked me to turn off my tape recorder. Then she started to cry in earnest, saying to me, "I'm sure you know about my mother, right?" Upset myself at her tears, I mumbled something noncommittal and kept patting her shoulder. "My mother's not *frum*! She's living a double life," she said. She was afraid, she told me, that her mother was teaching her to live a double life, too, showing her how to cheat the system because she knew Toby wanted her to be like her. With the brutal honesty of a teenager (in fact, she was exactly the same age as my son), she said, "Well, wouldn't you be upset if your son became *frum*?" To which I could only nod and blush because indeed I would be if he embraced a way of life that excluded me, our family, our values, and our way of life. Leyeh described how her mother tried to encourage her to push the envelope of modesty. When they went shopping, Leyeh told me, her mother tried to convince her that a hem just grazing her knee looked better, while she begged her mother to buy extra material to lengthen her skirts.

Leyeh was angry that her mother had made her feel so confused about faith. I ventured that maybe confusion could be productive, helping her make up her own mind. "That's what my mother always says too," Leyeh retorted. She was emphatic that a Jew could never rely exclusively on their own authority or trust themselves. "It says that in the Torah," she said. Moral ambiguity, competing voices of authority, reliance on her own judgment, were all the dangers she felt her mother had exposed her to.

A year and a half later, I was very surprised when she called me from her kosher phone, asking to meet again because she wanted to explain why she had gotten so upset. This time we met in my university office, and she confronted me, "Is your research really about people living double lives?" When I admitted it was, explaining I hadn't known how much she knew about her mother when we first spoke, she said, "I knew it! Talking about my mother is pure *loshn hora* [gossip], but maybe it's a little like therapy too." I reminded her that I was not a therapist and that I was writing a book. She said, "That's fine, as long as you don't write my name. That's why I wanted to meet you again. Because I want people to know this. Because people from double lives are going to read it." This was what she wanted to tell parents living double lives:

> Parents out there, you're being utterly cruel . . . because you're really, really confusing the kids. *Frum* in our perspective is like our life. . . .

It's not like you're Christian and you believe in Jesus. It's a whole way of life. We live with *Hashem* [God] every single day, and either you're *frum* or you're not *frum*. You cannot be both. Do you know what I'm saying? . . . They're so selfish. They think they're being unselfish but they're really being selfish, because they're letting the kids be so confused.

Leyeh described what it had been like for her to grow up with moral contradictions, which she understood as the danger of confusion. She remembered that when she was in ninth grade her mother took her and some of her younger brothers on a trip to an amusement park in Pennsylvania. Toby took off her wig once they got there, shaking out her long dark hair. Leyeh told her she wouldn't go out of the hotel with her like that. Her mother said, "Leyeh, there are no Jewish people here. We're good." But for Leyeh, the hypocrisy of taking the wig on or off depending on context was unacceptable. She said to her mother, "Would you take it off at home?" Her mother answered, "You know I can't do that." Leyeh said, "Either you take it off or you wear it all the time." She told me how confusing it had been, since they had learned in school for years how "terrible" it was for a married woman to uncover her hair. Why, she wondered, was her mother spending thousands of dollars in school tuition and then telling her the exact opposite of what she had learned? "It was very painful," she told me. She began anxiously watching her mother's behavior more carefully after that trip, never quite sure what was her imagination and what was real, worried about her mother's transgressions and their impact on her.

A turning point for Leyeh came when she met that camp counselor, Mrs. Gold, with whom she spent many hours discussing faith, God, and eventually, her mother. Until then, she told me, she had felt something was amiss at home, but she was never sure what because she did not have the "terms." When she confided in her counselor, Leyeh remembered, "She got it right away. Your mother is living a double life." Leyeh had never heard that expression before, but the pieces suddenly fell into place for her. At the end of camp, she felt scared to go home. She wanted to stay religious, and she did not want to be influenced by her mother. Desperate, she called an aunt, who was very open with her, acknowledging that her mother had always been a "bit like a rebellious type."

Her aunt encouraged her to go home, but with her phone call, Leyeh had activated a network of religious relatives and educators who were all advocating for her. They consistently told her she had to respect her mother, but they made it clear that she also needed to make plans to leave.

Her aunt soon called another relative, and they told Leyeh's school principal, who recommended she go to therapy, something Leyeh's parents did not feel she needed. In her last year of high school, Leyeh continued to ask for advice from her principal, the camp counselor, and her relatives. When her mother wanted to take her to the movies, for example, Leyeh called her grandfather and asked his advice. Go, he said, it's *kibud av-v'em* (honoring your parents), but leave the theater if it gets too inappropriate. It was this grandfather who agreed she should go to seminary, in part to leave home.

Leyeh acknowledged to me that her mother was a good person but "selfish." What she meant, she said, was that "in our world, children come first, and I don't see that with my mother." Was her mother selfish, I wondered, or was she simply less willing to sacrifice herself for a system she no longer believed in, like other parents living double lives? Leyeh understood that her mother had had questions that were never answered and had resorted to living "in two worlds." What she found "immoral" was less about religious questioning and more about hypocrisy and lying, things like "cursing" or wearing immodest clothes, or taking off her wig.

At the same time, in an about-face that seemed the epitome of adolescence, she confessed that she felt she was a "horrible daughter" who was always angry at and critical of her mother. "She'll have a wonderful life when I'm not there to mix in," she predicted. About her own faith, Leyeh felt she had to remain vigilant, but she did acknowledge the power of choosing to be religious, saying, "I know I'm real. I chose it [being *frum*], so that's amazing." And that sense of choice, ironically exactly what her mother had hoped to cultivate, was something she planned to pass along to her own religious children one day.

"Mixed Marriages": Supporting Children's Choice or Creating Religious Confusion?

Conflicts with their children and teens were confusing and upsetting for double-life parents. Unlike religious parents, they could not ask their own parents or their spouses or friends for advice, because they were not trying to socialize their children into the same ideologies. Instead, many used virtual and face-to-face spaces to ask for advice from others living double lives, to encourage each other as they secretly tried to change some of the dynamics in their own families. Gavriel, for example, regularly posted on Facebook to ask other parents for recommendations for leisure English reading for his young son, who had minimal English instruction in his

Hasidic school. One of his recent posts asked about series similar to *Harry Potter* or *Magic Tree House*, both of which his son had loved. Friends posted multiple suggestions, providing a reading list that contributed to a new kind of Hasidic male literacy: leisure secular reading in English. More mainstream Hasidic boyhood valued memorization, concentration, fluency in liturgical Hebrew and Yiddish, logical argumentation, and limited contact with girls. It certainly did not include reading about the brother-sister team, Jack and Annie, who time traveled from a magic treehouse. Gavriel's son, who attended a Hasidic yeshiva, was simultaneously becoming literate in English and popular American young adult culture, with its emphasis on individuality, independence, and imagination.

Social media like WhatsApp or Facebook also created spaces where a double-life parent got recognition for the subtle changes they were making in their childrearing, changes that if successful went unnoticed by a spouse. Chavi, for example, told me her father had asked her sons to prepare two questions about the *khumesh* (Bible) they had studied in yeshiva that week. She shared the questions her children had written "with the guys" (a group of double lifers we both knew). She was gratified when they quickly and enthusiastically complimented her, saying, "You're training questioners."

Gavriel, similarly, posted an interaction in which another of his sons asked him if Moses was "real." Gavriel said he did not know and asked him what he thought. His son replied that he did not think he was real because he was just in the Torah portion (*parsha*). A Facebook friend commented, "You have this sewn up." Gavriel explained to me that the friend was complimenting him for having a son with "the skeptical gene," which would help him resist "superstition and stupidity."

Double-life parents also debated among themselves the ethics of their own efforts to introduce more liberal values at home, trying to perhaps legitimate the unusual arrangements they found themselves in. Tsiri, for example, told me how her seven-year-old daughter accepted that there were certain foods she could not eat at home because they did not have the correct rabbinical stamp of approval. Her daughter knew her mother ate those foods, though, so she explained it this way, "I'm allergic to OU [the Orthodox Union rabbinical stamp her mother regularly ate], right?" This was a simple explanation, using childhood allergies to explain why she and her mother held to different standards of kosher food.

Tsiri herself pushed back against the idea that children needed to have one consistent message, that any difference of religiosity between parents would be confusing. This was increasingly called a "mixed marriage." She told me, "I hear that you can't have the mixed marriage situation because the kids are confused a lot. I kind of disagree with it because I don't think my child is confused. I kind of have this feeling of telling people, 'You're confused. My child is not confused, you're confused.'" A mixed marriage disrupted the consistency that ultra-Orthodox children grow up with, where home and school support each other. Hearing or reading about different ideas, relationships with someone who was not a believer, all of these could be dangerous for the development of faith.

That mixed marriages confused children, potentially leading them astray from ultra-Orthodoxy, was explicitly expressed in a 2015 *Mishpacha* (Family) magazine article, "A House on Shaky Ground." The journalist, Malkie Schwartz, profiled four women whose husbands had become cool to Judaism. She told me, in a phone interview, that she had been unable to find any women heretics whose husbands had not ultimately divorced them. This was more evidence that custody battles were at least one reason why women double lifers might be warier about expressing and acting on their life-changing doubt. The article, Ms. Schwartz told me, went through many rounds of edits because the topic was so "controversial." She concluded in her article that the real issue of mixed marriages was the danger they posed to children:

> The million-dollar question for couples of different religious levels is how their relationship will impact their children. What would be better for the kids—staying together or breaking up? . . . living with someone who has undergone a serious spiritual lapse requires herculean effort. In some ways it's similar to living with someone with a debilitating illness, only it's a spiritual malady in this case.

Note that she compared a "spiritual lapse" to a debilitating illness, a kind of "spiritual malady." The remainder of the article focused on the heroic efforts of the still-religious spouse to keep children religious and their families together. The editors, she told me, wanted something inspirational.

Soon after the *Mishpacha* magazine article was published, I heard about the formation of a closed group on Facebook called, "Mixed Marriage." On that site, people supported and advised each other on parenting and legal matters in cases of divorce. Some in the group were openly OTD and others were in the closet. The group also met in real life and went out to socialize, usually hanging out in bars and restaurants together. After multiple attempts to get invited, it was finally Tsiri, unrecognizable to me without her wig and in jeans, who invited me to join a small gathering at a bar in Manhattan because she felt nervous going out alone with two guys.

The conversation that night focused on parenting and marriage. The two men, Ushy and Yankl, were clearly intrigued to hear about Tsiri's experiences as a woman living a double life. Sitting in a booth with beer, they updated each other about their children. Ushy, who was Yeshivish, was recently divorced and openly OTD. He told us that his teenage daughters had agreed to spend Shabbes with him, a real triumph since some children of divorced parents refused to stay at the nonreligious parent's home, a situation termed "parental alienation." Yankl, a Hasid who was still in the closet, fist-bumped him.

But then Ushy told another story, a heartbreaking one. That weekend at his house, his teenage daughter was working on a paper for school about Maimonides. Ushy offered to help her, since, as he said, "I know this stuff." His daughter politely refused his help, saying she did not want his help because he was "a hypocrite." Ushy mimed a knife being stabbed into his heart as the others expressed sympathy, patting him on the shoulder.

Tsiri described how her daughter had reacted to her increased use of English cursing, which had begun with her doubting. She had said, "*Nor a* mommy *ken zugn* 'fuck it.'" Everyone but Ushy, who did not speak Yiddish, laughed. Tsiri translated for him, "Only a mommy can say 'fuck it.'" In fact, Blimi had told me that she could tell who among her sisters was on the internet by the profanities they knew. One of her sisters innocently asked her what "bitch" meant, suggesting to Blimi that she had never gone online.

There was talk about their still-religious spouses. Yankl asked Tsiri if her husband was worried she would have an affair because his wife was terrified of that, more than any beliefs he might have or not. They asked Tsiri how it felt to wear pants the first time. She described how wearing them helped her "blend into" public places like bars or the train, so that she actually felt more protected, and not constantly sticking out. Perhaps this was part of the shift in publics that having life-changing doubt led to. It was common for those living double lives to want to blend in more with other New Yorkers, to look less marked as ultra-Orthodox. Yankl shyly asked Tsiri if she was a good cook, to which she replied that her husband no longer ate her food because he did not trust her to maintain a certain level of *kashrus*. She described how her husband's family had gone through him to ask her to buy a dessert this past Hanukah rather than make one, because again, they could not trust her.

There was a lot of playful joking around, especially about gender, perhaps because mixed-gender hanging out was a relatively new experience. Yankl quoted a Hebrew text against walking between two women and mentioned that he was sitting between Tsiri and me, which was supposed to harm his memory.[9] At one point, both men took their hidden yarmulkes out of their pants pockets, a small velvet blue one for Ushy and a big velvet black one for Yankl. They tried each other's on, laughing, and then Ushy put his on Tsiri, to their amusement, which led to Tsiri's telling of the family fallout when she had decided to publicly stop wearing a hat on top of her wig. Talk or teasing about clothing, hair, or head covering acknowledged the emotion-laden, gendered signs that double lifers performed as they walked a dangerous line between self-expression and risk of harming those they loved.

Tsiri, for example, described telling her daughter a half-truth about herself and her clothing that had upset her just that very evening. Her daughter had watched her getting ready to go out, putting on jeans under her skirt. She asked, "Why can't you just wear the pants, without the skirt?" Tsiri had answered, "A Jewish mother can't do that." And while that statement was true, at the same time Tsiri was a different kind of Jewish mother. Within twenty minutes, safely on the train, she would actually just be wearing her jeans. Another kind of Jewish mother would not wear jeans at all, let alone under her skirt. Tsiri felt she had to at least perform and uphold that truth for her daughter, if she was going to stay married, live in their community, and send her daughter to the "right" schools, so she could eventually make a match with a nice family.

Changing and Staying the Same: Double Life Matchmaking

One day I got a private message on Facebook inviting me to Moishy's son's wedding. Moishy was one of the first of his double-life generation to "marry off" a child. His double-life friends had all watched closely to see what, if any, effects his double life had on his son's chances at a good match. Moishy had sent invitations on Facebook to many of his double-life friends, along with his OTD friends, work colleagues, and of course, Blimi. I asked him on WhatsApp about the decision to invite his secret heretical friends to this most public of family celebrations. It was not, he told me, such a risk. Some were Hasidic men "who looked *chassidish* [Hasidic] and no one knows they're RM [Reverse Marranos]." Others who were OTD could be mistaken for his work associates.

He said he was a little "concerned" about someone like Zalman, a prominent OTD person whom many would recognize. But Moishy figured Zalman would probably understand and not come, though he told me he would welcome him happily if he did. The same applied to some of the double-life and OTD women he invited. He wanted to let them know about the *simkha* (celebration), but he did not expect most of them to come. In fact, it turned out that a WhatsApp group had exactly this discussion about attending the wedding, with each member letting the others know if they were going to go. Zalman read between the lines of Moishy's invite and posted, "I wouldn't be doing him any favors if I went, so I won't."

Blimi had to be at the wedding. "This woman is my life!" Moishy wrote to me. They knew everything about each other's children. In fact, Blimi had been very involved in the matchmaking and planning the wedding for Moishy's son. He wrote to me, "She acted as a sounding board and helped me analyze every *shiddukh*. All that said, she's the one person who must be there for her sake and mine. But I can't have her come to the dancing [after the ceremony] because it'll ruin the night for my wife," implying that his wife knew or at least suspected something. When I asked Blimi why she was going, she texted me to explain, a bit impatiently, "It's a huge event in his life. I have to be there. Did you feel it was important for your husband to be in the delivery room when you gave birth?"

I bumped into Blimi just as I arrived. She told me she would not actually be going into the hall at all, just watching the ceremony from the street. Hasidic weddings take place outside, under the stars and under a *khuppa* (wedding canopy); every wedding hall has an outdoor space or a ceiling that opens to the sky. That evening, the veiled bride walked outside, holding tightly to the arms of her mother and future mother-in-law, each holding a candle, to meet the groom waiting under the *khuppa*. I followed along with the other guests. Then, I remembered to look out at the street. There, leaning against a chain link fence stood Blimi, silhouetted against the purple-pink twilight sky, watching the wedding. No one else looked her way or noticed. She could easily have been a curious onlooker, and not the intimate she was, the lover of the father of the groom.

The celebration followed the ceremony, with a big meal and dancing. There was a shadowy double-life celebration alongside the official one, which included secret texting and surreptitious meetings for men and women. For example, I had an ongoing WhatsApp thread with Blimi, who remained outside on the street. She wrote, "It if isn't too much trouble, can you send me pictures?" She wanted to see the bride dancing, and the dress of the sister of the bride she had heard all about. I took pictures and sent them to her, feeling both a thrill and a twinge of guilt at my complicity. Then Blimi sent another text telling me to make sure to check out

Moishy's wife's fancy diamond necklace, which she had helped pick out. Yitsy and Gavriel texted me from the men's section, suggesting we meet up by the *mekhitsa*, the wall separating the men and women, where we chatted and watched the men's dancing. Shmuel texted next, and I went outside to find him and Blimi on the street hanging out together.

Moishy had made a good match for his son. Apparently, Moishy's secret life had not been the issue he and Blimi had feared it might be. He had kept under the radar sufficiently and had been successful enough in his job, making money and getting promotions, that his family's reputation had not suffered. Somehow, he told me, everyone thought he was *davening* (praying) at another synagogue, and no one really caught on that he wasn't *davening* much at all.

Moishy, for his part, had done what he could to make sure his son would be happy even as he stayed in the system: small things, Blimi told me, to create a romantic setting for the new couple, like putting a loveseat in the dining room for the couple to curl up on and chat. Blimi told me she had been involved in every step, helping Moishy find a girl who seemed like a good fit for his son. Despite Moishy's disillusionment with the system, despite his doubts, Moishy had embraced arranged marriage for his son, which he wanted, too, although he was also talking about maybe going to college after studying in a *kollel* for a year or two. Moishy had not made revolutionary changes, just subtle small ones designed to ensure his son's happiness in his marriage, while keeping open the possibility of higher education and even a professional degree.

Exactly six months later, Blimi invited me to her daughter's wedding. Despite her own fears that her reputation had suffered, she felt, she told me, "vindicated" by the match with a "very nice boy" from a "good family."[10] Indeed, a friend had predicted that Blimi would have problems finding a good family because of her reputation, especially her tight clothing. However, Blimi's daughter was a "top girl," earnestly pious, smart, and pretty, and it didn't hurt that Blimi herself was from a popular, wealthy family, known for their scholarship and piety. This wedding was in a different, fancier hall—a cream and gold Louis XIV dream, with women in swirls of silk, feathers, sequins, jewels, and furs. Soon after arriving, we all went outside into the frosty air, where the black-velvet wedding canopy was set up on the icy sidewalk. The groom was waiting, flanked by his father and father-in-law-to-be, *shukling* (swaying) back and forth, praying, and crying. Then the bride came out, covered in her veil, clinging to Blimi and her future mother-in-law, who each held candles. They were all wrapped in white fur stoles and matching muffs.

Standing there, I suddenly recognized Moishy by himself across the street, wearing his everyday hat, no special occasion *shtraymel*. I gave what I hoped was a discreet wave, and he beckoned me over. "I could use the company," he said. He had snuck into the hall to see Blimi all dressed up. He said, "She looks amazing. It's such an emotional time for her." "Is it for you too?" I asked. "Of course it is, but I feel excluded," he said. He told me that he knew all about Blimi's daughter, the match and wedding, but even more, he knew how Blimi was feeling, and he wished he could share in the celebration with her. I mentioned that I had seen Blimi look across the street a number of times during the ceremony, and Moishy lit up. As the newly married couple and their parents went back into the hall, Moishy predicted Blimi would look back at him one last time. But she didn't, and he was left alone outside in the cold. And yet, Blimi and Moishy's secret love affair had been important to the matchmaking of both of their eldest children. Despite never meeting each other's children, they felt they knew them intimately. Their relationship, with all its secrets and betrayals, had ended up reproducing some form of ultra-Orthodoxy after all, but perhaps with the potential for change.

The Morality of Individual Choice

Rearing children to participate in a dominant public ideology, while simultaneously and secretly undermining that ideology, was ethically complicated. The compromise many living double lives made was to claim that they were creating "choices" for their children, the opportunity to choose what their lives would be like. But the concept of choice for children in particular was also complicated. Children have agency, but their agency is constrained in ways that are different from adults because they are not fully culturally competent adults; rather, they are fully culturally competent children, at least for a time.[11]

Further, choosing to be religious or not, even as a young adult, was not simply a matter of deciding between a Christmas tree or a Hanukah menorah, a Passover seder or an Easter basket. As Leyeh herself pointed out, children's entire socialization through adulthood was bound up with ultra-Orthodoxy. Their social and economic worlds, whom they might marry, the languages they spoke or read, all were forged in ultra-Orthodox institutions that had a consistent message. The choice to follow a heretical parent and choose a different way of life would be fraught with the loss of all that children were taught was good and true, along with their means to earn a living, a chance to get married and to live among family and friends.

Individual choice that went against the status quo was not something to be undertaken lightly. Perhaps the choice to live an ultra-Orthodox life, to feel that one had chosen it, maybe that was enough for double lifers.

Yet even those living double lives were often ambivalent about what kind of choices they were providing for their children, and how they would feel if their children ended up too different from them. Yanky, for example, a man living a double life, told me a little wistfully over a beer that he would not mind if his son ended up living a secular life. If he is a lawyer, he said, that would be fine, except then we might have very little in common. Double lifers' ultra-Orthodox habitus—their embodied, cultural sensibilities—continued to be important and to color their efforts at making changes at home.

Similarly, Pessy, a woman who had left her Hasidic group but remained Orthodox, told me that she couldn't really understand why she still so strongly wanted her son to go to a Hasidic yeshiva, but she did. "Maybe I was brainwashed," she said, "and I don't exactly understand it, but I want him to have the experience of feeling special." Special is a word that many Hasidic Jews use to reference a high spiritual level, going beyond what was required by Jewish law. When a girl chooses to wear tights when she could be wearing knee socks, her teacher might say she was "special." In Pessy's case, I understood that she wanted her son to feel that he, as a Jew, was specially chosen by God. She and her husband planned to supplement their son's Hasidic education with a tutor for secular subjects; however, she wanted her son to experience the moral certitude and the feeling of Jewish triumphalism of her own Hasidic upbringing.

Her father actually had had to step in and use his leverage when the Hasidic yeshiva rejected them for being too different, too modern, but it was worth it for Pessy to involve him. She told me, in a flash of insight, "If I put my son in public school, he also won't have a choice. He will just be secular. Maybe I'm fooling myself. I don't know." Neither a public school nor a yeshiva provide children with much choice, since each have an explicit ideological slant, be it Hasidic or secular. The actual choice Pessy wanted for her sons, then, was access to an ultra-Orthodox education with its claims to Jewish exceptionalism, supplemented by exposure to secular subjects (i.e., English and math). Perhaps this was the way that "Hasidic lite" or more "enlightened" ultra-Orthodoxy would actually be created (see next chapter).

My exchange with Pessy reminded me of another conversation I had had with Nosson, in which his own awareness of an irreconcilable moral conflict between individual choice and ultra-Orthodox claims to Jewish authenticity was exposed in a slip of the tongue. We had been having coffee one fall afternoon, and our conversation touched on holiday preparations for the upcoming Rosh Hashana, the Jewish new year. I mentioned something about my own family preparations, and he said, "Oh, you remembered you were Jewish!" By the time I had walked the few blocks home, he had texted me to apologize for what he said was his "judgmental" comment. In truth, I understood his slightly sarcastic comment to me, someone whose Judaism really was about choice and very little sense of obligation. Nosson had grown up in an ultra-Orthodox community where consistency, moral certitude, and a sense of being "special" were reinforced in every institution. His apology was yet another example of his self-taught awareness, his effort to both live in and reject aspects of his own moral universe.

The stuff of small everyday exchanges between and among children, mothers, and fathers, amid domestic mundanity—around supper tables, in bedtime stories, and holiday celebrations—were actually the very basis for unexpected social transformations. These transformations were lived in gendered realms of authority, where mothers, fathers, sons, and daughters all had different stakes in what constituted an ethical person. What exactly constituted change was subtle and partial; nevertheless, the tension between ultra-Orthodox moral authority and double lifers' gendered ethics of choice opened up the possibility for other ways of being Jewish.

8

Endings and Beginnings

Motti sent me an original English-language poem he had originally shared with friends on WhatsApp. His "The Road Never Travelled " explicitly riffed on Robert Frost's "The Road Not Taken":

The Road Never Traveled
A single road was set before me
A road that climaxed in a dead-end
Where you face the Wailing Wall
I looked back and turned around
And paved a new road that diverged
From all roads that ever were
I proudly traveled my new road
For it was never traveled before
And that has made one hell of a difference

Motti turned Frost's classic poem, one that so many American high school students read, into a double-life manifesto, harnessing the power and possibilities of forging an independent life. This resonated across the diversity of double-life experiences. Other men and women similarly rejected that "Wailing Wall," the authority of contemporary ultra-Orthodoxy, claiming the individual autonomy to make their own choices, within limits. They had to travel that new road in secret, though, and that brought anxieties and anguish. Indeed, those living double lives, their spouses, and their children all paid an emotional toll. There was a mix of pain and hope that came from choosing a different life path from those one loved the most, and the necessity of keeping that choice a secret created distance in the most intimate of relationships.

Double lifers like Motti were part of the loud heretical counterpublic that contributed to the contemporary ultra-Orthodox crisis of authority that was publicly fought over ultra-Orthodox Jewish hearts, minds, and souls. There were ongoing struggles to understand life-changing religious doubt, its causes, and its cures. Some rabbis and activists blamed the internet, others, including many religious therapists, blamed an ultra-Orthodoxy that had become too stringent and too rigid. Over time, many of the faithful and those living double lives came to a shared conclusion: that the real threat of the medium of the internet was its new possibilities for interaction with like-minded others, its avenues to alternative truths, and its spaces for anonymous, yet public dissent that directly challenged ultra-Orthodox authority.

Endings and Beginnings, Part I

Life keeps going, but ethnographic research must end. By 2019, some, like Leyzer, Shimon, Yitsy, Boruch, Yonah, Gavriel, Motti, Toby, Zisi, and Shmuel, remained more or less in the same familial situations in which I first met them. However, except for Zisi, they had all become less observant in private and bolder in their secret explorations. Leyeh, Toby's daughter, was at a teachers' seminary, waiting for the perfect match. Moishy and Blimi were still in love and still married to other people. Chavi had figured out how, as she described it, "to take a little happiness for herself" without "rocking the boat" or hurting her kids. Esty remained with her husband, while she slowly pursued that college degree online. Indeed, others who were able to access higher education, including master's and even doctorates for some, or land well-paid, high-level jobs especially outside of their communities in fields such as technology, healthcare, or finance often had more bearable double lives. One thing that all double lifers shared was that almost none had had more children since I first met them. Indeed, this was one of the first major decisions that they had all negotiated with their still-religious spouses and sometimes their spouse's rabbis.

Making bigger changes were Menashe and Tamar, each of whom had convinced their spouses to move to more diverse New York neighborhoods where they felt less social pressure and fewer neighbors' eyes on them. Perhaps most dramatically, Chaim had been kicked out of his community, divorced by his wife, and had gone OTD. Bentsy's wife had divorced him, as well, once she discovered he had been having an affair. Miriam had finally come clean to her parents about her doubt, gotten a divorce, and had very happily gone off to university, driven cross-country by Chaim and a few other OTD friends in loco parentis. Those who stayed and those who left often remained in touch, continuing to get together online and in person.

Technologies on which the heretical counterpublic grew continued to change as well. There were double-life threads on newer social media platforms, like Reddit, Instagram, Tumblr, and Snapchat. Some on WhatsAppville Yinglish even lamented that they had a hard time keeping up with all the changes. Menashe posted, "Apparently there's a whole charedi [ultra-Orthodox] Instagram/Snapchat alternate universe that I'm not privy to. There are famous young yingerleit and balebustes [married men and women] with thousands of followers that we old geezers never heard of." Maybe every generation eventually feels left behind as technology changes, and with it, affordances for the creation of different publics.

Ultra-Orthodoxy was changing too. I began to hear from those on WhatsAppville Yinglish and other double-life friends about a new category for Hasidic families, "Modern Hasidish"[1] or "Hasidish Lite." Modern Hasidish fell somewhere between Modern Orthodoxy and ultra-Orthodoxy. For example, couples who experienced life-changing doubt together might slowly, over years, change their levels of observance. These families could not be labeled bums or tuna baygels. That is, they were not simply too undisciplined to live up to the stringencies of ultra-Orthodoxy, just wanting to be "cool" or more modern (i.e., to fit in more with Gentile society). Nor did these families go completely OTD or embrace another denomination, like Modern Orthodoxy. Instead, they kept up aspects of a Hasidic lifestyle and ties to their families, while they made their own decisions about adopting more lenient stances to Jewish practice. For example, Chaya-Rivke and her husband, both of whom had grown up Hasidic in Brooklyn, quietly moved further and further away from their extended families as their children were growing up. First, they went to another Brooklyn neighborhood, then upstate to Monsey, where they put their children into a non-Hasidic Orthodox school; eventually, they decided to spend more and more time out of New York altogether, where they had more "freedom," Chaya-Rivke explained to me at a party. Looking at her teenage daughter (one of only two children) wearing a short skirt, no stockings, and crocs, I gathered that freedom meant no family or neighbors watching as they slowly changed their levels of observance, together. The united front of their marriage was critical, as was the fact that they continued to maintain extended family ties, including going to *simkhes* (celebrations) like weddings or bar mitzvahs, where they dressed to fit in. I knew because many posted pictures of themselves at Hasidic weddings looking more or less like everyone else. The new category of Modern Hasidish or Hasidish Lite was a grudging acknowledgment that for those who doubted or had questions as a couple and a family (never an individual), there might be more than one way to be ultra-Orthodox.

There was a perception for some that ultra-Orthodoxy was, as two Hasidic therapists told me, "opening up." In response, they too mobilized the modern American value of individual choice, but they did so to uphold structures of ultra-Orthodox authority. One of the Hasidic therapists, for example, told me that that he "chose" a simple faith that asked no questions (*emuna peshuta*). He explained that he was *temimesdik* (pure, innocent) because he chose not to question, "consciously as an intellectual person." He explained that he would rather not read certain critiques of ultra-Orthodoxy online, so he simply avoided them. He had, he told me, an "intellectual understanding of conformity." He valued the system, and as he said, "I want not to question. I choose not to be exposed."

Perhaps growing opportunities for participation in wider American society in the digital age actually made remaining in the fold and submitting to hierarchies of authority more of an ethical, individual choice. This reminds us that when people perceive that they have a choice, they might, in fact, choose to reject secularism—viewing certain freedoms or avenues for individual expression as undesirable or morally wrong. At the same time, using the language of choice simultaneously acknowledged a kind of unwitting participation in those same liberal values of individualism and autonomy, even by rejecting them.

These ongoing changes to ultra-Orthodoxy and to those living double lives were all on display in a celebration I attended for Zalman's second marriage. On Facebook, Zalman and his new bride (Jewish but not Orthodox) invited their OTD, double-life friends, and me to a "post-*chuppa* [bridal canopy] boogie." The wedding itself had been in a Hasidic hall in Williamsburg, where men and women celebrated separately divided by a *mekhitsa* (divider). After the wedding, the Hasidic and liberal Jewish families left the hall and spilled out onto the city sidewalks, *shtraymels* (high, fur holiday hats for men) unusually mixing in among sleeveless summer cocktail dresses. Then, a second celebration began in the same hall. A huge Russian bouncer stood at the entrance to a ballroom, blocking it so no one would see that there was mixed dancing inside. The guests were dressed to the nines, though not all modestly, and I watched as women and men celebrated together. The party itself was less remarkable, with its pop music, vodka, canapés, and disco ball, than the fact that it happened at all. In the heart of Hasidic Brooklyn, an ex-Hasidic man's second marriage to a liberal Jewish woman was attended by her family and his, all toasting the union. Afterwards, their OTD and double-life friends danced with them in the same hall, albeit hidden from the ultra-Orthodox public. Later, though, congratulatory pictures and good wishes were posted on the heretical counterpublic of Facebook.

The Ethics of a Double Life

Life-changing doubt for double lifers was not what philosopher Charles Taylor dubbed "a subtraction story," a disenchantment ending in secularism.[2] Those living double lives did not experience a radical conversion from belief to disbelief, which transformed their everyday lives into a "before" and an "after." Instead, living a double life was a drawn-out, messy process, one that continuously tacked among emotional commitments, moral dispositions, and changes of many kinds. Such a life necessitated picking and choosing between competing yet related moral systems, simultaneously inhabiting two different ways of being in the world. This meant that life-changing doubt was not necessarily a process that always ended in certainty.[3] Indeed, even when life-changing doubt reached a point of intellectual certainty, there was an ongoing emotional entanglement with ultra-Orthodoxy, with its habitus, and with a legacy of loss and disillusionment. This entanglement persisted not only because double lifers continued to participate in the everyday rhythms of the life of ultra-Orthodoxy, but also because their experiences of life-changing doubt—of anger for women or sadness for men—had changed their minds, their hearts, their languages, and their bodies.

Double lifers elaborated a contingent morality, one that straddled contradictions and hypocrisies, in order to protect their families and themselves. Perhaps unsurprisingly, many drew on North American liberal values, always refracted through and in conversation with the moralities of ultra-Orthodoxy. Because their life-changing doubt was kept secret, there were complicated ethical judgments and moral compromises, guilt and ambivalences. As Leyzer texted me when I asked him why he stayed, "There's sacrifices either way you go. . . . I'm either too lazy, copping-out to do what makes me happy. Or doing what's right." It was not always clear what the right thing was, which way happiness lay, or who might get hurt along the way. Double lifers' ongoing struggle was to reconcile their changing, sometimes ambivalent individual desires and beliefs with their steadfast love for and moral obligations to their families.

As we have seen, differences of gender were critical to double lifers' moral struggles. Ultra-Orthodox men and women, for example, not only had distinctive emotional experiences of life-changing doubt, but structurally, women and men had different access to technology, languages, and knowledge, along with different responsibilities for their children and homes. Men framed their life-changing doubt in intellectual terms, aligning themselves with illustrious heretics of a shared, more moral Jewish past. Using their skills as Jewish male scholars, they read, studied, and reasoned until they came to other truths. The change, however, was rarely a happy one. It was experienced instead as emotional despair, loss, and personal torment. In contrast, women's intellectual doubting was not even a communally recognized part of Jewish history, so that their life-changing doubt was exclusively interpreted by their families and religious authorities in emotional or sexual terms, rarely in intellectual ones. Where men experienced loss with life-changing doubt, women were angry because they had made so many personal sacrifices for a system they no longer believed to be true. Even for those women who did manage to live double lives, there were fewer opportunities for participation in the heretical counterpublic, for socializing in person, and for elaborating an alternative morality with changing relationship to authority. However, double-life women could and did try to subtly influence their children, just like men did.

The moral struggles of double-life men and women occurred first and foremost in their families. Families are moral units, especially in orthodox religious communities where parents, children, and relatives all pull together to fulfill shared goals and values. When one member of an ultra-Orthodox family was no longer completely on board with those shared goals and values, there were ripple effects for all. Especially in the intimacy of the nuclear family, children, teens, and still-religious spouses were affected by double lifers' changes in all kinds of ways, reminding us that morality and ethics are shaped by age, generation, gender, and of course, temperament. Each ultra-Orthodox family member had their own distinctive ethical obligations, feelings, and desires, which shaped how each responded to a double-life parent or spouse. Some still-religious spouses, for example, were forced to make ethical judgments and decisions anathema to their own faith and morality. Some had to take on religious authority that violated what they perceived to be the moral order of the world. Others had to lower their religious standards in order to keep the peace at home. Most had to lie to those they loved or pretend they did not see what was going on in their own homes.

Children and teenagers have been particularly absent in anthropological accounts of religiously orthodox worlds and recent work on morality and ethics. However, children and teens were key players in the ultra-Orthodox crisis of authority with their own forms of ever-changing agency. They were implicated in both of their parents' ethical dilemmas: the parent living a double life and the still-religious parent. Parents' dilemmas often led to teens' own dilemmas the older they got. Their emergent moralities, forms of expression, and gendered relationships to authority of all kinds will shape where and how ultra-Orthodox Judaism will continue to change.

Belief and Doubt

This ethnography has implications for the study of faith, doubt, and change in other religious worlds. John Patrick Shanley, the playwright of *Doubt: A Parable*, writes, "Conviction is a resting place and doubt is infinite."[4] However, my study of ultra-Orthodox life-changing doubt reveals that conviction is not always a stable state, either. Spending time with ultra-Orthodox Jews has taught me that both belief and doubt are "worked on," as the ultra-Orthodox like to say, in all kinds of ways over the course of a lifetime. Further, sometimes belief and doubt are worked on in private, silent invisible interiors, and other times they are worked on in very public imaginaries.

Belief and doubt, what people think and feel, should be considered complementary rather than opposed to what people actually do. Anthropologist Talal Asad showed, through an analysis of Christianity and Islam, that the social science category of religion, with its focus on interior belief, was in fact shaped by a specific set of Protestant assumptions about the nature of religion, persons, language, and God. In response, many scholars of religion over the past few decades have turned away from private, immaterial belief and instead studied religious life through materiality, embodiment, and the senses.

However, I think we might recuperate belief into these newer, productive approaches to religious life. Anthropologist Danilyn Rutherford, for example, offers a helpful way of rethinking belief. She draws on philosopher Charles Sanders Peirce's insight that "belief is a habit, a habitual practice of the mind, that intervenes in history."[5] The same is true, I submit, of doubt. Conceptualized this way, belief and doubt are practices of thought, processes like any other, open to historical, individual, and institutional change.

Understanding those living double lives required I attend to both beliefs and behaviors precisely because they were in conflict: dramatically changing interior belief battled with the continuity of embodied religious practice. Many double lifers described this conflict using a term coined by social psychologist Leon Festinger in 1957, "cognitive dissonance," the uncomfortable state of simultaneously holding conflicting attitudes, beliefs, or behaviors. Conflicts between beliefs and behaviors may take many forms and are dependent on all kinds of factors. Open-minded Yitsy had different opportunities and challeges than the atheist Motti or the disillusioned, but still spiritual Esty. If belief and doubt are practices, they can be ethnographically studied to account for the diversity of experiences afforded by age, gender, piety, or social class.

Double lifers' cognitive dissonance of many kinds was mediated—that is, made visible, audible, discursive, and public—by bodies, material objects, technology, and language. For example, trimmed beards, different colored stockings, English and Enlightened Hasidic Yiddish, online forums, Facebook, and in-person parties all mediated life-changing doubt. Moments of change and conflict are especially productive times to study belief and doubt because what is so often implicit is made explicit in all kinds of unexpected ways. Methodologically, focusing on mediation foregrounds the everyday processes by which interior life-changing doubt can be made public. And it was that publicity that was so challenging to ultra-Orthodox authority because it was ultimately political: whose version of truth would prevail?[6]

Mediation and Crises of Authority

Broader struggles over contemporary ultra-Orthodox authority and change in New York converged around the internet. Rabbis and those with life-changing doubt integrated this new medium into their shared historical narratives of Jewish survival in the face of change. Familiar battles and schisms were reanimated by contemporary generations of men over whose version of Jewish Orthodoxy was closer to a more moral past. Women, who had been peripheral to those past battles, continued to be peripheral in contemporary struggles as well, except when rabbinic authorities appealed to them to enforce new rulings.

The reactions of rabbinic authorities to the internet—their continued efforts to harness it to serve ultra-Orthodoxy, while keeping out forbidden ideas and images, were not novel. All kinds of media are routinely subjected to the scrutiny of ultra-Orthodox religious hierarchies of authority and either made Jewish or censored. These practices have been in place for decades and more, speaking to the creative flexibility necessary for the maintenance of a community that explicitly rejects the secular world to which it is inextricably bound. However, the internet has become central to sustaining ultra-Orthodox livelihoods, implicated in global networks of all kinds. Ultra-Orthodox accountants, business owners, matchmakers, and real estate agents all had to use the internet in order to be viable in an increasingly connected world.

Rabbinic authorities began calling the internet their *nisoyen ha-dor*, their generation's challenge in the timeless Jewish struggle for survival. They claimed that the religious stringencies that had kept religious doubt quietly and appropriately inside individuals so successfully in the United States from the 1950s on, when all were preoccupied with rebuilding what the Holocaust had destroyed, were no longer enough. Ultra-Orthodox rabbinic authorities blamed the medium of the internet for contaminating pure Jewish interiors, for making public and social what should have remained a private ethical struggle with oneself. When Hasidic and Yeshivish rabbinic leadership began requiring kosher filtering enforced by ultra-Orthodox schools, many of the less cynical Yeshivish men and women capitulated. However, many Hasidic men who were disillusioned with their rabbinic leadership balked, so their rabbis deputized women to protect their families and the coming generations.

Ultra-Orthodox rabbis bolstered their own religious authority with appeals to secular experts' growing concerns over the effects of digital media. In particular, they turned to old and new experts on interiority to protect the Jewish faithful and cure those "sick" with doubt. They integrated two distinctive discursive traditions, each with its own form of authority: Jewish ethical writings and contemporary American psychology. As rabbis and therapists worked together, life-changing doubt could be treated as an emotional illness, so that rabbis remained moral authorities over the soul; yet another example of the flexibility of a community that defines itself by its strict adherence to tradition.

Those living double lives and those who had gone OTD rejected these explanations for life-changing doubt and its cures. They argued that their intellectual and emotional reasons for doubting were homegrown and not a result of any new medium. They also rejected explanations that they were addicted to social media or traumatized by sexual abuse. Their questioning came, they said, from reading books and learning more compelling truths, both valuable currency among the ultra-Orthodox. They were dissatisfied with the answers they had received from rabbis, angry that secular truths (like science) had been kept from them, and bitter that they had made sacrifices for a system they no longer believed in. Most told me that the internet had merely been a support in all of this, a medium that connected them to others so they did not feel so lonely or so "crazy."

My own understanding of the medium of the internet in the ultra-Orthodox crisis of authority lies somewhere in between rabbinic positions and those of double lifers. While double lifers did not credit the internet with their life-changing doubt, there is no denying that the heretical counterpublic enabled by the internet made questioning, doubting, and ultimately the very option of living a double life more possible. Life-changing doubt and double lives were not new, but previous generations often had to look outside of their own communities, to more liberal Jewish institutions or intellectual spaces like the Jewish Theological Seminary or the Jewish Reading Room of the New York Public Library. However, the heretical counterpublic emboldened those with doubts, who quickly realized that there were "normal," admirable people in their very own communities who shared their questions and critiques. Supported by networks of online and in-person friends and lovers similarly closeted or even publicly "out," a double life became more viable for those who could not or would not leave, despite the very real costs. In this sense, the ultra-Orthodox rabbis were quite right to warn, as Rabbi Wachs thundered at the Citi Field anti-internet rally, "The internet is changing who we are!"

As those with life-changing doubt moved beyond their screens, many experimented with all kinds of media, including their bodies, writing and speaking, and material objects, to explore their changing senses of themselves. They did so while they secretly broke Jewish laws that no longer felt binding or obligatory. And yet, though they sought out new worlds with their own values, aesthetics, and norms, they continued to hold fast to their families and the familiarity of ultra-Orthodoxy. Ultimately, the medium of the internet allowed those with life-changing doubt to remain at home, while they simultaneously changed who they were, their perceptions of language, of morality, and even what constituted religion. These underground rumblings of dissent and change have affected the faithful as well, who now know that their neighbor or a family member, no matter how they look or act, might just not be who they seem. This is further evidence that ultra-Orthodoxy is changing. As Leyzer posted on Whats-

Appville Yinglish, "Change is constant. It's a continuous tug of war, competing forces pushing and pulling, the fanatics in one direction, others to another direction, the masses being pulled along the strongest currents. . . . Change is here. Embrace it."

The ultra-Orthodox crisis of authority ultimately provokes a more general question: When does a medium become a political public concern, a proxy for wider struggles over authoritative religious truth? And when do religious authorities resort to public talk about interiority in their efforts to protect the integrity of their institutions and narratives? The answer lies in moments when interior belief becomes social and public through communication with others, laying the foundation for the creation of a counterpublic. Think about Yisroel, whose story began this book. Eventually his rabbis gave up on him, but they told him that if he was determined to eat nonkosher food or break the Sabbath, he should do so in secret and at home where other religious Jews, including his own family, would not see him and be influenced. As long as Yisroel kept his heretical ideas to himself, he and his family would be allowed to stay.

When heretics will not stay quietly at home, when they will not keep their ideas to themselves, when they spread their new ways of seeing the world to reading or listening publics, religious authorities may resort to excommunication and ejection. In 1656, philosopher Baruch Spinoza was formally excommunicated from his Jewish community in Amsterdam for spreading his heretical ideas about God and nature. His rabbis denounced him on the threshold of the Torah's ark in the synagogue, putting him in *kherem* (excommunication) for the rest of his life. The double lifers in these pages are not, of course, as well known or as revolutionary as Spinoza, or for that matter, others famously charged with heresy, such as Martin Luther or Galileo Galilei. Yet double lifers offer us an important, sometimes overlooked perspective on religious change. In contrast to those heretics whose world-altering ideas disseminated to others changed the course of history, double lifers remind us that everyday individuals and their engagement with a new medium can also bring about change. Perhaps these changes are more gradual, and they take place in the intimacy of families or illicit romances and friendships, but they are important nonetheless. What ultra-Orthodox rabbinic leadership came to understand was that the real threat to their authority was not just a new technology or individual loss of faith, but rather that the internet enabled those heretics and fellow travelers to stay hidden, secretly supporting each other and sharing their ideas as they searched for new ways of being in the world. And though double lifers and their explorations might remain secret, in the intimacies of domestic life, even subtly, they could not help but effect changes in all kinds of unpredictable ways.

The internet or any medium is never determinative, of course. We cannot say that the internet always causes heresies or that it reinforces existing structures of authority in religious communities. There are plenty of ethnographic and historical examples of both.[7] Rather, we can say that in particular historical moments and places a new medium with its own affordances may be drafted in times of conflict to further religious agendas or challenge them. But to understand these dynamics and their implications requires ethnography. People of all political and religious stripes, including me, worry that the internet is changing us, our ability to concentrate, to spend time together, to be creative, think deeply, or maintain our privacy. The ultra-Orthodox worry about these very same things, but against a different backdrop, one with metaphysical dramas and redemptive stakes. When rabbinic authorities turned out to be too flawed or too rigid, when ultra-Orthodox life in New York became too economically difficult to maintain or too restrictive, a medium that gave voice to dissent became central to struggles over what all community members held most dear. In the end, the conflict over the internet and life-changing doubt among the ultra-Orthodox was one piece in a bigger puzzle that centered on how to account for competing notions of persons, authority, and truth.

Endings and Beginnings, Part II: Yisroel and Rukhy Eighteen Months Later

When I last met up with Yisroel, whose story opens this book, I almost did not recognize him. He was wearing a white polo shirt, slacks, and his long *peyos* (side curls) were tucked up under a baseball cap with his company's logo, so no one he knew might potentially spot him. He also sported wire-rimmed glasses, not the usual Hasidic plastic ones, and his beard was noticeably shorter. "Did you trim your beard?" I asked, knowing that trimming was forbidden. "Nah," he said, "I pull it out. It's a work around." Pulling at a beard was not technically a breaking of Jewish law, often excused as a "nervous" behavior.

Over beer, Yisroel told me that since I had last seen him his life had not changed as much as he had hoped it would. He was still "fighting for his freedom," still living in the same neighborhood, outwardly keeping all the commandments in front of his kids. His wife was still religious, and he was still keeping secrets from his parents and friends. He was less worried, though, that his children would be expelled from school, since the *vaad* (the Committee on Purity) had stopped harassing him and his wife once they realized he was not going to publicly defy too many community norms.

What he called "freedom" threaded through our long conversation. He had been working feverishly on developing his own business, while he held down his day job, since he felt his financial independence was essential to making any life decisions. He had also stopped socializing almost completely with others living double lives, online or in person. His secret "second life," he had decided, was not really solving any of his problems, and he did not really yearn to explore secular life. He knew, he told me, that secular life and religious life "both have upsides and downsides." He was just trying to find a place for himself and his family, where it wasn't dangerous to be what he called "an independent thinker."

Yisroel's life-changing doubt, especially his acceptance of evolution, had gradually changed his outlook on life, making him, he told me, much more "cynical to the world." He was sure that people were just animals after all, not created by God. And he was just as sure, he said, that there was no afterlife, no Garden of Eden (*gan eydn*), where, as he had learned, pious Jewish men sat at God's feet and learned Torah (women, in that scenario sat at their husbands' feet listening). These changes to his belief system made him feel there was nothing to look forward to, that nothing mattered, that everything was a joke. Yisroel's cynicism even extended to how he felt about his wife. He still loved her and needed her, of course. He still found her "cute," he told me with a shy smile. However, he wished that they shared more intellectual interests, like philosophy or science. "If I met her at college, I don't know if we would have dated. We're very different," he said.

Yisroel encouraged me to talk with his wife, to get her perspective. Rukhy and I arranged to meet in her small, spotless kitchen one summer afternoon. After looming so large in my conversations with Yisroel, Rukhy was surprisingly young. A petite matron who barely took a breath during our four-hour conversation, she had bright blue eyes and wore a matching turban, something many Hasidic women wear to relax at home.

Spending time with her was fascinating and troubling. Too often she asked me for advice or reassurance that I was not qualified to give. Despite setting the parameters explicitly at the outset of our interview that I could not share information from her husband's interview, she asked, for example, if he had happened to mention that he still loved her. She wanted me to confirm that he had a "heart of gold," that he put her and the kids above everything. I had no problem truthfully agreeing with any of this, to which she replied, "Yes, I think so, but I always want to hear it from someone else, because of his loss of belief."

Initially, her husband's loss of belief had rattled her own, but eventually, after numerous visits to multiple therapists, activists, and rabbis, it was her uncle, a respected rabbi, who helped her find her own strong belief. She described debating with her husband at first, both because she was curious and because she wanted to understand his motivations. She said, "Although I would want to debate, I know it's not good . . . I want the closeness and I'm curious . . . but lately I'm trying not to get pulled." Rukhy described her own conflicted feelings toward Yisroel, "I felt he made me weak in my *emuna* . . . I have my own life, my own *emuna* . . . why do I have to be weaker because of him? And I felt like, 'who gave him permission?'" In effect, Rukhy replaced her husband's authority with her uncle's, one authoritative man for another whose authority was compromised. Nevertheless, out of this relationship she was able to claim authority for her own belief. As she said, "I learned I cannot rely on my husband, that I should not, in spirituality."[8]

Her uncle and another rabbi she spoke with advised her to just "love Yisroel" and to stop watching him all the time, worrying that he might sin. Rukhy, though, could not stop trying to understand why Yisroel had lost his belief. She told me that for a time she had worried that she was to blame because she was too "modern." Unlike her sisters, she wore makeup and lighter seamed stockings and even had a smartphone. Perhaps Yisroel's doubt was all a punishment for her inability to give up certain desires, she suggested. At the same time, she was angry that Yisroel had had to go so far. "I am not some *frummy* [overly pious woman]," she wanted me to know, "Why couldn't he have become a little more modern, but still believed?" They had been on the same page when they had stood under the wedding canopy together, she remembered sadly. Eventually she decided, with her uncle's help, that "100 percent it doesn't have to do with me," though she remained anxious and sad about her new challenges.

Over time, she decided that she should be confident enough in her own beliefs. As she said, "I became more *frum* because I see this is what I want . . . I made up my mind. I'm here. My heart belongs here." Rukhy qualified her decision to remain a believer. She explained to me that even though some rules did not make sense to her, like shaving her head under her wig, she had decided they did not bother her enough to actually stop. Her decision made her feel proud of her own strength. She told her uncle that she wished her mother, whom she still wanted to please, knew how strong she was. Even though she was "modern" and had a husband that "doesn't believe," she was still "keeping her family together."

But keeping her husband's secret from her friends, family, and her children was hard. To tell anyone else would be an admission of failure, a humiliation. Rukhy described sharing such "sensitive" information as "below her dignity." I took this to mean that she would be on the receiving end of others' pity; she would be a *nebekh* (a pity case, a loser). However, this meant that she had almost no one to confide in besides her uncle. Rukhy told him, "I'm carrying a burden until forever." Nobody knew, she said, and she told her husband that she was going to go to her grave with this secret. She dreamed of telling her favorite cousin or her eldest daughter, who was close to her father. Instead, she pressed her hand to her heart and said, "It stays here."

Her uncle had advised Rukhy and Yisroel to make some ground rules in their home life. Yisroel should not be permitted to talk to the children about certain topics or break Jewish law in front of them. Her uncle gave her the right to speak firmly to him if he did. Rukhy was worried, though, that the mixed messages Yisroel sometimes sent to the children confused them, which for ultra-Orthodox children was believed to be dangerous to their faith. She told me how much she pitied her children for having a father who was "off."

Rukhy eventually found some comfort in the explanation her uncle had given her for her situation. Her husband, he said, had lost his belief because he was "sick," something was wrong with his brain. In his efforts to convince Rukhy to stay with her husband, he said, "If your husband had cancer, would you leave him?" Believing her husband to have what she called a "funny brain," made Rukhy feel that she was less morally compromised by staying. Indeed, that explanation convinced her that she was doing the right thing.

And yet, Rukhy continued to worry, grieving at how different she and her husband had become. Unlike him, she believed in the afterlife. But would she and Yisroel end up there together? As I was packing up my bag to go home, she quietly told me:

I'm thinking, how will *gan eydn* be if he's like that, and I'm worrying. But I shouldn't worry because *hashem* [God] knows. Because if he gave it to me, it's his business not mine. I, how's it called in English? *Ikh farloz zikh af bashefer*, I'm leaning on God. I'm relying on him.

There's a Crack in Everything / That's How the Light Gets in (Leonard Cohen)

As I left Rukhy's house and made my way to the subway, I thought about how her husband's life-changing doubt had forced her into the position of making her own decisions about religious authority and truth. Yisroel's rejection of ultra-Orthodox rabbinic authority had led her to recommit herself to believing and upholding the system, even if everything did not always make sense to her, or she fell short of her religious obligations. Sometimes, she confessed to me, she fell asleep before she finished praying. She knew she shouldn't, but she kept wearing lipstick and using her smartphone in private. She was determined, however, to keep trying to do what she had decided was the right thing. Even though that decision, legitimized by her rabbi uncle, separated her from her beloved husband and made her the religious authority at home, a state of affairs that turned her moral world upside down.

During our afternoon together, Rukhy had asked me, like teenage Leyeh had, to imagine how I would feel if my husband suddenly became religious. As I did, I began to understand the everyday conflicts that kind of change would entail. My husband, Adam, would no longer eat the food I cooked or even eat in our apartment; he might ask me to change how I dressed or to go to synagogue with him on Saturday mornings when I much preferred going for a run. I was not interested in that kind of journey, and he would undoubtedly have to go it alone. Even worse, I knew that he and I would eventually come to hold different understandings of the very nature of the world, politically, socially, ethically, and religiously. And that would separate us. People change in marriage all the time. They change what they want or how they see the world and themselves. But what happens when someone you love, a spouse or a child, embraces a radically distinct way of understanding humanity and themselves? Can you support someone who you think is morally wrong? Can love be maintained across the divide of what have become different moral world views? These are questions double lifers, ultra-Orthodox rabbis, and religious therapists are all struggling with, but they have, I think, universal resonance.

Dramatic personal changes come with shifting alignments to sources of authority. For example, when Yisroel rejected the truth of divine revelation, he also rejected the entire way of life that had been built to live out that truth. Eventually, as he came to believe in the authority of science instead, he felt at sea, without a sense of purpose. When he rejected the authority of ultra-Orthodoxy, he also lost his moral compass. Like Yisroel, individuals can decide to choose a way of life that aligns them with different authorities than those of their families. Children, for example, grow up to inhabit sexualities, political positions, careers, or marriages that their parents or extended families don't approve of or worse. However, these kinds of personal changes have a very different valence in religiously orthodox communities. I remember a Hasidic friend, a very pious woman, who told me, "In the secular world your family doesn't obligate you to anything and your community. You could have grown up, moved to Alaska and become a hermit and you'll just be the funny uncle at the Christmas party. But here, there is so much more weighing on the conformity."[9] Among the ultra-Orthodox, where there is one authoritative truth, publicly rejecting the system or doubting its religious authorities can be tantamount to heresy, and certainly a death knell for hopes of any arranged marriages, the point where families reproduce themselves. For those living double lives, morally constrained from living their changing beliefs openly because of familial loyalties and perhaps fear of the unknown, there were consequences and costs for entire families.

Ultimately, the ultra-Orthodox crisis of authority and the ethical predicaments of double lifers, though so unique in many ways, speak to broadly human concerns in the digital age. These include shared moral endeavors in families and the consequences when a family member changes belief, with the cultural and political effects that follow. I think of Menashe, who wrote on WhatsAppville Yinglish that he had played Leonard Cohen's "Hallelujah" for his children on the piano. His son sang the song for the rest of the day at the top of his lungs, though Menashe told us he had hoped he wouldn't sing it in yeshiva the next day, with its sexy lyrics about biblical King David and the forbidden Batsheva, who "tied him to a chair and made him sing the hallelujah." When his son later that day changed the refrain to "hallelu*kah*," Menashe mused that perhaps his wife had told him to at least stop singing "Yah," (God's Hebrew name in that Gentile word, "hallelu*jah*"). A secular song with biblical allusions taken up by a double lifer, taught to his son, and made a little more kosher by his still-religious mother. Who knows how or where these interactions will go?

The stories of those living double lives and those who minister to them tell us about the historical and cultural vicissitudes of faith and doubt, especially when individual doubt expressed publicly with others has the potential to provoke wider social change. There are ethical dilemmas in the intimacy of families that come from the moral burden of dramatically rejecting what you were reared to believe. And there is the potential of a new medium and its affordances to provoke struggles over authority, changing sociality and interiority in unexpected ways and with unexpected consequences. While these were dynamics among ultra-Orthodox Jews in twenty-first-century New York, they are surely relevant for all of us who confront flexible morality as we strive to live our truths.

APPENDIX

What You Need to Know about
Ultra-Orthodox Jewish Languages

Jewish Multilingualism

Ultra-Orthodox Jewish communities today are multilingual, as religious Jews have been for millennia. Their multilingualism can be defined as "triglossia," meaning their linguistic repertoire includes three languages, each used for a distinctive communal activity:[1] (a) *loshn koydesh* (holy language; ancient Hebrew and Aramaic) is the language of the Torah and Talmud, used for prayer and religious study; (b) A Jewish language, such as Yiddish or Ladino, is spoken and written as a vernacular or everyday language among Jews; (c) A "coterritorial" language, such as English or Polish, is used for communicating with non-Jews in the wider state or empire where Jews lived and among themselves too. *Loshn koydesh* is considered a sacred language and has remained constant over time and space, distinctive from other forms of Hebrew, including Modern Hebrew in Israel (*ivrit*). In contrast, Jewish vernaculars and coterritorial languages have changed as Jews settled in different places. Examples of just a few Jewish vernaculars beyond Yiddish or Ladino include Judeo-Arabic and Judeo-Greek spoken in areas where the coterritorial languages have been respectively Arabic and Greek.

In the post–World War II United States, in addition to reading, praying, and studying *loshn koydesh,* some ultra-Orthodox Jews (Hasidim) speak and read in Yiddish (Yid=Jew, Yiddish=Jewish), a language that developed initially during contact between Jews and Gentiles living along the Rhine beginning in the year 1000. As Jews migrated east over hundreds of years throughout Europe, Yiddish expanded to include linguistic elements from wherever they settled, though it remained written in the Hebrew alphabet.

The major components of Yiddish are *loshn koydesh*, Germanic, and Slavic languages. In the United States, the Yiddish of Hasidic Jews has acquired a great deal of English, too, though it generally remains written in the Hebrew alphabet.[2]

Other ultra-Orthodox communities (the Yeshivish) in the contemporary United States use a different Jewish language, Yeshivish English: a variety of English written in the English alphabet that incorporates Yiddish and *loshn koydesh* words and expressions. An example of Yeshivish English is the expression, "I'll eat by you," where the use of "by you" is a direct translation from the Yiddish construction, *Ikh'l esn bay dir*, meaning, "I'll eat at your house." Yeshivish English can be more or less intelligible to speakers of Standard English, depending on how much or how little Yiddish and *loshn koydesh* are integrated.

Triglossia is shaped by gendered schooling among the ultra-Orthodox, with boys and girls learning and using these three languages differently. All ultra-Orthodox boys learn to read *loshn koydesh* in private religious schools. For Yeshivish boys, the language of instruction and discussion of *loshn koydesh* texts is Yeshivish English. In Hasidic schools, in contrast, the language of instruction and discussion is Hasidic Yiddish, Yiddish with *loshn koydesh* and English components. Some Hasidic schools offer boys very little secular education, and boys may not speak or write much English through adulthood.

In contrast, private Jewish schools for girls are divided into religious and secular studies in the morning and the afternoon. In their religious studies Yeshivish and Hasidic girls learn to read *loshn koydesh,* too, but their religious study is much less extensive than for boys, and does not include Talmud study. For Yeshivish girls the language of instruction is Yeshivish English or Standard English.[3] In Hasidic schools, girls are taught in Yiddish in the mornings for religious subjects and English in the afternoon for "secular" subjects. Some girls' schools teach basic Yiddish grammar and literacy as well. At home, many Hasidic families speak a variety of Yiddish, but even within families, girls and women often speak a Hasidic variety of English (English mixed with Yiddish and *loshn koydesh*) and boys and men speak Hasidic Yiddish (Yiddish mixed with English and *loshn koydesh*). Hasidic Jews often call their spoken, Yiddish-inflected variety of English, "Yinglish" (playing, of course, on the term "Spanglish").

Both Yeshivish and Yinglish are part of a broader ultra-Orthodox project of recovering a sacred Jewish spark from a Gentile medium and making it Jewish. English, for example, is transformed into an ultra-Orthodox Jewish language by integrating the sounds, orthographies, and words of Yiddish and *loshn koydesh*. Changing the form of a language or any other secular object, a hemline of a skirt, a melody or a storyline, for example, uplifts the non-Jewish medium and makes it kosher.[4]

Transcription and Translation Conventions

In this book, Yiddish and *loshn koydesh* terms are italicized, transliterated and translated in parentheses as they appear once per chapter, to make reading easier. I have also included a glossary after this appendix as a reference for key terms in *loshn koydesh*, Yeshivish, and Yiddish. When Yiddish or *loshn koydesh* appear in a digital text or post, I leave them as originally rendered by the author, which is rarely italicized and may use a different orthography than my transliteration or incorporate multiple alphabets. Writers on social media or blogs generally did not translate Jewish terms and concepts into English at all, hinting that their primary audiences were other ultra-Orthodox Jews. In these cases, I note where I added my own translations in brackets.

Readers will therefore experience orthographic variation throughout this book, since transcribing Hasidic Yiddish from its Hebrew alphabet into the English alphabet can be a challenge given the diversity of speakers and limited Hasidic Yiddish standardization. Hasidic Jews speak different regional dialects of Yiddish, and in general there is little concern with standardization of Yiddish spelling, transcription, or grammatical correctness in either Hebrew or English alphabets. I decided to transcribe Yiddish from its Hebrew alphabet using a modified YIVO Institute for Jewish Research system, which differs from some of the few conventionalized Hasidic spellings for Yiddish and *loshn koydesh* words. For example, ultra-Orthodox Jews (Hasidic and Yeshivish) generally write "ch" for the sound of *Ch*anukah or Ru*ch*el (the woman's name, Rachel); in contrast and in order to be clearer to English speakers, I use "kh" to write *Kh*anuka and Ru*kh*el. Another English-language convention I also adopted for readability is the conventional "Hasidic" instead of "Chassidic," as well as adding double consonants to transliterate words such as *Yiddishkayt* or *Shabbes*.

In my transcriptions of spoken language I have mostly chosen a single rendering of Yiddish and *loshn koydesh* words. I do this to make reading easier, even though this may not always accurately reflect the diversity of spoken language. For example, an important word in this book is *emuna* (belief). The *loshn koydesh* word is written as אמונה in the Hebrew alphabet. When this word is spoken it is pronounced differently in different communities based on regional variations. For example, Hasidic Jews, especially Hungarian Hasidim, say, *emine* (e-MIN-a). Israeli Hebrew speakers use the Sephardic pronunciation and say, *emunah* (e-moo-NA).

Yeshivish and Modern Orthodox therapists and life coaches most often said, *emuna* (e-MOO-na).

A SELECTIVE GUIDE TO YIDDISH PRONUNCIATION
AND TRANSCRIPTION

a	similar to a in "father"
u	similar to oo in "boot" but may also be like oo in "cook"
e	similar to e in "get"
i	similar to ee in "feet" or i in "big"
ou	similar to ow in "low"
oy	similar to oy in "boy"
ay	similar to i in "fine"
ey	similar to e in "hey"
dzh	similar to g in "George" or j in "Jessica"
zh	similar to s in "measure"
kh	like the German ch in "Bach"
tsh	like ch in "church"
ts	like ts in "cats"
r	produced by tapping the tip of the tongue to the roof of the mouth, similar to producing the English "udder" or "utter."

Three Notes

1) Some Yiddish syllables have no vowels. At the end of a word a cluster of consonants ending in "l" or "n" constitute a syllable. For example, the word for language, *loshn,* has two syllables: lu-shn or lo-shn.

2) An "e" at the end of a Yiddish word is not silent, but is pronounced as a short English "e," which is sometimes written in English as "eh." For example, the Yiddish word for a difficult question, *kasha,* is pronounced ka-sha, rhyming with "Sasha." Again, for ease of reading, when a word ends with an "e" in Yiddish I generally use an "a." For example, my transcription of the word for faith, is *emuna,* not *emune* or *emunah,* which some community members write. A few exceptions to facilitate recognition include my spelling of the name Leyeh (two syllables Ley-eh) and Toyre and Kave Shtibl.

3) Some words inhabit both English and Yiddish simultaneously. For example, the word "bum" (feminine, *bumte*) has become part of American Hasidic Yiddish, with the feminine incorporating a Yiddish gender marker (-te). I decided not to italicize "bum" simply because the phonology is the same as English. I do italicize *bumte* though because an English speaker would not understand the term. Note that *bumte* is two syllables (bum-te).

GLOSSARY

Agudas Yisroel: Orthodox Jewry's national umbrella organization that is guided by a council of Torah sages (Moetses Gedolei Hatorah).

Apikoyrus (plural, apikorsim): a skeptic, someone who denigrates the sages/rabbis, reads heretical literature, rejects specific doctrines. From the Greek, Epicurean.

Askn (plural, askonim): a self-appointed activist in an ultra-Orthodox community.

Bitl toyre: a waste of time, specifically time that could have been spent by men and boys studying Torah.

Bum (fem. bumte): an ultra-Orthodox Jew who is lax with observance and just wants to have a good time. Bums do not necessarily challenge the system. They are simply too lazy or selfish to take on the obligations of religious stringency. See also tuna baygel.

Emuna: faith, belief, trust in God.

Frum: religious, observant.

Glitsh: slip or slide.

Hasidic Judaism: a spiritual revival movement founded in the eighteenth century in contemporary Ukraine, which spread throughout eastern Europe. Hasidic Judaism was a radical movement for its time and emphasized individualized connection to God. Decimated in the Holocaust, Hasidic Jews rebuilt their communities worldwide. Each Hasidic community known as a court (*hoyf*) is led by a rebbe, who acts as an intermediary between his Hasidim (male adherents) and God. Courts are named after their eastern European country or town of origin, and leadership is inherited through male lines of descent.

Haskalah: Jewish Enlightenment, a mid-eighteenth-century to mid- to late nineteenth-century intellectual movement among central and eastern European Jews. Inspired by the European Enlightenment, the Jewish Enlighteners (*maskilim*) attempted to both preserve and renew Judaism, espousing rationalism, liberalism, and freedom.

Haymish: homey, implying ultra-Orthodox sensibilities and tastes.
Kalt tse yiddishkayt: cool to Judaism, a distancing from Judaism, where religious practices cease to create feelings of warmth (*varemkayt*) and closeness to God and community.
Kfira: heresy.
Klal Yisroel: the Jewish people, meaning Jews all over the world.
Koyfer (plural, kofrim): a heretic, denying God or Torah.
Loshn koydesh: holy language, the ancient Hebrew and Aramaic used in the Torah and its commentaries. *Loshn koydesh* is distinct from other variants of Hebrew, including the language in in Israel (*ivrit*) and the Hebrew *maskilim* used.
Maskil (plural, maskilim): an adherent of the Haskalah, the Jewish Enlightenment (see above). *Maskilim* created a modern, secular form of Hebrew in their writings and publications and fought vigorously against the growing Hasidic movement and the Yiddish language.
Matn toyre: God's revelation of the Torah to Moses and the Jews standing at Mount Sinai.
Mesoyra: Jewish tradition handed down from parents to children.
Mitsva (plural, mitsves): commandments. There are 613 commandments. 248 are positive (to do) and 365 are negative (not to do).
Mosdos: Ultra-Orthodox schools and institutions of learning.
Mussar: ethical and philosophical writings of nineteenth-century Lithuanian Jews.
Ofgeklert: open-minded, enlightened.
OTD: off the *derekh* (path), those who leave their Orthodox Jewish communities.
Peyos: side curls worn by ultra-Orthodox men.
Pnimiyus/khitsoynius: theological terms referring to the interior or exterior of an object or person.
Rabbi: Jewish scholar and teacher.
Rebbe: male leader of a Hasidic sect.
Rov: A prominent rabbi who advises on issues of Jewish law.
Sheytel: Wigs worn by married ultra-Orthodox women, for whom exposing their hair is forbidden except to their husbands.
Shtraymel: a high fur hat worn by Hasidic married men on holidays and the Sabbath.
Talmud: A key text in Rabbinic Judaism, the Talmud provides guidance on Jewish religious law and theology. The Talmud is composed of both the Mishnah (oral law) and the Gemora (commentary on the Mishnah, the Hebrew Bible, and other writings).
Tayves: lust, urges.
Toyre (Torah): The five books of Moses, the Pentateuch.
Tsnius: modesty.

Tuna Baygel (tuna beigel, tuna bagel): Similar to a bum. A tuna baygel is an ultra-Orthodox Jew who gives in to his lusts for pleasure, trying to be more like Gentiles. Tell-tale signs of a tuna baygel include wearing colored instead of white button-down shirts, gelling sidecurls, tucking them under a baseball hat, and generally looking less distinctively Jewish. However, a tuna baygel's true Hasidic background, with limited English fluency, is exposed when he orders a tuna salad sandwich on a bagel, using the Hasidic Yiddish pronunciation to say "baygel" instead of "bagel."

Vaad ha-tsnius: a shadowy, self-appointed committee that enforces communal practices more generally, but especially women's modesty, sometimes violently.

Yeshiva/kollel: Orthodox Jewish institutions of higher men's learning. Yeshivas are the equivalents of middle and high schools, while *kollels* are post-high school.

Yeshivish or Litvish: Ultra-Orthodox Jews who follow the nineteenth-century traditions of the Lithuanian yeshivas. In their opposition to the contemporaneous Hasidic movement, these observant Jews were also called *misnagdim* (those against, i.e., against Hasidim).

Yeytser hora: inclination for evil, innate at birth.

Yeytser hatov: inclination for good, develops only after bar or bat mitzvah age.

Yiddish: a postexilic Jewish language that developed during contact between Jews and Gentiles in different areas of Europe over hundreds of years of migration and resettlement. The three major components of Yiddish are *loshn koydesh*, Germanic, and Slavic languages. Yiddish is generally written in the Hebrew alphabet, although there are English transliterations (see appendix).

NOTES

Chapter 1: Life-Changing Doubt, the Internet, and a Crisis of Authority

1. Talal Asad. *Genealogies of Religion.*
2. An online survey sponsored by Footsteps, a nonprofit organization supporting ultra-Orthdox Jews who are questioning or who leave, reported that out of 885 respondents, 33 percent (290 respondents) claimed they were living double lives (Trencher 2016). However, given the problematic of self-reporting, it is unclear if these statistics are reliable. My sense is that even if the numbers of those living double lives are not very large, there is a growing concern about them and this itself merits investigation.
3. Statistics are from the Berman Jewish Policy Archive's 2011/2012 Jewish community population study. https://www.bjpa.org/search-results /publication/14341 and from the 2013 Pew Research Center's "A Portrait of Jewish Americans." https://www.pewforum.org/2015/08/26/a-portrait-of -american-orthodox-jews/
4. Anthropologists of religion of late have studied religious life through materiality, the body, the senses, and politics (e.g., Mahmood 2005; Hirschkind 2006; Keane 2007). This important body of work provoked new questions and directions. As so often happens, more recently and in response, some argued that these approaches overemphasized discipline and individual ethical cultivation at the expense of religious institutions (e.g., Ammerman 2016; Handman 2017). Others noted that with the focus almost exclusively on religious study, texts, and ritual, we had missed the ways that aspirations for piety might occur simultaneously with other less transcendent desires and dreams (e.g., Liberatore 2015; Mittemaier 2012; Schielke 2012). Particularly relevant for this book are those who suggest that there has not been enough attention to uncertainty, failure, skepticism, and religious doubt over the course of the lifecycle and beyond, though there have been exceptions (e.g., Engelke 2005; Keane 2003; Pelkmans 2014).

5. Tanya Luhrmann. *When God Talks Back.*
6. Mathijs Pelkmans. *The Ethnography of Doubt.* This edited volume lays out what an ethnography of "lived doubt" might include. I originally used the idea of lived doubt, because it reminded me of a lived religion approach, although Pelkmans does not cite that literature. Lived religion comes out of religious studies and sociology and includes the work, for example, of Robert Orsi, Nancy Ammerman, and Courtney Bender. I have decided to use the term "life-changing doubt," which more accurately captures the case of those living double lives, while distinguishing between different types of doubt.
7. Philip Salim Francis. *When Art Disrupts Religion.*
8. Hella Winston describes the process of leaving and living a double life in *Unchosen: The Hidden Lives of Hasidic Rebels,* as does Lynn Davidman in *Becoming Unorthodox.* E. Marshall Brooks in *Disenchanted Lives* writes about Mormons who experience crises of faith.
9. Medium/media are tricky words with a diversity of disciplinary histories and attendant meanings. Anthropologist Patrick Eisenlohr (2011) notes a tension in contemporary anthropological thinking about media, especially new media and the circulation of culture: on the one hand, a medium may be thought of as any material object that stands between humans and their world, including the body, language, or any other form of technology. On the other hand, a medium and its material properties may also creatively shape worlds for humans, influencing communication, and social and political arrangements. The ultra-Orthodox crisis of authority offers a grounded case study to explore this tension. See chapter 2 for a definition of mediation.
10. Faranak Margolese. *Off the Derech.* Margolese, an observant Jew, wrote this prescriptive book in an attempt to understand why some leave Orthodox Judaism. The book was enthusiastically recommended to me by several religious therapists, and it even included letters of support (*haskamas*) from several prominent rabbis. Margolese uses the book as a platform to make an argument for returning to a more authentic Judaism, one that is about emotional connection to God, rather than a focus on *halakhic* (Jewish law) practice.
11. See Henry Goldschmidt, *Race and Religion among the Chosen Peoples of Crown Heights.* There is press coverage of upstate (New York) battles over school districting, funding, and real estate, a topic that could surely use more research.
12. Jeffrey Blutinger suggests that in the eighteenth century the term "Orthodox" was used by German Enlighteners for Jews and Christians who were against the Enlightenment. It was only in the nineteenth century that the term was used as a religious denomination for Jews exclusively. There is a rich literature on histories of both the Hasidic and the Yeshivish. See, for

example, the classics, such as Hundert 1991; Rosman 1996, or more recent work such as Biale et al. 2018.

13. Ashkenazic Jews lived for over a thousand years in western and then eastern Europe. Mizrachi and Sephardic Jews, in contrast, include diasporas from the Mediterranean, North Africa, and the Middle East.

14. Hasidic Jews today, as they were in eastern Europe, continue to be led by a rebbe, a divine mediator. Each Hasidic court (*hoyf*) has its own schools, synagogues, and other ritual institutions. Hasidic-dominated neighborhoods in New York include Williamsburg, Borough Park, and upstate Palm Tree (formerly Kiryas Yoel). Those who are Yeshivish, in contrast, follow prominent rabbis who are affiliated with a yeshiva, a Jewish institution of higher learning. Lakewood, New Jersey, is a well-known stronghold for Yeshivish Jews as is Flatbush, Brooklyn. There are a range of religious stringencies among Yeshivish Jews; however, compared to Hasidic Jews, the Yeshivish generally have more flexibility in terms of participation in the secular world. There is a rich ethnographic literature on both the Yeshivish and Hasidic Jews in New York and Israel (see, for example, El-Or 1994, 2004; Goldschmidt 2005; Kranzler 1995; Levine 2005; Mintz 1968, 1993; Poll 2006; Stadler 2010, among others).

15. I used "nonliberal" in most of my own earlier writing, but found that it was confusing for nonacademics and required too much historical contextualizing to be that helpful. The term "fundamentalism" has acquired racist undertones, especially since 9/11. *Haredi*, a Hebrew term meaning "those who tremble (before God)," is used most often in Israel, although it is commonly used by Jewish studies scholars, and so has spread to some ultra-Orthodox Jews in the United States too. I feel, however, that the Hebrew term precludes comparison with other religious traditions and minimizes differences between Israeli and North American ultra-Orthodox, both of which have led to a marginalization of Jewish studies scholarship in anthropology more widely.

16. See Ayala Fader. "The Counterpublic of the J(ewish)Blogosphere."

17. See Samuel Heilman, *Who Will Lead Us?*, for a discussion of leadership among Hasidic Jews.

18. For example, see Heilman 2006; Heilman and Friedman 2012; Mintz 1993; Rubin 1997.

19. Ayala Fader. "Is the Internet the Problem?"

20. Ayala Fader. "Nonliberal Jewish Women's Audiocassette Lectures in Brooklyn."

21. Graham Jones. "Secrecy."

22. There is a rich body of literature on the politics of fieldwork in religiously orthodox contexts. See, for example, Harding 2000; Belcove-Shalin 1995; Kugelmas 1988; Stadler 2010, among others.

23. Studies of Hasidim have included Bobover, Lubavitcher, and Satmar groups

(e.g., see Fader 2009; Fishman 2005; Rubin 1972; 1997). Studies of the Yeshivish include Finkelman 2011, in Israel; and Helmreich 1980, in New York.

24. Tom Boellstorff, *Second Life*. For a review of digital anthropology see Coleman 2010.

Chapter 2: The Jewish Blogosphere and the Heretical Counterpublic

1. *Ami Magazine*, 2011.
2. Immanuel Etkes, "Haskalah."
3. Angela Zito, "Culture."
4. For discussions of counterpublics and publics see Cody 2014; Fraser 1990; Warner 2002.
5. The small body of scholarship on Orthodox Jewish bloggers in North America and Israel finds that while blogging created spaces for self-expression, the authority of the rabbinical establishment was not directly challenged. See, for example, Baumel-Schwartz 2009; Campbell and Golan 2010; Lev-On and Neriya-Ben Shachar 2011; Lieber 2010.
6. Ilana Gershon and Paul Manning note that the introduction of a new medium can change communication itself. The medium of language used on a new technology of communication can be equally significant, as Janet McIntosh notes, "Code switching may confer certain qualities onto speakers, suggesting that the medium may be as transformative as the message" (2005, p.1941).
7. Hussein Ali Agrama, "Ethics, Authority, Tradition." Agrama suggests exploring not only why religious authority becomes binding to people, but how. He focuses on interactions between muftis and petitioners in Egypt, suggesting that religious authority is negotiated through shared conceptions of time and tradition that shape ideas about people and their sensibilities. My focus, in contrast, are the contexts and reasons why religious leadership loses its authority to bind. The Jblogs that formed a heretical public, show that shared notions of time, tradition, and persons can become the grounds for rejecting religious authority.
8. Of course, this is a play on Marshall McLuhan's famous phrase, found in *Understanding Media*.
9. See Bambi Schieffelin, Kathryn Woolard and and Paul Kroskrity, *Language Ideologies*.
10. Marcus Moseley, "Autobiography and Memoir." See also Jeffrey Shandler, *Awakening Lives*.
11. Recent research, though, has recovered examples of women who gained access to Enlightenment ideas through their reading in non-Jewish languages, such as Russian, Polish, or German. See for example, Tova Cohen's "Por-

trait of the Maskilah as a Young Woman," or Iris Parush's *Women Readers as Agents of Social Change.*

12. Marcus Moseley, "Autobiography and Memoir."

13. Jewish Enlighteners' negative attitudes to Yiddish were directly related to their anxieties at the rise of the Hasidic movement. One way that Hasidism spread so quickly was through the publication of Yiddish stories and sermons about and by Hasidic rebbes.

14. Ilana Gershon attributes the term to psychologist James Gibson (1986).

15. Ken Moss, "Printing and Publishing."

16. Adam Reed describes how technological innovations made blogging much more accessible to anyone with a computer, using his case study of bloggers in London in "My Blog Is Me."

17. http://zootorah.com/controversy/.

18. The Kuzari proof makes a case for the undeniable truth of the revelation at Sinai. The argument goes that God revealed the Torah to 600,000 Jews standing at Mount Sinai in a public setting. Such a large number of eyewitnesses could not have made up the revelation and passed it on to successive generations. Thus, it is true.

19. Michael Warner, *Publics and Counterpublics*, 68.

20. Warner, *Publics and Counterpublics,* 52, 57.

21. Webb Keane, *Christian Moderns.*

22. Janet McIntosh (2005) calls this process "linguistic transfer." In the ultra-Orthodox case, the language ideology of sacred *loshn koydesh* casts some of its holiness onto Yiddish, the language used to interpret *loshn koydesh.* Yiddish simultaneously indexes memories of a lost pre-Holocaust European past.

23. Psalm 1:1: "Blessed is the man who walks not in the counsel of the wicked, nor stands in the way of sinners, nor sits in the seat of scoffers."

24. Janet McIntosh (2005) describes linguistic essentialism as a linguistic equivalent to religious essentialism. In this case, linguistic essentialism is used to challenge religious essentialism through parody.

25. All the translations from Yiddish are by Zachary Sholem Berger, 2009 and 2014. Zacharysholemberger@Blogspot.com.

26. In *Mitzvah Girls* I suggest a number of different reasons why community members were not concerned with linguistic purity or standardization. These included issues of gender, generation, and diversity of Jewish ultra-Orthodoxy. Mothers of girls I worked with emphasized "ways of talking" rather than which language was chosen, Yiddish or English.

27. I describe Hasidic language ideologies and language use in *Mitzvah Girls.*

28. The reference to "dry bones coming alive" is from "The Valley of Dry Bones" prophecy, Ezekiel 37. Thanks to Shimon Steinmetz for the reference.

29. http://www.kaveshtiebel.com/viewtopic.php?f=24&t=2123.

30. Nicholas Harkness and Lily Chumley (2014) and Susan Gal (2013) describe Peirce's notion of *quale*, which is useful to this analysis. Quale are signs that incorporate sensory experiences across semiotic registers. For example, the quality of *haymish*-ness, the sensual aspects of comfortable ultra-Orthodox familiarity, includes *haymish* food, music, people, language, dress, style of home furnishings, and religious practice. *Haymish*-ness was a way to experience the moral distinction between Orthodox Jews and others, who include other Jews (not religious, not Ashkenazic, not ultra-Orthodox) and Gentiles.

31. Carmel Vaisman, "Beautiful Script," 69.

32. Ayala Fader, "The Counterpublic of the J(Blogosphere)."

33. Shulem Deen, *All Who Go Do Not Return*.

34. The food is kosher, but the restaurant stays open on the Sabbath so they do not have a reputable *hekhsher* (certificate of approval).

35. *Times of Israel*, 2012.

36. *Matzav*, 2014, "The Truth about Those Who Feed the Anti-Frum Bloggers." The author is Rafael Gebrili. https://matzav.com/the-truth-about-those-who-feed-the-anti-frum-bloggers/

37. Birgit Meyer, "Mediation and Immediacy."

38. Ilana Gershon and Paul Manning, "Language and Media."

39. Faye Ginsburg, Lila Abu-Lughod and Brian Larkin, *Media Worlds*, 19

40. Hannah Arendt, *On Violence*, 45.

41. Annabelle Sreberny and Gholam Khiabany, *Blogistan*, 59.

42. https://www.washingtonpost.com/news/monkey-cage/wp/2014/04/11/the-decline-of-irans-blogestan/?utm_term=.43d6ba814a3c.

43. Jon Bialecki, n.d.

Chapter 3: Ultra-Orthodox Rabbis versus the Internet

1. Though I use the terms double lifers did, I want to acknowledge the diversity of rabbinic positions on religious stringencies and leniencies that shaped specific rulings on access to media and technological innovations. Further, these differences among rabbis gave individuals and their families a certain flexibility in making decisions. For example, anthropologist Lea Taragin-Zeller (2019) has shown how Orthodox couples in Israel making decisions about family planning choose certain rabbis they know in advance will give them the decision about birth control that they want.

2. For more on the Jewish family, see Jonathan Boyarin, *Jewish Families*.

3. Talal Asad, *Genealogies of Religion*.

4. Dr. Rosenberg posted on the Ruach listserv that Rav Kook identified two approaches to religious doubt articulated by major rabbis, one that embraced simple faith (*emuna peshuta*) and another that did not. Dr. Rosen-

berg summarized that the more normative view "accepts that there are serious doubts and questions that Jews face in their emuna [faith] . . . and that this approach does not cherish emuna peshuta [simple faith]." He contrasted that view to what he called the "not mainstream" Jewish view. From this perspective simple faith is highly valued and doubt is frowned upon. He notes, "In some communities, doubts are forbidden and are considered to be the effect of *shedim* [demons] or the result of not being careful enough with kashrus or other ritual observances."

5. See for example, Birgit Meyer, *Religion in the Public Sphere.*
6. Matthew Engelke, *A Problem of Presence.*
7. Patrick Eisenlohr, "What Is a Medium?"
8. Ayala Fader, *Mitzvah Girls*, 36–41.
9. Gerson Bacon, http://www.yivoencyclopedia.org/article.aspx/Daas _Toyre.
10. See Summerson Carr, *Scripting Addiction*, for a discussion of contemporary understandings of addiction and wellness.
11. The name GYE invokes the more general concept of *shmiras eynayim* (guarding one's eyes), whereby Orthodox and ultra-Orthodox Jews are expected to discipline themselves from exposure to images or interactions that could lead to sinful thoughts or deeds. The visual for GYE, two hands forming eyelids, cradling the eye, emphasized that the digital age might require, even more than usual, the helping hands of others.
12. Don Seeman, "Coffee and the Moral Order," 737.
13. Tsuriel Rashi, "The Kosher Cell Phone."
14. http://www.nytimes.com/2012/05/18/nyregion/ultra-orthodox-jews-will -meet-at-citi-field-to-discuss-internet-dangers.html.
15. https://www.timesofisrael.com/rabbis-get-rid-of-the-internet-if-you-know -whats-good-for-you/.
16. Hebrew translations are by Shimon Steinmetz.
17. I did not hear about parallel appeals to Yeshivish women. Perhaps, as a member of my WhatsAppville Yinglish group suggested when I asked, "The *temimes* [simple, innocent] chasm between the sexes we [Hasidim] have, where girls are more *temimesdig* [simple, innocent] than men doesn't exist in the Litvish world." Perhaps, as Shmuel told me, Yeshivish men tended to willingly "opt in" to rabbinic decrees more than Hasidim did. There was also the point Blimi made, that Litvish women were frequently the family breadwinners while their husbands learned, so rabbis could not target women as not needing the internet.
18. "On the merit of righteous women, the Jews were redeemed from Egypt".
19. Ayala Fader, "Nonliberal Jewish Women's Audiocassette Lectures." This was a media ideology (a cultural belief about media and what it is good for) I had heard in other women's inspirational lectures. The words of a sincere

speaker, even if one did not understand them, could enter one's heart and strengthen faith.

20. For a discussion of Hasidic matchmaking see Ayala Fader, *Mitzvah Girls*, chapter 7.

21. https://motherboard.vice.com/en_us/article/8q8k45/kosher-internet -filters.

22. א בעל מסחר וועלכער איז אמת'דיג איבערצייגט אז ס'איז אים א צורך גדול צו האבן א סמארט־ פאון אדער א טעבלעט פאר זיין פרנסה, איז פארפליכטעט זיך צו באניצן נאר מיט אזא כלי וואס איז געפילטערט דורכ'ן ''גדר פילטער'' שע''י קהלתינו הק'.

עס איז ריכטיג אז בעלי מסחר זאלן האבן א באזונדערע כשר'ע סעלפאון, אין צוגאב צו די ביזנעס-סמארטפאון, כדי צו פארמיידן דאס זיך באניצן מיט'ן סמארטפאון—אפילו מיט א פיל־ טער—אין שטוב אדער אין ביהמ''ד, און אוודאי זאל מען בשום אופן דאס נישט איבעגעבן פאר די קינדער.

23. https://www.youtube.com/watch?v=nvj1rq0s9rk.

24. The WhatsAppville Yinglish group called this term "slang," coined by un-married yeshiva students (*bokherim*). It has a number of meanings including disoriented, drunk, stoned, out of it.

Chapter 4: The Morality of a Married Double Life

1. Georg Simmel, *The Sociology of Secrets and of Secret Societies*.
2. Tanya Luhrmann, *Persuasion of the Witch's Craft*, 161.
3. While almost all became more politically progressive, most remained less progressive on the topic of feminism and almost all actively supported Is-rael. I understand support of Israel in particular as a liberalizing move to support the secular state in contrast to some in their ultra-Orthodox com-munities, and as part of an inculcated assumption that the world was antisemitic.
4. The documentary, *One of Us* (2017), similarly recounts gendered struggles over divorce.
5. We see this, for example, in Saba Mahmood's 2005 work on Egyptian wom-en's veiling and religious study as disciplinary practices aimed at becoming closer to God.
6. Didier Fassin, "The Ethical Turn in Anthropology." Fassin also critiques readings of Durkheim that do not acknowledge his sensitivity to the ways that duty or obligation can become something desirable. A reading in that vein might recoup human agency in Durkheim's writings through the con-cept of duty. More recently but along similar lines, Mara Benjamin (2018) elaborates the idea of obligation, while shifting the focus to the family rather than religious texts or rabbinic leadership.
7. Michael Taussig, *Defacement*.
8. The term tuna baygel refers to Hasidic men who try to look and act "cool and modern." However, their limited Hasidic education, particularly their

lack of English fluency, outs them for what they really are (bummy Hasidic Jews). See appendix.

9. http://killingthebuddha.com/mag/confession/raised-by-jews/.

10. Hugh Gusterson, *Nuclear Rites*.

Chapter 5: The Treatment of Doubt

1. Phillip Rieff, *The Triumph of Therapy*.

2. Tanya Erzen, *Straight to Jesus*, 162; for other relevant discussions of the role of the therapeuetic framework and religion see also Yoram Bilu and Yehuda Goodman, "What Does the Soul Say?," and Ellen Herman, *The Romance of Psychiatry*, or Stephania Pandolpho, *Knot of the Soul*.

3. In this model, homosexuality was named as a sickness or an addiction that could be healed by personal effort (discipline) and a healthy relationship with Jesus.

4. See also James Hoesterey, *Rebranding Islam,* and Ayala Fader, "Ultra-Orthodox Jewish Interiority."

5. In fact, the Lubavitcher *mashpia* concept has become increasingly popular with other Hasidic groups.

6. Religious law dictates that a man who does not keep the commandments cannot make the Sabbath blessing over the wine. His very touch would taint the wine and make it nonkosher.

7. Andrew Heinze, "The Americanization of Mussar," 5.

8. Heinze, "The Americanization of Mussar," 9.

9. http://www.timesofisrael.com/topic/nechemya-weberman/.

10. For example, on the online chat site *Yeshiva World-Coffee Room*, someone began a thread asking about master's programs for observant Jews:
A: I'm wondering how frum people deal with the obvious conflicts between the social work code of ethics and Torah?
B: Find a mentor in the field, AND a rav [a rabbinic adviser]. The obvious conflicts include but are not limited to: working in an agency and having to give someone the option to have an abortion, or completely accept any sexual orientation as legitimate plus tons more like examples. December 2009. http://www.theyeshivaworld.com/coffeeroom/topic/social-work -school.

11. For example, https://reliefhelp.org/mental-health-101/types-of-mental -health-providers/.

12. In fact, cognitive behavioral therapy was a particularly easy fit for the *halakhic* (Jewish law) notion that religious practice could cultivate desired faithful interiors, something that Friedman and Yehuda noted (2003) and my own fieldwork supported.

13. See, for example, journalist Batya Unger Sargon's pieces, 2016, 2015.

14. This is the Hebrew acronym for Rabbi Shlomo Yitzchaki, a medieval French

scholar and one of the most prominent commentators on the Talmud and Torah.

15. JONAH was the organization that recently was closed by the State of New Jersey for its breach of contract: it promised to change homosexuals into straight Jews, but was unable to do so. Ruach, in fact, was going to sponsor a seminar on SSA with the deposed head of JONAH invited to speak, until the mainstream media heard about it. The seminar was quietly and quickly cancelled.

16. Tanya Luhrmann, *Between Two Minds*.

17. For a historical discussion of Freud, Jewishness, and the development of psychoanalysis, see Stephen Frosh, "Freud and Jewish Identity."

18. E.g., Michel Foucault, *Discipline and Punish*.

19. See Lila Abu-Lughod, "Do Muslim Women Need Saving," for example, or Nancy Scheper-Hughes, *Death without Weeping*.

Chapter 6: Double-Life Worlds

1. Tanya Luhrmann, *Persuasion of the Witch's Craft*. See also Lilith Mahmud, *The Brotherhood of Freemason Sisters*.

2. In a series of articles for the *Forward*, Judy Brown (under her then-pseudonym, Eishes Chayil) critiqued Hasidic childhood particularly for girls. https://forward.com/author/judy-brown-eishes-chayil/.

3. Pierre Bourdieu, *Outline of a Theory of Practice*.

4. This is something that Lynn Davidman (2014) and Hella Winston (2005) each noted.

5. Sarah Benor makes a similar argument in *Becoming Frum*, for those who return to the faith (BTs), though her argument is more expansive, including changes to the body, material culture, and language.

6. In response to the generative critique of the category of religion with its Protestant legacy of interior belief (Asad 1993, 2003), many turned to the material and sensory dimensions of religion and publics (e.g., Engelke 2012; Houtman & Meyer 2012; Shandler 2017). Those who have addressed language in a framework of religion and media include Eiesenlohr (2009) and Stolow (2010), who have each shown how written/printed and spoken language, for example, religious poetry recorded on cassettes or the rise of an Orthodox Jewish publishing empire, is constitutive of mediated faith, creating distinctive dynamics among the material, the discursive, and the sensual.

7. The categories of niks are real, but the examples are not in order to protect anonymity. Think of them as pseudonymous niks or niks upon niks.

8. These kinds of written interactions created, I think, exactly the kind of public sphere political theorist Jurgen Habermas (1989) described, where the bourgeoisie (well, men) hanging out in coffeehouses, reading and discuss-

ing, created a sense of belonging to the nation-state. Habermas, as many have noted, not only excluded women, but all kinds of others and their languages. Habermas more recently revised the concept of the public sphere to include religion in an important volume edited by Edourdo Mendieta and Jonathan VanAntwerpen (2011).

9. Asch's play written in Yiddish (*Got fun Nekomeh*) in 1907 is about a Jewish brothel owner, who attempts to make himself respectable by commissioning a Torah and marrying off his daughter to a Torah scholar. His daughter, meanwhile, is having a love affair with one of the prostitutes.

10. If a couple signed a "Hasidic upbringing agreement" as part of their divorce proceedings in Jewish religious court, a secular state court might give custody to the parent who remained Hasidic. The issue for the court to decide was around contract violation. For more on "spiritual custody" in cases of divorce and Hasidic upbringing agreements, see Nomi Stolzenberg, "Spiritual Custody."

11. Janet McIntosh, "Mobile Phones and Mipoho's Prophesy."

12. Isaac Bleaman, "Syntactic Variation in Hasidic Yiddish on the Web."

13. Isaac Bleaman, personal communication, May 10, 2018.

14. http://www.kaveshtiebel.com/viewtopic.php?f=24&t=8207.

15. http://www.kaveshtiebel.com/viewtopic.php?f=10&t=8086&p=246551 #p246551.

16. http://kaveshtiebel.com/viewtopic.php?p=129267#p129267.

17. http://www.kaveshtiebel.com/viewtopic.php?f=7&t=3599.

18. Yiddish translator Rose Waldman, personal communication.

19. Ms. Waldman translated a Yiddish poem on KS by "Copernicus" as an example of the one poet's individualized, emotional expression, noting that it rhymed in the original Yiddish. In her translation she chose not to rhyme.

Poverty: A Gift
I am the owner of two things
Burning love and an empty stomach
Both of these things
Smolder and boil
The empty stomach so famished
The great love so searing
I seek a pretty gift
To bequeath to my love
I give my dearest all I own
My love wrapped in my poverty

20. Yiddishists are proponents of secular Yiddish literature and culture, which is modelled on Lithuanian Yiddish and standardized. YIVO, for example, was founded by one of the most prominent Yiddishists and linguists, Max Weinreich.

21. http://www.kaveshtiebel.com/viewtopic.php?f=50&t=8276&hilit=
    שלום+בערגער

22. Yiddish has gendered nouns requiring gendered articles, including a neuter case: *der, di, dos* (masculine, feminine, neuter). Because vernacular Yiddish is mostly spoken or has been, usually the article is merely de, avoiding gendering the noun. One of the founders of KS, Avi, told me that it would be an "impossible" task to edit for each noun, so *Der Veker* has grammatical errors for much of their article use. A more formal and strictly religious Yiddish educational magazine, *Maalos*, does edit for gendered articles.

23. Thanks to Isaac Bleaman for sharing this quote from his dissertation with me.

Chapter 7: Family Secrets

1. See Mara Benjamin's *The Obligated Self* for a discussion of choice and obligation in families.

2. See Ayala Fader, *Mitzvah Girls*, chapters 2 and 3.

3. To use anthropologist Joel Robbins's (2007, 2012) language, double lifers socialized their children into both "the morality of reproduction," the moral action that reproduces already existing patterns of behavior, and the "morality of freedom," people's need to make difficult moral choices between hierarchies of values. Robbins lays these out as opposing tendencies within different societies, but we can see that these could easily be tendencies within the same society, maybe even within the same person.

4. Just a few examples of this approach include Robbins 2004; Laidlaw 2014; Mahmood 2005.

5. There has been much debate about what should constitute the terrain of the anthropology of morality and ethics. Jared Zigon makes the compelling point that the underlying approach in much of philosophy, which forms the basis for anthropological work on morality and ethics, is a rational actor who strives for the good. Instead, he advocates for an emotional person who sustains relationships. This seems to me to be unnecessarily polarizing, since morality and emotions are mutually constitutive (see Shohet 2017).

6. Cheryl Mattingly, *Moral Laboratories*. See also Shohet 2017; Das 2010.

7. Veena Das's analysis tracks the everyday moral decisions made over time by parents and children when a Hindu young man and Muslim young woman in a Delhi neighborhood fall in love and marry. Community members struggled, weighing consequences and outcomes, in their attempts to make sense of a forbidden love. She writes, "What moral projects might be embedded in everyday life in the context of the agonistic belonging of Hindus and Muslims as neighbors in the same local worlds—local worlds that are,

however, inflected with national and even transnational imaginaries that shape Hindu and Muslim identities," 395.

8. Julie Archimbault, "Cruising through Uncertainty," 97.

9. Pesokhim 11a and Horayos 13b both note that walking between two women harms a man's memory (*kosha leshikkhoh*). https://judaism.stack exchange.com/questions/1875/.

10. For a discussion of the intricacies of Hasidic matchmaking see Fader, *Mitzvah Girls*, chapter 7.

11. Elise Berman (2019) argues for the term "aged agency," the agency relevant to particular points on the lifecycle.

Chapter 8: Endings and Beginnings

1. "Modern" is a complicated term among Hasidic Jews, which I have discussed, see Fader, *Mitzvah Girls*. It generally refers to any behavior that aligns with Hasidic understandings of the Gentile world, but more often refers to someone who does not conform to the standards set in a particular community. Having a pet dog is often considered modern, as might be wearing lipstick or wearing black stockings (if you only wear thick, flesh-colored seamed stockings). Similarly, Hasidic children I knew from Borough Park often called Yeshivish Jews "modern," despite their being equally religiously stringent. In short, any style or form of observance that seems to be more like Gentiles or even different from one's own could be labeled with the pejorative "modern."

2. Charles Taylor, *A Secular Age*.

3. Pelkmans (2013) suggests that methodologically doubt must be "caught in mid-air" before it turns to certainty.

4. John Patrick Shanley, *Doubt: A Parable*.

5. Danilyn Rutherford, https://tif.ssrc.org/2009/12/01/an-absence-of-belief/. In this review of Webb Keane's book, *Christian Moderns* (2007), Rutherford not only points to the possibilities for recuperating the concept of belief, but also for its implications for the concept of semiotic ideologies. She suggests, and I agree, that semiotic ideologies, with its focus on cultural beliefs about signs, smuggled belief back into many linguistic anthropological accounts as a privilege of the analyst.

6. The analytic category of religious orthodoxies, with an emphasis on correctness, "ortho," and belief, "doxa," can accommodate both religious practice and interior doubt and belief, individual experiences and larger political structures. Anthropologists Andreas Bandak and Tom Boylston (2014), who each study Christian orthodoxies, make a similar argument, writing, "Our aim is to promote a way that orthodoxy can be used as an analytic foray into how religious worlds come into being, how they are structured,

and how they become attenuated in people's practices," p. 26. Further, orthodoxies of religion as an analytical category draws attention to more marginalized traditions in the anthropology of religion, which has of late focused on Protestantism. However, widening the scope to include Orthodox Jews or Muslims, the Christian Orthodox or Mormons, not to mention non-Abrahamic religions, challenges how we think about the very category of religion itself, since these religions often cross lines and categories of anthropological analytical frameworks.

7. See, for example, Susan Harding on televangelists (2000) or Arsalan Khan's work with Tablighi Muslims in Pakistan (2015), which describes the anxieties over the new public sphere constituted by mass media, including online communities, with their "egalitarian ethos" that threatens the "ethics of pious hierarchies."

8. This has had far reaching ramifications, since the man of the household is supposed to lead in issues of spirituality. In reality, of course, there are plenty of men who were less serious about religion than their wives might have wished. I have gone to many inspirational lectures intended to instruct women on the best ways to encourage their husbands to be more serious about, for example, learning some Talmud with the boys on long Shabbes afternoons. Rukhy similarly reported that in her marriage, her husband had always been the lenient one in religious issues, not praying too often and never being very strict with the children.

9. Ayala Fader, *Mitzvah Girls*, 59.

Appendix

1. Sociolinguist Charles Ferguson developed the notion of diglossia. Joshua Fishman (1981) extended Ferguson's model to include a third language and defined it as triglossia.

2. There is a rich body of scholarship on the history of Yiddish in particular, but also on Jewish languages and literacies. See, Joshua Fishman, *Never Say Die*; Michael Wex, *Born to Kvetch;* or Chaim Weiser's *Frumspeak,* among many others.

3. In some Yeshivish Bais Yaakov schools for girls, a gendered idiolect of Hebrew, *ivris*, is used for morning instruction of religious subjects. Naomi Seidman describes this in her book, *Sarah Schenirer and the Bais Yaakov Movement.*

4. I discuss this process in depth in *Mitzvah Girls.*

REFERENCES

Abu-Lughod, Lila. 2002. "Do Muslim Women Need Saving?" *American Anthropologist* 104(3): 783–791.

Agrama, Hussein Ali. 2010. "Ethics, Authority, Tradition: Towards an Anthropology of the Fatwa." *American Ethnologist* 37 (1): 2–18.

Ammerman, Nancy. 2016. "Denominations, Congregations, and Special Purpose Groups." In *Handbook of Religion and Society*, edited by David Yamaneed, 133–54. New York: Springer.

Archimbault, Julie Soleil. 2013. "Cruising through Uncertainty." *American Ethnologist* 40 (1): 88–101.

Arendt, Hannah. 1970. *On Violence*. Boston: Houghton Mifflin Harcourt.

Asad, Talal. 1993. *Genealogies of Religion*. Baltimore, MD: Johns Hopkins University Press.

———. 2003. *Formation of the Secular: Christianity, Islam, Modernity*. Stanford, CA: Stanford University Press.

Bacon, Gershon. "Daas Toyre." The Yivo Encyclopedia of Jews in Eastern Europe https://yivoencyclopedia.org/article.aspx/Daas_Toyre.

Bandak, Andreas and Tom Boylston. 2014. "The 'Orthodoxy' of Orthodoxy: On Moral Imperfection, Correctness and Deferral in Religious Worlds." *Religion and Society: Advances in Research* 5: 25–46.

Barzilai-Nahon, Karine and Gad Barzilai. 2005. "Cultured Technology: Internet & Religious Fundamentalism." *The Information Society* 21(1): 25–40.

Baumel-Schwartz, Judy. 2009. "Frum Surfing: Orthodox Jewish Women's Internet Forums as a Historical and Cultural Phenomenon." *Journal of Jewish Identities* 2 (1): 1–30.

Belcove-Shalin, Janice. 1995. *New World Hasidim: Ethnographic Studies of Hasidic Jews in North America*. New York: SUNY Press.

Bender, Courtney. 2010. *The New Metaphysicals: Spirituality and the American Religious Imagination*. Chicago: The University of Chicago Press.

Benjamin, Mara H. 2018. *The Obligated Self: Maternal Subjectivity and Jewish Thought*. Bloomington: Indiana University Press.

Benor, Sarah. 2012. *Becoming Frum: How Newcomers Learn the Language and Culture of Orthodox Judaism.* Rutgers, NJ: Rutgers University Press.

Berman, Elise. 2018. *Talking Like Children: Language and the Production of Age in the Marshall Islands.* Oxford: Oxford University Press.

Biale, David, David Assaf, Benjamin Brown, Urel Gellman, Samuel Heilman, Moshe Rosman, Gadi Sabiv, Marcin Wodzinski, and Arthur Green. 2018. *Hasidim: A New History.* Princeton: Princeton University Press.

Bialecki, Jon. "Religious Speculation and the Belief/Discipline Complex: Transhumanism, Crisis, Leniency in the Mormon Church, *or* the Return of Speculative Thought." Unpublished manuscript.

Bilu, Yoram and Yehuda Goodman. 1997. "What Does the Soul Say? Metaphysical Uses of Facilitated Communication in the Jewish Ultraorthodox Community." *Ethos* 25 (4): 375–407.

Bleaman, Issac. 2018. "Big Data in a Low Resource Language: Syntactic Variation in Hasidic Yiddish on the Web." Talk given at the Linguistic Society of America meeting, Salt Lake City, UT, January 6, 2018.

Blutinger, Jeffrey C. 2007. "So-Called Orthodoxy: The History of an Unwanted Label." *Modern Judaism* 27 (3): 310–28.

Boellstorff, Tom. 2010. *Coming of Age in Second Life: An Anthropologist Explores the Virtually Human.* Princeton, NJ: Princeton University Press.

Bourdieu, Pierre. 1977. *Outline of a Theory of Practice.* Cambridge: Cambridge University Press.

Borges, Rafael [pseud.]. 2011. "Imposters among Us." *Ami Magazine*, April 6, 2011.

Boyarin, Jonathan. 2013. *Jewish Families.* New Brunswick, NJ: Rutgers University Press.

Brooks, E. Marshall. 2018. *Disenchanted Lives: Apostasy and Ex-Mormonism among the Latter-day Saints.* Rutgers, NJ: Rutgers University Press.

Brown, Judy (Eishes Chayil). 2013. https://forward.com/author/judy-brown-eishes-chayil/

Campbell, Heidi. 2007. "What Hath God Wrought? Considering How Religious Communities Culture (or Kosher) the Cell Phone." *Continuum* 21 (2): 191–203.

———. 2012. "Understanding the Relationship between Religion Online and Offline in a Networked Society." *Journal of the American Academy of Religion* 80 (1): 64–93.

Campbell, Heidi and Oren Golan. 2011. "Creating Digital Enclaves: Negotiation of the Internet among Bounded Religious Communities." *Media Culture Society* 33 (5): 709–24.

Caplan, Kimmy. 1997. "God's Voice: Audio Taped Sermons in Israeli Haredi Society." *Modern Judaism* 17 (3): 253–80.

Carr, E. Summerson. 2010. *Scripting Addiction: The Politics of Therapeutic Talk and American Sobriety*. Princeton, NJ: Princeton University Press.

Cody, Francis. 2011. "Publics and Politics." *Annual Review of Anthropology* 40: 37–52.

Cohen, Tova. 2008. "Portrait of the Maskilah as a Young Woman." *Nashim: A Journal of Jewish Women's Studies & Gender Issues* 15 (Spring): 9–29.

Coleman, E. Gabriella. 2010. "Ethnographic Approaches to Digital Media." *Annual Review of Anthropology* 39: 487–505.

Das, Veena. 2010. "Engaging the Life of the Other: Love and Everyday Life." In *Ordinary Ethics: Anthropology, Language, and Action*, edited by Michael Lambek, 376–99. New York: Fordham University Press.

Davidman, Lynn. 1993. *Tradition in a Rootless World: Women Turn to Orthodox Judaism*. New Brunswick, NJ: Rutgers University Press.

———. 2014. *Becoming Un-Orthodox: Stories of Ex-Hasidic Jews*. Oxford: Oxford University Press.

Deen, Shulem. 2015. *All Who Go Do Not Return*. New York: Greywolf Press.

Deutsch, Nathaniel. 2009. "The Forbidden Fork, the Cell Phone, the Holocaust and Other Haredi Encounters with Technology." *Contemporary Jewry* 29: 3–19.

Eickelman, Dale and Jon Anderson, eds. 2003. *New Media in the Muslim World: The Emerging Public Sphere*. Bloomington: Indiana University Press.

Eisenlohr, Patrick. 2009. "Technologies of the Spirit: Devotional Islam, Sound Reproduction, and the Dialectics of Mediation and Immediacy in Mauritius." *Anthropological Theory* 9 (3): 273–96.

———. 2011. "What Is a Medium? Theologies, Technologies and Aspirations." *Social Anthropology* 19: 1–5.

El-Or, Tamar. 1994, *Educated and Ignorant: Ultraorthodox Jewish Women and Their World*. Boulder, CO: Lynne Rienner Press.

———. 2002. *Next Year I Will Know More: Identity and Literacy among Young Orthodox Women in Israel*. Detroit, MI: Wayne State University Press.

Endelman, Todd. 2014. *Leaving the Jewish Fold: Conversion and Radical Assimilation in Modern Jewish History*. Princeton, NJ: Princeton University Press.

Engelke, Matthew. 2005. "The Early Days of Johane Masowe: Self-Doubt, Uncertainty, and Religious Transformation." *Comparative Studies in Society and History* 47(4): 781–808.

———. 2007. *A Problem of Presence: Beyond Scripture in an African Church*. Berkeley: University of California Press.

———. 2010. "Religion and the Media Turn: A Review Essay." *American Ethnologist* 37 (2): 371–77.

———. 2012. "Angels in Swindon: Public Religion and Ambient Faith in England." *American Ethnologist* 39 (1): 155–70.

Erzen, Tanya. 2006. *Straight to Jesus: Sexual and Christian Conversions in the Ex-Gay Movement*. Berkeley: University of California Press.

Etkes, Immanuel. 2010. "Haskalah." *YIVO Encyclopedia of Jews in Eastern Europe*. http://www.yivoencyclopedia.org/article.aspx/Haskalah.

Fader, Ayala. 2007. "Reclaiming Sacred Sparks: Syncretism and Gendered Language Shift among Hasidic Jews in New York." *Journal of Linguistic Anthropology* 17 (1): 1–23.

———. 2008. "Reading Jewish Signs: Multilingual Literacy Socialization with Hasidic Women and Girls in New York." *Text and Talk* 28 (5): 621–41.

———. 2009. *Mitzvah Girls: Bringing Up the Next Generation of Hasidic Girls in Brooklyn*. Princeton: Princeton University Press.

———. 2012. "Is the Internet the Problem? Sexual Abuse Scandals and Ultra-Orthodox Jews in Brooklyn." *The Revealer: A Daily Review of Religion and Media*. The Center for Religion and Media, New York University. http://therevealer.org/archives/14351.

———. 2013. "Nonliberal Jewish Women's Audiocassette Lectures in Brooklyn: The Crisis of Faith and the Morality of Media." *American Anthropologist* 115 (1): 72–84.

———. 2017a. "The Counterpublic of the J(ewish) Blogosphere: Gendered Language and the Mediation of Religious Doubt among Ultra-Orthodox Jews in New York." *The Journal of the Royal Anthropological Institute* 23 (4): 727–47.

———. 2017b. "Ultra-Orthodox Jewish Interiority, the Internet and the Crisis of Faith." *Hau: The Journal of Ethnographic Theory* 7 (1): 185–206.

Fader, Ayala and Owen Gottlieb. 2015. "Occupy Judaism: Religion, Media and the Public Sphere at Occupy Wall Street." *Anthropological Quarterly* 88 (3): 759–93.

Fassin, Didier. 2012. *Companion to Moral Anthropology*. Malden, MA: Wiley.

———. 2014. "The Ethical Turn in Anthropology: Promises and Uncertainties." *Hau: Journal of Ethnographic Theory* 4 (1): 429–35.

Fishkoff, Sue. 2005. *The Rebbe's Army: Inside the World of Chabad-Lubavitch*. New York: Schocken Books.

Fishman, Joshua, ed. 1981. *Never Say Die! A Thousand Years of Yiddish in Life and Letters*. The Hague: Mouton.

Foucault, Michel. 1979. *Discipline and Punish: The Birth of the Prison*. New York: Vintage Books.

———. 1997. "On the Genealogy of Ethics: An Overview of Work in Progress." In *Ethics: Subjectivity and Truth*, vol. 1, *Essential Works of Foucault, 1954–1984*, edited by Paul Rabinow, translated by R. Hurley, 281–301. New York: New Press.

Francis, Philip Salim. 2017. *When Art Disrupts Religion: Aesthetic Experience and the Evangelical Mind*. Oxford: Oxford University Press.

Fraser, Nancy. 1990. "Rethinking the Public Sphere: A Contribution to the Critique of Actually Existing Democracy." *Social Text,* nos. 25/26: 56–80.

Friedman, Michelle and Rachel Yehuda. 2016. *The Art of Jewish Pastoral Counseling: A Guide for All Faiths.* Routledge: Abingdon.

Frosh, Stephen. 2008. "Freud and Jewish Identity." *Theory & Psychology* 18 (2): 167–78.

Gal, Susan. 2013. "Tastes of Talk: Qualia and the Moral Flavor of Signs." *Anthropological Theory* 13 (12): 31–48.

Gershon, Ilana. 2010. "Media Ideologies: An Introduction." *Journal of Linguistic Anthropology* 20 (2): 283–93.

Gershon, Ilana and Paul Manning. 2014. "Language and Media." In *The Cambridge Handbook of Linguistic Anthropology,* edited by N. J. Enfield, Jack Sidnell, and Paul Kockelman, 559–76. Cambridge: Cambridge University Press.

Gibson, James Jerome. 1986. *The Ecological Approach to Visual Perception.* New York: Hove.

Ginsburg, Faye, Lila Abu-Lughod, and Brian Larkin, eds. 2002. *Media Worlds: Anthropology on New Terrain.* Berkeley: University of California Press.

Goldschmidt, Henry. 2006. *Race and Religion among the Chosen People of Crown Heights.* New Brunswick, NJ: Rutgers University Press.

Gurock, Jeffrey. 2009. *Orthodox Jews in America.* Bloomington: Indiana University Press.

Gusterson, Hugh. 1996. *Nuclear Rites: A Weapons Laboratory at the End of the Cold War.* Berkeley: University of California Press.

Habermas, Jurgen. 1989. *The Structural Transformation of the Public Sphere: An Inquiry into a Category of Bourgeois Society.* Cambridge, MA: The MIT Press.

Handman, Courtney. 2017. "Language without Subjects: On the Interior(s) of Colonial New Guinea." *Hau: Journal of Ethnographic Theory* 3 (3): 107–37.

Harding, Susan. 2000. *The Book of Jerry Falwell: Fundamentalist Language and Politics.* Princeton, NJ: Princeton University Press.

Harkness, Nicholas and L. H. Chumley. 2013. "Special Issue: Qualia." *Anthropological Theory* 13 (1–2).

Heilman, Samuel. 2006. *Sliding to the Right: The Contest for the Future of American Jewish Orthodoxy.* Berkeley: University of California Press.

———. 2017. *Who Will Lead Us? The Story of Five Hasidic Dynasties in America.* Berkeley: University of California Press.

Heilman, Samuel and Menachem Friedman. 2012. *The Rebbe: The Life and Afterlife of Menachem Mendel Schneerson.* Princeton, NJ: Princeton University Press.

Heinze, Andrew. 1999. "Jews and the Americanization of Mussar: Abraham

Twersky's Twelve Steps." *Judaism: A Quarterly Journal of Jewish Life and Thought* 48 (4): 450–69.

Heinze, Andrew. 2006. *Jews and the American Soul: Human Nature in the Twentieth Century*. Princeton, NJ: Princeton University Press.

Helmreich, William. 1980. *The World of the Yeshiva: An Intimate Portrait of Orthodox Judaism*. Jerusalem: Ktav Press.

Herman, Ellen. 1996. *The Romance of American Psychology: Political Culture in the Age of Experts*. Berkeley: University of California Press.

Hirschkind, Charles. 2006. *The Ethical Soundscape: Cassette Sermons and Islamic Counterpublics*. New York: Columbia University Press.

Hoesterey, James. 2015. *Rebranding Islam: Piety, Prosperity, and a Self-Help Guru*. Palo Alto, CA: Stanford University.

Houtman, Dick and Birgit Meyer. 2012. *Things: Religion and the Question of Materiality*. New York: Fordham University Press.

Hundert, Gershon, ed. 1991. *Essential Papers in Hasidism*. New York: New York University Press.

Hutchby, Ian. 2001. "Technologies, Texts, and Affordances." *Sociology* 35 (2): 441–56.

Jones, Graham. 2014. "Secrecy." *Annual Review of Anthropology* 43: 53–69.

Keane, Webb. 2002. "Sincerity, 'Modernity,' and Protestantism." *Cultural Anthropology* 17 (1): 65–92.

———. 2007. *Christian Moderns: Freedom and Fetish in the Mission Encounter*. Berkeley: University of California Press.

Khan, Arsalan. 2015. "Islam and Pious Sociality: The Ethics of Pious Sociality in the Tablighi Jamaat in Pakistan." *Social Analysis* 6 (4): 93–113.

Kranzler, George. 1995. *Hasidic Williamsburg: A Contemporary American Hasidic Community*. Lanham, MD: Jason Aronson Press.

Kugelmas, Jack. 1988. *Between Two Worlds: Ethnographic Essays on American Jewry*. Ithaca, NY: Cornell University Press.

Laidlaw, James. 2002. "For an Anthropology of Ethics and Freedom." *Journal of the Royal Anthropological Institute*, 8 (2): 311–32.

Lambek, Michael, ed. 2010. *Ordinary Ethics*. Bronx, NY: Fordham University Press.

Lehmann, David and Batya Siebzehner. 2006. "Holy Pirates: Media, Ethnicity, and Religious Renewal in Israel." In *Religion, Media and the Public Sphere*, edited by B. Meyer and A. Moors, 91–114. Bloomington: Indiana University Press.

Lev-On, Azi and Rivke Neriya-Ben Shachar. 2011. "A Forum of their Own: Views about the Internet among Ultra-Orthodox Jewish Women who Browse Closed Fora." First Monday 16(4), https://firstmonday.org/ojs/index.php/fm/article/view/3228/2859

Levine, Stephanie. 2004. *Mystics, Merrymakers and Mavericks: An Intimate Journey among Hasidic Girls*. New York: New York University Press.

Liberatore, Giulia. 2013. "Doubt as a Double-Edged Sword: Unanswerable Questions and Practical Solutions among Newly Practicing Somali Muslims in London." In *Ethnographies of Doubt: Faith and Uncertainty in Contemporary Societies,* edited by Mathijs Pelkmans, 225–50. London: I. B. Tauris.

Lieber, Andrea. 2010. "A Virtual Veibershul: Blogging and the Blurring of Public and Private among Orthodox Jewish Women." *College English* 72: 621–38.

Lopez, Jr., Donald S. 1998. "Belief." In *Critical Terms in Religious Studies,* edited by Mark C. Taylor, 21–35. Chicago: University of Chicago Press.

Luhrmann, Tanya. 1989. *Persuasion of the Witch's Craft.* Cambridge, MA: Harvard University Press.

———. 2002. *Of Two Minds: An Anthropologist Looks at American Psychiatry.* New York: Vintage Press.

———. 2004. "Metakinesis: How God Becomes Intimate in Contemporary US Christianity." *American Anthropologist* 106 (3): 518–28.

———. 2012. *When God Talks Back: Understanding the American Evangelical Relationship with God.* New York: Random House.

Mahmood, Saba. 2005. *Politics of Piety: The Islamic Revival and the Feminist Subject.* Princeton, NJ: Princeton University Press.

Mahmud, Lilith. 2014. *The Brotherhood of Freemason Sisters.* Chicago, IL: University of Chicago Press.

Margolese, Faranak. 2005. *Off the Derech: How to Respond to the Challenge.* CreateSpace Independent Publishing Platform.

Mattingly, Cheryl. 2014. *Moral Laboratories: Family Peril and the Struggle for a Good Life.* Berkeley: University of California Press.

McIntosh, Janet. 2010. "Mobile Phones and Mipoho's Prophecy: The Powers and Dangers of Flying Languages." *American Ethnologist* 37 (2): 337–52.

———. 2005. "Language Essentialism and Social Hierarchies among Giriama and Swahili." *Journal of Pragmatics* 37 (12): 1919–44.

McKinnon, Susie and Fenella Cannell, eds. 2013. *Vital Relations: Modernity and the Persistent Life of Kinship.* Santa Fe, NM: SAR Press.

McLuhan, Marshall. 1964. Understanding Media: The Extension of Man. Boston, MA: MIT Press.

Mendieta, Eduardo and Jonathan VanAntwerpen, eds. 2011. *The Power of Religion in the Public Sphere.* New York: Columbia University Press.

Meyer, Birgit, ed. 2009. *Aesthetic Formations: Media, Religion, and the Senses.* New York: Macmillan.

———. 2011. "Mediation and Immediacy: Sensational Forms, Semiotic Ideologies and the Question of the Medium." *Social Anthropology* 19 (1): 23–39.

Meyer, Birgit and Annalies Moors, eds. 2006. *Religion, Media, and the Public Sphere.* Bloomington: Indiana University Press.

Miller, Daniel and Don Slater. 2000. *The Internet: An Ethnographic Approach.* London: Berg Press.

Mintz, Jerome. 1968. *Legends of the Hasidim*. Chicago: Chicago University Press.

——. 1993. *Hasidic People: A Place in the New World*. Cambridge, MA: Harvard University Press.

Mittemaier, Amira. 2012. "Dreams from Elsewhere: Muslim Subjectivities beyond the Trope of Self-Cultivation." *Journal of the Royal Anthropological Institute* 18 (2): 247–65.

Morgan, David, ed. 1998. *Key Words in Religious Studies*. Chicago, IL: University of Chicago Press.

Moseley, Marcus. 2010. "Autobiography and Memoir." The YIVO Encyclopedia of Jews in Eastern Europe. https://yivoencyclopedia.org/article.aspx/Auto biography_and_Memoir

Moss, Kenneth B. 2010. "Printing and Publishing: Printing and Publishing after 1800." *YIVO Encyclopedia of Jews in Eastern Europe*. http://www .yivoencyclopedia.org/article.aspx/Printing_and_Publishing/Printing_and _Publishing_after_1800.

Nissim, Leon. 2011. "The Political Use of the Teshuva Cassette Culture in Israel." *Contemporary Jewry* 31: 91–106.

Orsi, Robert. 2005. *Between Heaven and Earth*. Princeton, NJ: Princeton University Press.

Otterman, Sharon. 2012. "Ultra-Orthodox Jews Hold Big Meeting on Internet Risks." *New York Times*, May 17, 2005.

Pandolfo, Stefania. 2018. *Knot of the Soul: Madness, Psychoanalysis, Islam*. Chicago: University of Chicago Press.

Parush, Iris. 1997. "Women Readers as Agents of Social Change among Eastern European Jews in the Late Nineteenth Century." *Gender and History* 9 (1): 36–59.

——. 2004. *Reading Jewish Women: Marginality and Modernization in Nineteenth-Century European Jewish Society*. Waltham, MA: Brandeis University Press.

Pelkmans, Mathijs, ed. 2013. *Ethnographies of Doubt: Faith and Uncertainty in Contemporary Societies*. London: I. B. Tauris.

Poll, Solomon. 2006. *A Hasidic Community in Williamsburg*. New York: Kessinger Press.

Rashi, Tsuriel. 2013. "The Kosher Cellphone in Ultra-Orthodox Society: A Technological Ghetto within a Global Village." In *Digital Religion: Understanding Religious Practice in New Media Worlds*, edited by H. Campbell, 173–81. Philadelphia, PA: Routledge.

Reed, Adam. 2005. "'My Blog Is Me': Texts and Persons in United Kingdom Online Journal Culture." *Ethnos* 70 (2): 220–42.

Rieff, Philip. 1968. *The Triumph of the Therapeutic: Uses of Faith after Freud*. New York: Harper Torchbooks.

Robbins, Joel. 2004. *Becoming Sinners: Christianity and Moral Torment in a Papua New Guinea Society*. Berkeley: University of California Press.

———. 2007. "Between Reproduction and Freedom: Morality, Value, and Radical Cultural Change." *Ethnos* 72 (3): 299–308.

———. 2012. "Cultural Values." In *A Companion to Moral Anthropology*, edited by D. Fassin, 117–32. Malden, MA: Wiley.

Rosman, Moshe. 1996. *Founder of Hasidism: A Quest for the Historical Ba'al Shem Tov*. Berkeley: University of California Press.

Rubin, Israel. 1972. *Satmar: An Island in the City*. New York: Quadrangle Books.

———. 1997. *Satmar: Two Generations of an Urban Island*. New York: Peter Lang.

Rutherford, Danilyn. 2009. "An Absence of Belief." The Immanent Frame: Secularism, Religion, and the Public Sphere https://tif.ssrc.org/2009/12/01/an-absence-of-belief/

Salamon, Michael. 2012. "The Great Internet Asifa." *Times of Israel* https://blogs.timesofisrael.com/the-great-internet-asifa/.

Sargon, Batya Unger. 2015. "Undercover Atheists." *Aeon Magazine*. https://aeon.co/essays/secretly-seduced-by-science-hasidic-atheists-lead-a-double-life.

———. 2016. "Healing Hasidic Masturbators and Adulterers with Psychiatric Drugs." *Narratively*, August 23 2016.

Scheper-Hughes, Nancy. 1993. Death without Weeping: The Violence of Everyday Life in Brazil. Berkeley: UC Press.

Schieffelin, Bambi, Kathryn Woolard and Paul Kroskrity, eds. 1998. *Language Ideologies: Practice and Theory*. Oxford: Oxford University Press.

Schielke, Samuli. 2012. "Being a Non-Believer in a Time of Islamic Revival: Trajectories of Doubt and Certainty in Contemporary Egypt." *International Journal of Middle Eastern Studies* 44 (2): 301–20.

Seeman, Don. 2015. "Coffee and the Moral Order: Ethiopian Jews and Pentecostals against Culture." *American Ethnologist* 42 (4): 734–48.

Seidman, Naomi. 2002. "Raised by Jews." *Killing the Buddha: Old Gods, New Tricks*. May 24 2002 http://killingthebuddha.com/mag/confession/raised-by-jews/

———. 2019. *Sara Schenirer and the Bais Yaakov Movement: A Revolution in the Name of Tradition*. Liverpool: Littman Library of Jewish Civilization with Liverpool University Press.

Shamah, David. 2012. "Rabbis Tell 60,000 in NY: Get Rid of the Internet If You Know What's Good for You." *The Times of Israel*, May 12.

Shandler, Jeffrey, ed. 2002. *Awakening Lives: Autobiographies of Jewish Youth in Poland before the Holocaust*. New Haven, CT: Yale University Press/YIVO Institute.

———. 2017. *Holocaust Memory in the Digital Age*. Stanford: Stanford University Press.

Shanley, John Patrick. 2005. *Doubt: A Parable*. Theatre Communication Group.

Shohet, Merav. 2017. "Troubling Love: Gender, Class, and Sideshadowing the 'Happy Family' in Vietnam." *Ethos* 45 (4): 555–76.

Simmel, Georg. 1906. "The Sociology of Secrets and Secret Societies." *American Journal of Sociology* 11: 441–98.

Soloveitchik, Hayyim. 1994. "Rupture and Reconstruction: The Transformation of Contemporary Orthodoxy." *Tradition* 28 (4): 64–130.

Sreberny, Annabelle and Gholam Khiabany. 2011. *Blogistan: The Internet and Politics in Iran*. London: I. B. Tauris.

Stadler, Nurit. 2010. *Yeshiva Fundamentalism*. New York: New York University Press.

Stolow, Jeremy. 2010. *Orthodox by Design: Judaism, Print Politics, and the ArtScroll Revolution*. Berkeley: University of California Press.

Stolzenberg, Nomi. 2004. "Values: 'Spiritual Custody': Religious Freedom and Coercion in the Family." In *The Jewish Role in American Life, An Annual Review*, vol. 3, edited by Barry Glassner and Hillary Lachoff, 1–22. USC Casden Center, Study for the Jewish Role in American Life, UCLA.

Taragin-Zeller, Lea. 2019. "Toward an Anthropology of Doubt: The Case of Religious Reproduction in Orthodox Judaism." *Journal of Modern Jewish Studies* 18 (1): 1–20.

Taussig, Michael. 1999. *Defacement: Public Secrecy and the Labor of the Negative*. Palo Alto, CA: Stanford University Press.

Taylor, Charles. 2007. *A Secular Age*. Cambridge, MA: Harvard University Press.

Trencher, Mark. 2016. "Starting a Conversation: A Pioneering Survey of Those Who Have Left the Orthodox Community." http://nishmaresearch.com /social-research.html.

Vaisman, Carmel. 2014. "Beautiful Script, Cute Spelling, and Glamorous Words: Doing Girlhood through Language Playfulness on Israeli Blogs." *Language and Communication* 34: 69–80.

Warner, Michael. 2002. "Publics and Counterpublics." *Public Culture* 14 (1): 49–90.

Weiser, Chaim. 1995. *Frumspeak: The First Dictionary of Yeshivish*. Northvale, NJ: Jason Aronson.

Wex, Michael. 2006. Born to Kvetch: Yiddish Language and Culture in all its Moods. P.S. Harper Perennial.

Winston, Hella. 2005. *Unchosen: The Secret Lives of Hasidic Rebels*. Boston: Beacon Press.

Woolard, Kathyrn. 1998. "Simultaneity and Bivalency as Strategies in Bilingualism." *Journal of Linguistic Anthropology* 8 (1): 3–29.

Zigon, Jared. 2007. "Moral Breakdown and the Ethical Demand: A Theoretical Framework for an Anthropology of Moralities." *Anthropological Theory* 7 (2): 131–50.

Zito, Angela. 2008. "Culture." In *Keywords in Religion, Media and Culture*, edited by David Morgan, 69–82. New York: Routledge.

INDEX

Abu-Lughod, Lila, 58
activists. See *askonim*
addiction, 62, 64–68, 70, 123–24, 130
Adelphi University, 131
adolescence, reclaiming of, 159–63
agnosticism, 13, 91, 96–97
Agudas Yisroel, 18
Alcott, Louis May, *Little Women*, 12
Amazon (online retailer), 178
American culture. *See* popular American culture
American Psychological Association, 131, 150
Ami Magazine, 6, 31, 55, 115, 116
anusim (the forced), 24
apikorsim (skeptics), 12–13, 57
apikorsus (heresy), 31, 93, 134
Archimbault, Julie, 191
Arendt, Hannah, 59
Aristotle, 93
arranged marriages: of double lifers' children, 204–7; double lifers' experience of, 95, 96; schools' role in, 8, 77–78; smartphone use as factor in, 86
art, 176–77
Asad, Talal, 6, 216, 246n6
Asch, Sholem, *God of Vengeance*, 168, 247n9
askonim (self-appointed activists), 6, 55, 62, 107, 122, 124–25, 128, 137, 138
atheism, 13, 53, 98, 116, 124–25, 137, 187
authority: as ally in struggle against evil, 65–67; autonomy in relation to, 33, 87, 92–93, 101, 113–14, 144, 182, 198, 209, 213, 225; crises of, 4–5, 7, 10–11, 17–18, 26, 32–34, 55–58, 63–64, 211, 217–21, 225–26; double lifers' challenge to, 75, 87, 96, 99, 101,

210; gendered nature of, 73, 75, 87, 114, 186–87; generational, 81–86; in Hasidic Judaism, 114, 138; Jbloggers' challenge to, 32–33, 37–39, 55–59; in marriage, 97–98, 103, 112, 113–14; parental, 83, 85; rebellion against, 17; religious therapy as site for contention over, 124; smartphones as site of contention over, 77–87; sources of rabbis', 17, 64
autonomy: authority in relation to, 33, 87, 92–93, 101, 113–14, 144, 182, 198, 209, 213, 225; of children, 181–82, 189–90, 207–9; of double life couples, 212–13; of double lifers, 4, 5, 33, 75, 87, 92, 96–97, 101, 107–8, 112–14, 143–44, 210, 221–22; liberal conception of, 5, 182, 213; morality and, 207–9; ultra-Orthodox conception of, 182, 198; of women, 104, 107–8

bahaltena apikorsim (hidden heretics), 2, 24. *See also* double lifers
Bandak, Andreas, 249n6
bars, 166–67
beards, 3, 11, 14, 94, 96, 98, 101, 113, 115, 221
belief, in relation to doubt, 216–17
Bialecki, Jon, 60
bicycles, 164
Bieber, Justin, 197
Bina Magazine, 141–42
bipolar disorder, 138–39
birth control, 106–7, 135
bitmojis, 154
Blackberry, 113
Blogger (software), 37, 40
blogosphere. *See* Jewish blogosphere